Alan Pipes

Drawing for Designers

LAURENCE KING PUBLISHING

Published in 2007 by Laurence King Publishing Ltd
361–373 City Road
London EC1V 1LR
United Kingdom
Tel: + 44 20 7841 6900
Fax: + 44 20 7841 6910
e-mail: enquiries@laurenceking.co.uk
www.laurenceking.co.uk

A catalogue record for this book is available
from the British Library

ISBN-13:   978-1-85669-533-6
ISBN-10:   1 85669 533 6

Editor: Richard Mason
Designers: Newton Harris Design Partnership and John Dowling
Picture research: Alan Pipes and Anna Frohm
Printed in China

Front cover: Karim Rashid, *Plomb* Umbrella stand/Flower pot, 2001.
Courtesy Karim Rashid.

Drawing for Designers

Contents

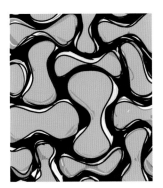

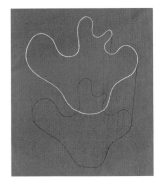

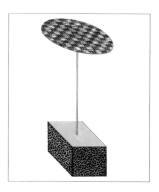

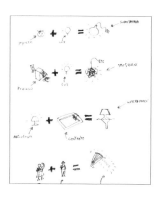

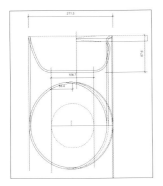

7 From general arrangement drawing to production

8 Technical illustration

9 The future of the design drawing

Preface

Designers have helped create the visual appearance of most aspects of civilized life today. They are now working on what the future might look like. They do it by thinking, conceptualizing, and drawing. The drawing is the visible manifestation of their thought processes. But the designer's drawing is often a private and hidden art, the marks on paper treated merely as a means to an end. This book aims to reveal those hidden images and give them the respect and appreciation they deserve, for designers' drawings are more than mere instructions on how to make objects. They are beautiful artefacts in their own right.

Of course, there have always been designers (mostly from architectural backgrounds) who are proud enough of their drawings that they want to display them whenever they can. But equally there are designers whose drawings have never been seen outside their studios, who say that they prefer to let the final product shots speak for themselves. In a way they are teasing us, like conjurors, by keeping the design process that led to the finished object shrouded in mystery. But all designers draw, whether with a pencil on paper or pixels on a computer screen, and this book celebrates them by showing drawings from all stages of the design process, from back-of-envelope sketches to fully rendered 3D computer models.

Drawing for Designers grew out of a book that I wrote in 1990 entitled *Drawing for 3-Dimensional Design*. A lot has changed since then. At that time, presentation drawings were still made with marker pens, technical illustrations were airbrushed, and engineering drawings were rendered by pencil or ink on Mylar; even CAD drawings were made with real ink, on pen plotters. Many 3D modeling and rendering techniques now commonplace on the lowliest desktop PC were then research projects requiring supercomputers. Today almost every drawing, except perhaps the simplest sketchbook concept, has been touched and modified by the computer. Many drawings do not even exist in a physical form until they are printed out as hard copy.

Compared with books on drawing for architects, there are still very few good books covering drawing for product designers. *Drawing for Designers* fills this gap, offering a comprehensive guide to drawing for product and industrial designers and students at all levels. The book also encompasses drawings of cars and household products such as furniture, lamps, clothing, and jewelry.

This book covers drawing at all stages of the design process, from concept sketches through to presentations and production drawings. It is a practical guide to drawing techniques that includes Step-by-Step sequences, tips and tricks, and Case Studies featuring international designers. It is essential reading for all students on product and industrial design courses as well as practising designers wishing to refresh and update their drawing skills.

The book is constructed chapter-by-chapter around specific themes: A brief history of designers' drawings; Basic drawing skills; Tools and materials; Computer systems; Concept design; Presentation drawings and visuals; From general arrangement drawing to production; Technical illustration; and The future of the design drawing.

I was brought up in the northwest of England, an area with a great engineering heritage. Sadly, most of the huge factories there that exported machinery to the world have closed down. My father was a draughtsman for a firm that manufactured papermaking equipment, and I often wondered what draughtsmen actually did. All I knew was that they made straight lines in hard pencil on blue-tinted linen, or they used one of many fascinating instruments from a geometry set. I hope this book will be a tribute to all those unsung heroes. I have no idea how much actual designing they did, but everything has to be designed by someone, whether it's a small cog in a big machine or an iconic designer chair.

Many old drawings are in a terrible condition, for they were never meant to be framed and hung on a wall. Instead, they served a practical purpose; they were intended to be handled and used to make parts in a workshop. I sincerely hope that many of these artistic relics from a bygone age will be liberated from their dusty storage areas, unrolled, conserved, exhibited, and marveled at to provide inspiration for today's designers. I also hope that the new generation of designers will not become utterly enslaved by the computer, but will continue to be taught the art of drawing and feel the joy and exhilaration of making marks on a blank piece of paper.

I should like to thank all the designers from around the world who contributed images to this book. My only regret is that we were unable to use them all. Of the roughly 300 we did choose, many had to be selected for utilitarian reasons—to illustrate points in the text—rather than for their intrinsic beauty. But I couldn't resist using some just because they are so beautiful. I would particularly like to thank those designers commissioned to create the Step-by-Step sections: James Wright and Mark Jones, both graduates of Central Saint Martins College of Art and Design; Etienne Salomé, Royal College of Art graduate; internet tutor Thomas Parel; and Ryan Whittaker (student) with John Fox (tutor) of Blackpool and The Fylde College. I should also like to express my gratitude to Raysan Al-Kubaisi for creating computer renderings

especially for me. My thanks also to the Case Study participants for allowing me some of their precious time: Dick Powell, Nelson Au, David Goodwin, and Linda Andersson.

This book would never have existed were it not for Jo Lightfoot, my commissioning editor at Laurence King Publishing. I'd also like to thank Anne Townley for nursing the project through its early stages and making valuable suggestions for improving the text; Richard Mason for his thorough and patient management of the editorial, design, pictorial and cover processes; and Anna Frohm for her enthusiastic picture research in which she targeted today's hot-shot designers and persuaded them to part with their best images. Finally, I thank the designers Nick Newton and John Dowling for displaying all these wonderful drawings to their best advantage.

Alan Pipes, February 2007

Picture Credits

Grateful acknowledgement is extended for use of the following images. Every effort has been made to trace and contact all copyright holders. The publishers apologise for any unintentional omissions or errors and will be pleased to insert the appropriate acknowledgement in any subsequent edition of this book.

p. 10 Ron Arad Associates; 1 Tokujin Yoshioka; 2 V&A Images; 3 Michael DiTullo; 4 Ron Arad Associates; 5, 6 Michael Graves and Alessi spa; 7 King and Miranda Design, Milan; 8 Thomas Gardner; 9 Karim Rashid; 10 Youmeus Design Ltd; 11 Motoring Picture Library, National Motor Museum, Beaulieu, England; 12 Shin Azumi; 13 Marcel Wanders; 14 Iittala Group, Helsinki, Finland; 15 Springtime-USA, New York, Springtime Industrial Design, Amsterdam, The Netherlands, and Studio Red at Rockwell Group, New York; 16 BMW Group; 17, 18 Karim Rashid; 19 Dassault Systèmes; 20 RIBA Library Drawings and Archives Collections, London; 21 UGS, Huntsville, AL, USA; 22, 23 Mathias Bengtsson; 24, 25 SowdenDesign, Milan; p. 26 Iittala Group, Helsinki, Finland; 1.1 Bridgeman Art Library, London; 1.2 Institution of Mechanical Engineers, London; 1.3 Bibliothèque Nationale de France, Paris; 1.4 National Maritime Museum, London; 1.5 Pepys Library, Magdalene College, Cambridge; 1.6 Photo © Hunterian Museum and Art Gallery, University of Glasgow. Mackintosh Collection; 1.7 Georg Jensen, Denmark; 1.8 Bibliothèque de l'Institut de France, Paris, France. Lauros/Giraudon/Bridgeman Art Library; 1.9 Georg Jensen, Denmark; 1.10 Bauhaus Archiv; 1.11 Rietveld Shröder Archive, Utrecht; 1.12 Sottsass Associati EEIG, Milan; 1.13 Cooper-Hewitt, National Design Museum, Smithsonian Institution; p. 42 Alessi spa, Italy; 2.1 SolidWorks Corporation; 2.2 Pepys Library, Magdalene College, Cambridge, England; 2.3, 2.10 RIBA Library Drawings and Archives Collections, London; 2.4–2.9, 2.11, 2.13, 2.15–2.16, 2.20–2.23, 2.31, 2.40, 2.42 Alan Pipes; p. 48 James Wright; 2.12, 2.17, 2.24 SowdenDesign, Milan; 2.14 SolidWorks Corporation; 2.18 Steve Summerskill, Design Ergonomics Group, Loughborough University; 2.19 Dassault Systèmes; 2.25 SolidWorks Corporation; 2.26, 2.27 Ron Arad Associates; 2.28 Mario Bellini Associati; 2.29 Raysan Al-Kubaisi; 2.30 Héctor Serrano; 2.32–2.35 Raysan Al-Kubaisi; 2.36 Stuart Lawson; 2.38, 2.39 Rio21 Design and Ashlar Inc.; 2.37 Jaguar Cars, Coventry, England; pp. 62–3 Thomas Gardner; 2.41 Pearson Lloyd Design Ltd; pp. 66–9 SeymourPowell; p. 70 Sottsass Associati EEIG, Milan; 3.2 Alan Pipes; 3.3 Etienne Salomé; 3.4 Derwent Cumberland Pencil Company; 3.6 James Wright; 3.7 Pilot Pen Corporation; 3.8 Isao Hosoe; 3.10 King and Miranda Design, Milan; 3.11 Mathias Bengtsson; 3.13 Ford of Europe; 3.14 Héctor Serrano; 3.16 Tombow Pencil Co Ltd, Tokyo; 3.17 Rotring GmbH; 3.18 Michael Graves and Alessi spa; 3.20 Alexander Åhnebrink; 3.21 Greg Vedena and Tim Thayer; 3.22 Shin Azumi; 3.23 John Fox; 3.24, 3.25 Jan Frohm; 3.26 Letraset Limited; 3.27 Iittala Group, Finland; 3.28 King and Miranda Design;

3.29 El Ultimo Grito; 3.30 Héctor Serrano; p. 90 Thomas Gardner; 4.1 Hewlett-Packard; 4.2 Apple, Inc.; 4.3 SolidWorks Corporation; 4.4 LaCie; 4.5, 4.6 Wacom Company, Ltd.; 4.7 Ron Arad Associates; 4.8, 4.9 Wacom Company, Ltd.; 4.10, 4.11 Logitech; 4.12 SensAble Technologies; 4.13 Seiko Epson Corp; 4.14 PiliPili Product Design and UGS; 4.15 Seiko Epson Corp; 4.16 Hewlett-Packard; 4.17 Canon Inc.; 4.18, 4.19 Roland Corporation; 4.20, 4.21 3D Systems, Inc.; 4.22, 4.23 Alan Pipes; pp. 106–07 David Goodwin; p. 108 Héctor Serrano; 5.1 King and Miranda Design; 5.2 SowdenDesign, Milan; 5.3 Sony Ericsson; 5.4 Karim Rashid; 5.5 BMW AG; 5.6 Braun GmbH; 5.7 Oscar Tusquets Blanca; 5.8 Paul Sayers, Drum Design Studios; 5.9, 5.10 Alessi spa; 5.11, 5.12 Priestman Goode; 5.13 Youmeus Design; 5.14 Pearson Lloyd Design; 5.15 Autodesk Inc.; 5.16 Dassault Systèmes; 5.17 Force Dimension, Switzerland; 5.18 Parametric Technology Corporation; 5.19 Pearson Lloyd Design; 5.20, 5.21 Iittala Group, Helsinki, Finland; 5.22 William Latham; 5.23 El Ultimo Grito; pp. 125-7 Linda Andersson; p. 128 Mario Bellini Associati; 6.1 Michael DiTullo; 6.2 Factory Design; 6.3 Pilipili Product Design and UGS; 6.4 Georg Baldele; 6.5 Factory Design; 6.6 Science Museum, London, and Science and Society Picture Library; 6.7 TEST Institution, Washington, DC.; 6.8 Daniel Weil and Pentagram; 6.9 Braun GmbH; 6.10 Sony Ericsson; 6.11 Jonas Hultqvist; pp. 138–40 Etienne Salomé; 6.12 Paul Collicut; 6.13 Mark Jones; 6.14 Alexander Åhnebrink; pp. 143–5 Mark Jones; 6.15–6.18 Raysan Al-Kubaisi; 6.19 UGS and Solid Edge; 6.20 SolidWorks Corp; 6.21 Next Limit Technologies, Madrid; 6.22, 6.23 Rio21 Design and Ashlar Inc.; 6.24 David O'Connor; 6.25 El Ultimo Grito; p. 154 Torsten Neeland; 7.1 RIBA, London; 7.2 BMW AG; 7.3, 7.4 Alan Pipes; 7.5 Brompton Bicycle Ltd.; 7.6 Ron Arad Associates; 7.7, 7.8 Bang & Olufsen; 7.9 RIBA, London; 7.10 UGS; 7.11 Rio21 Design and Ashlar Inc.; 7.12 Ron Arad Associates; 7.13 Institution of Mechanical Engineers, London; 7.14–7.16 Alan Pipes; 7.17 Héctor Serrano; 7.18 Alexander Åhnebrink; 7.19, 7.21 Torsten Neeland; 7.20 Ora Ito; pp. 172–5 Nelson Au and Seagate Technology; p. 176 SolidWorks Corporation; 8.1 SolidThinking Ltd.; 8.2 Brompton Bicycle Ltd; 8.3 Anglepoise Ltd, Waterlooville, Hampshire, England; 8.4 Science Museum, London; Science and Society Picture Library; 8.5 Alan Pipes; 8.6 Cooper-Hewitt National Design Museum, Smithsonian Institution, Washington, DC.; 8.7 Jan Frohm; 8.8 Torsten Neeland; 8.9 Institution of Mechanical Engineers, London; 8.10 Jaguar Cars, Coventry, England; 8.11 Ford Motor Company; 8.12 co-lab*; 8.13 Volkswagen AG; 8.14 UGS; p. 188 Ryan Whittaker and John Fox; 8.15 Ford Motor Company; 8.16 Mario Bellini Associati; 8.17 Jan Frohm; 8.18 UGS; 8.19 Youmeus Design; p. 192 James Wright; 8.20 UGS; 8.21, 8.22, 8.24 ITEDO & Granthams; 8.23 Corel Corp; p. 198 Ron Arad Associates; 9.1 Karim Rashid; 9.2, 9.3 Alessi spa; 9.4 Mathias Bengtsson; 9.5 UGS; 9.6 Dassault Systèmes; 9.7 Daniel Weil and Pentagram; 9.8 Héctor Serrano; 9.9 El Ultimo Grito.

"In the design process, drawing is the act of thought."
Sir Richard MacCormac

Introduction

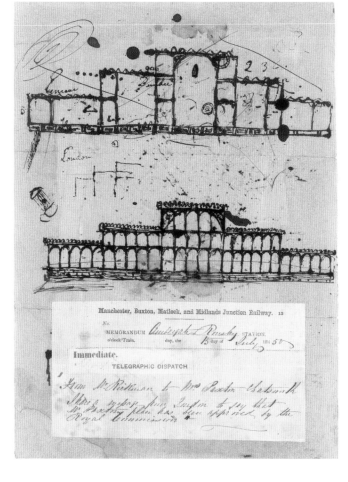

It's that Eureka moment: you have a brilliant idea and must get it down onto paper, using whatever is to hand (Fig. 1). That usually means the back of an envelope, or like Victorian engineer Joseph Paxton daydreaming about the design for the Crystal Palace during a boring committee meeting, a sheet of blotting paper (Fig. 2). Despite the ubiquity of computer systems, the humble pencil or ballpoint pen still has a place in the designer's toolkit. And that's not the end of it. The act of drawing stimulates another thought, and that demands another drawing, and so on (Fig. 3). Unlike today's computer model that insists on precision and finality, the sketch depicts perhaps a fuzzy idea of what could be before it actually exists. As designer Richard Seymour (*see* Case Study 1, p. 66) puts it: "A complex ballet of information processing, two-way non-verbal dialogue and extreme fine motor control allows us to process emotion, space, reality, and imagination, and offer it up to ourselves and others in a form that is instantly and universally understandable, regardless of what language you speak or how old you are."

Interest in the act of drawing has seen a resurgence—in design, as well as in art. Multidisciplinary drawing courses have appeared in colleges with titles such as

Above 3   Jordan B'2rue, 2004. Michael DiTullo produced this set of concept sketches and presentation drawings for Brand Jordan, a division of Nike. He used a Prisma pencil, markers and pastel on graphics paper, plus Illustrator finished in Photoshop.

Right 4   London-based Israeli designer Ron Arad uses a Wacom Cintiq graphics tablet and Corel Painter to draw directly into the computer. In this sketch, complete with still life, he has drawn the 2004 "Lo-Res-Dolores-Tabula-Rasa" table made from blank white Corian plastic and brought to life with film, music and images.

Right 5   American designer
Michael Graves designed the
Post-Modern but practical Kettle
with Bird for Alessi in 1985.
This is one of his initial concept
sketches.

Above 6   Kettle with Bird,
1985. The wide base fits a stove
top and the handle is blue where
it is cool to the touch. The red
ends signify heat and, of course,
a red bird whistles when the
kettle boils.

"Drawing as Process", aiming to demonstrate drawing as a necessary tool in the thinking process across the boundaries of art, design and technology. At final-year art school shows it is heartening to see that graduating students are still taught drawing along with how to use 3D computer modeling software—and using marker pens too, albeit the drawings are finished, fine-tuned and "airbrushed" later using a computer. The drawings of product designers such as James Dyson and Terence Conran can be seen in lifestyle magazines, alongside photographs of the real objects. Some of the most enthusiastic drawers are architects turned product designers, such as Ron Arad (Fig. 4), Michael Graves (Figs. 5 and 6) and Aldo Rossi. And many designers, for example Perry King (Fig. 7), Philippe Starke and Ross Lovegrove, take great joy in exhibiting their drawings whenever they can.

In this book, "design" encompasses product and industrial design, what American designer Raymond Loewy said ranged "from the toothbrush to the locomotive ... the lipstick to the ocean liner", so we include vehicle/automotive design and the design of other 3D artefacts such as jewelry, footware and furniture.

The chapters of this book follow the progress of the design process: from initial concept sketches, where designers struggle for a solution while satisfying the constraints introduced by the client's marketing and production demands; through presentation drawings and visualizations to keep the client informed; to general arrangement and detail drafting; to fully dimensioned engineering production drawings for the parts themselves plus the tools, moulds, or dies required to manufacture them; and beyond—to technical illustrations and the exploded diagrams used for publicity and instructing the end user in the product's assembly, operation and maintenance. Each stage has its own type of drawing tools and methods.

What is a designer's drawing for?

Designers of products—be they automobiles, chairs,
industrial machinery or pasta shapes—like architects,
also have a special relationship with their drawings. For
them, drawings must embody and convey information
about complex three-dimensional shapes, endowing new
products that may be unfamiliar to the consumer with
personality and ease of use (Fig. 8).

> A designer's drawing has three main functions:
> – It is a means of externalizing and analysing thoughts
>   and simplifying multi-faceted problems to make
>   them more understandable.
> – It is a medium of persuasion that sells ideas to clients,
>   and reassures them that their brief is being satisfied.
> – It is a method for communicating complete and
>   unambiguous information to those responsible for
>   the product's manufacture, assembly and marketing.

In addition, once the product has been designed, the
designer may be expected to produce further drawings—
called technical illustrations—that instruct the end user
in the product's operation.

Drawing in product design

Product designers, unlike architects, can be self-deprecating about their drawings. They modestly say: "the drawing is just a means to an end, the important thing is the finished product." And when the project is over, early exploratory drawings are often destroyed, cleared away to make room for the next job. Nevertheless, when pressed, designers admit to deriving great pleasure from the act of drawing and are quick to praise a colleague's skill in representing on paper a three-dimensional object. The product designer's art is therefore often a hidden one.

A designer who cannot draw well is at a disadvantage. Despite the important role of the concept block model (many designers need something solid and tangible they can hold and move around), drawing is the fundamental means of externalizing ideas and then communicating those concepts to other members of the design team, to clients and managers and on to those responsible for production.

The importance attached to design as "functional problem solving" in the mid-twentieth century had the effect of relegating drawing to that of a frivolous activity, a necessary evil. Styling has been used as a derogatory term. Post-Modernism, by restoring colour, texture and ornamentation as deserving attributes of a design, has also emphasized the idea of design as differentiation. There is no such thing as the "ideal" car or jug kettle; the look of a product will change inevitably with fashion. Aesthetics are marketable commodities. And it follows that if a design cannot be generated automatically from a functional specification, it will have to be drawn (Fig. 9). Electronic goods, for example, are no longer restricted to the "form follows function" rule, and can be made in any shape that can be manufactured.

A designer needs to be a paragon, proficient in a whole range of apparently disparate drawing skills. At the concept stage, as well as being able to clarify on paper his or her own thoughts, it is crucial to be able to explain in a few economically placed lines, perhaps at a briefing meeting with the client, exactly how the as yet non-existent product will look, feel and fit together, demonstrating that all the various specifications imposed on the designer by the client's brief will be resolved within budget.

Designers must know how to convey information about complex, often freeform, shapes and are asked to demystify unfamiliar products, perhaps inspired by a quantum leap in technology—such as cell phones, digital cameras and MP3 players—giving them user-friendliness and perhaps making their shapes metaphors or clues for their efficient use.

Below 9   Is it an umbrella stand, or is it a flower pot? Karim Rashid, who was born in Cairo, raised in Canada, and now works in New York, designed the sculptural *Plomb* in 2001 for the Italian company Serralunga. This playful concept sketch was drawn in ballpoint pen. (*See also* figs. 17 and 18)

Right 10   This 3D rendering
of the Kenwood travel kettle,
2001, by the London design group
Youmeus was produced using
Autodesk AliasStudio (formerly
Alias StudioTools).

Drawing by hand or computer

Two-dimensional CAD (computer-aided design) was
once affordable by only the largest firms and practices.
Only a decade ago, solid 3D photo-realistic rendering
could only be attempted by supercomputers. Now it is
commonplace and, like it or not, the computer has become
an indispensable tool for the designer, integrated into the
design process at almost every stage (Fig. 10). It is an
enabling technology with the potential to restore to
designers complete control over their designs, something
that was temporarily denied them when the demands of
the Industrial Revolution led to the division of labour and
the fragmentation of the design-to-production stream.

CAD has proved a mixed blessing to the designer.
It can speed up, smooth out and concatenate the design
process, but it also makes the designer more responsible
and accountable for the integrity of the final design.
The mathematical efficiency of the CAD system eliminates
"draughtsman's license" from the drawings, when precision
could be sacrificed for the sake of appearance, with non-
square corners and bent "straight" lines joining up two
carelessly measured points. The designer has to work hard
to resolve any potential production problems upfront,
where the implications of any changes are cheaper, and

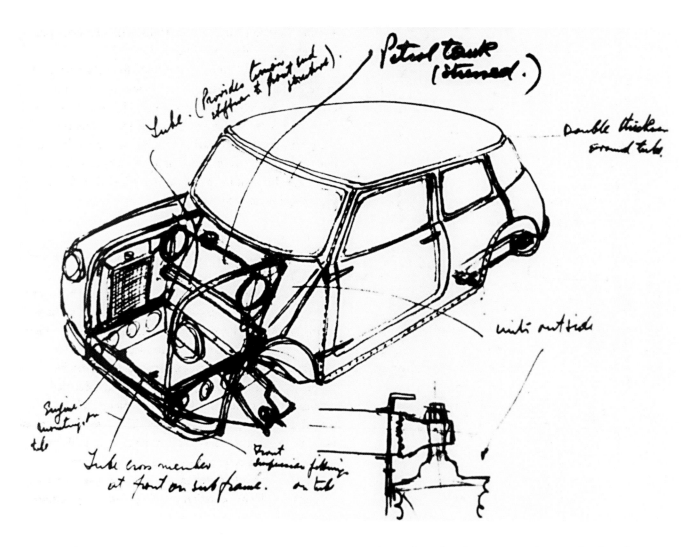

Above 11   The Austin Mini
of 1959 revolutionized small car
design and became a symbol for
the Swinging Sixties. This 1957
concept sketch by (Sir) Alec
Issigonis reveals his method
of working: His fluid drawings
were merely meant to communicate
engineering details to his assistants.
Courtesy Motoring Picture Library,
National Motor Museum,
Beaulieu, England.

not leave them for the patternmaker on the shopfloor
to inherit and sort out later.

Hand-drawn "artists' impressions" can still be seen,
however, to show the human hand of the designer and as
an expression of the lifestyle context in which the artefact
will exist. A rough concept sketch, executed in pencil or
ballpoint pen on paper, can also reassure a client that the
proposed design is still a work in progress and not yet
fixed and finished (Figs. 11, 12).

What is design?

What are we talking about when we say "design"? There
are lots of definitions. Is it simply "preparing for action"?
Or "a search process in a space of alternative solutions,
seeking one or more that satisfy certain design criteria"?
Or "a process of recursive conjecture-analysis operating
within the framework of abduction, deduction and
induction, proceeding on the basis of a series of paradigm
shifts to more detailed levels as the proposal becomes more

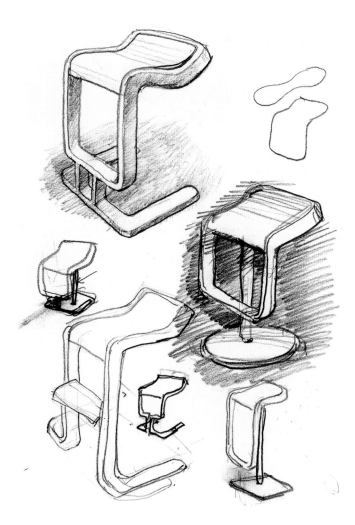

Above 12 Pencil sketches by the London-based Japanese designer Shin Azumi show him exploring concepts for the *Lem* high stool for Lapalma, Italy, 2000. The high stool won the FX International Design Award, UK Product of the Year 2000.

specific"? Or, to paraphrase surrealist Marcel Duchamp, is design what a designer does?

It is not the intention of this book to explore or review current thought on design methods and theories; there are several books on these topics listed in *Further reading*. This book is constructed on the assumption that the design process as practised proceeds along the following lines and that drawings are an integrated part of that process, a different form of drawing using the different tools required at each stage.

The design process

The designer or design practice first receives a commission from a client, in the form of a design brief. The client's marketing people have presumably identified the need for a new product. A team is then set up, comprising perhaps a project leader and various professionals: a stylist, a design engineer and so on. They meet the client and sort out a timescale with deadlines, talk about fees, and maybe negotiate a more detailed brief, preferably in a detailed document that spells out all the requirements, called a product design specification (PDS). The designers go away to think, search around for old envelopes to scribble onto the backs of, and eventually—according to the agreed schedule—submit to the client a series of proposals, usually accompanied by presentation drawings and physical models.

The concept sketch

The first stage is the concept sketch (Chapter 5). A concept sketch can be defined theoretically as "a collection of visual cues sufficient to suggest a design to an informed observer". It is likely to be executed in pencil or fibretip pen as the designer is exploring possibilities and doesn't yet want to be tied down to a particular approach (Figs. 13, 14).

Presentation drawings

The second stage, a presentation drawing (Figs. 15, 16), is something completely different (Chapter 6). Here the intention is to show the client or financier a selection of highly rendered images, as realistic looking as possible, so that a decision can be made to go ahead with the project. These once were marker or pastel drawings on board, but increasingly this will be a drawing started using manual methods but finished using a 2D image processing program, such as Adobe Photoshop, or even a fully rendered 3D "solid" computer model (Fig. 17). The drawings will consist of computer printouts, on-screen presentations, or even animations. Airbrush, once the preferred medium for special presentations, is no longer

Right 13   The *Zeppelin* lamp for Flos by Dutch designer Marcel Wanders was inspired by Achille Castiglioni's 1960 cocoon lamp. Here Wanders explored early concepts on squared paper, 2005.

Below 14   Alvar Aalto's almost abstract free-flowing shapes in three-dimensional form were drawn in crayon on cardboard for the 1937 Paris World's Fair. These concept sketches of glass vases for Iittala Glassworks, Finland, are the precursors of his *Savoy* vases, still in production, and were inspired by Eskimoerinden Skinnbuxa (the leather trousers of an Eskimo woman). Courtesy Iittala Group, Helsinki, Finland.

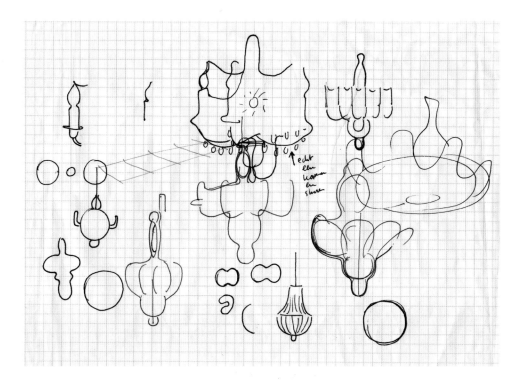

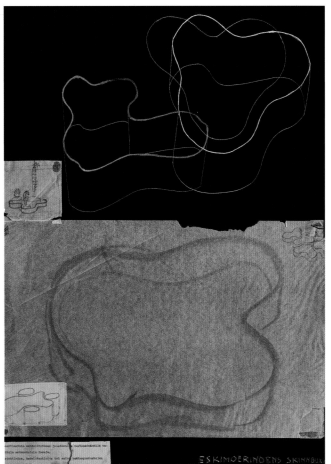

cost-effective or even necessary for design projects with tight deadlines.

The client deliberates and evaluates these proposals, and accepts one of the variations or a composite constructed from portions from two or more of them. For some designers and design studios, this may already be the end of the story and they will hand over the concept documentation (and maybe a computer model) to the client to progress and ultimately manufacture.

The general arrangement (GA) drawing

So-called "engineering design" is something that happens downstream of the concept design, or is concerned with the inner workings of more complex objects and systems, and is included here as an essential stage of the design process—the third stage (Chapter 7). Those designers who take the design process forward after the presentation then receive the go-ahead to get down to details—producing first a GA (general arrangement) (Fig. 18) drawing, and later all the detailed dimensioned drawings for production and assembly (Fig. 19). They will liaise with technical people, who may be subcontracted to be responsible for special requirements, such as stress analysis or the use of new materials. Some design consultancies will produce a working prototype.

In the past these engineering drawings were created using technical ink pens on vellum or tracing paper (Fig. 20). They are almost universally generated these days using 2D CAD. More progressive firms are using 3D solid

Right 15   The CC Cruiser, a Dutch/American collaboration between John Kock (Springtime Industrial Design) and Tucker Viemeister (Springtime, USA), is a battery-operated beverage delivery vehicle for Coca-Cola, on which the driver stands and rides, much like being on skis. This sketch, by Michiel Knoppert, was done using a black ballpoint pen, and was coloured and finished in Photoshop, 2001.

Below 16   The latest Mini Cooper S, a mixed media drawing by Frank Stephenson, employs pencils, markers, chalk, and gouache, 1998. Courtesy BMW Group.

Right 17   A computer rendering in SolidWorks of Karim Rashid's *Plomb* umbrella stand, 2001.

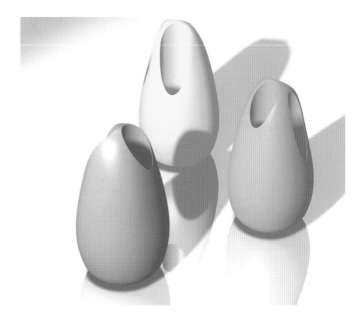

Below 18   These orthographic production drawings (using SolidWorks) for Karim Rashid's *Plomb* umbrella stand (for the Italian company Serralunga) show three different sections across the plan at the top of the drawing, 2001.

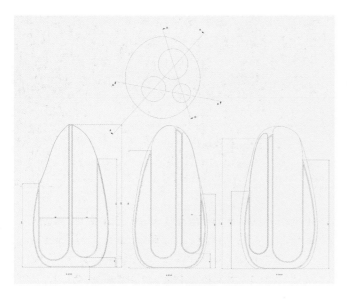

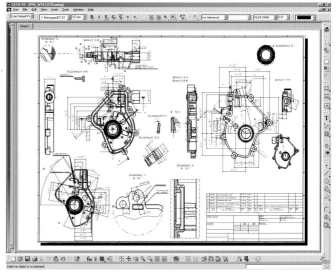

Above right 19   A screenshot showing 2D orthographic drawings produced by Dassault Systèmes and their CAD program Catia, 2006.

modeling, which encapsulates the complete geometry of the product, to ultimately drive the machine tools that will be used to make the product and all its parts. Producing a 3D computer model may be more akin to sculpture, but in this book it is treated as drawing, albeit in 3D space.

Technical illustrations

Finally, once the product is in production and all the design decisions are set in stone, technical illustrations (Chapter 8) will be required to inform the people responsible for assembling, maintaining, and using the product (Fig. 21). These drawings, again once produced using an airbrush, are now almost entirely created in the computer.

Right 20　A classic engineering drawing in ink on tracing linen by Sir Giles Gilbert Scott (1880–1960) for the iconic GPO telephone kiosk no. 2, 1924, showing a plan view, two elevations, and a section. Courtesy RIBA Library Drawings and Archives Collections, London.

Below 21　A 3D exploded technical illustration of a Dyson vacuum cleaner motor created using UGS NX (formerly known as Unigraphics) software, 2003. The carbon-free X020 has no brushes, no magnets and no commutator.

In a one-person practice, all these activities may be undertaken by the same person; in a multi-disciplinary practice, the job will be distributed to several specialists. The designers' involvement may end with the styling model, or the designers may be brought in after the package-constrained object has been sketched out, to do a "packaging" or styling job. All practices are different, and individual designers within a practice may work in different ways (see the case studies throughout this book that take a more detailed look at the day-to-day operation of various different design studios).

Design can be top-down: starting with a clean sheet of layout paper and producing a free-ranging solution that could be any shape as long as it satisfies certain functional criteria (Figs. 22, 23). Or design can be bottom-up: to design a new car or television set for example, the designer is given a collection of already engineered pre-sourced components, such as a motor or cathode-ray tube, with a standard printed-circuit board or two, and given the task of combining them and containing them into a unified aesthetic whole (Figs. 24, 25).

Right 22   Danish designer
Mathias Bengtsson's sculptural
Slice chair of 1999 combined
computerized laser-cutting
technology with handwork to
create a series of chairs and
chaise longues in plywood and
aluminum. This expressive
concept drawing was executed
in conté crayon.

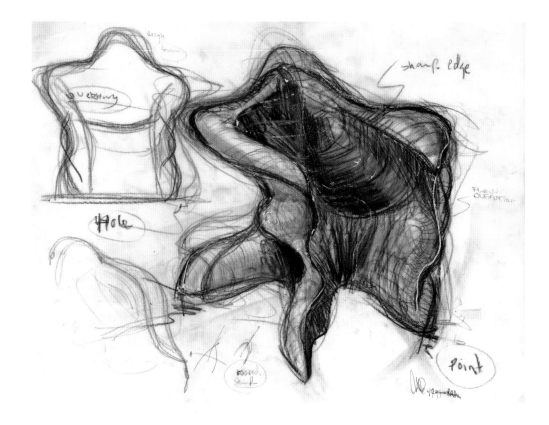

Left 23   The finished *Slice*
chair looks organic but could
only be realized using computer
technology. Each layer was cut out
of sheet material into complex
shapes by a computer-controlled
laser. The 2D layers were then
assembled by hand into a 3D
solid form, 1999.

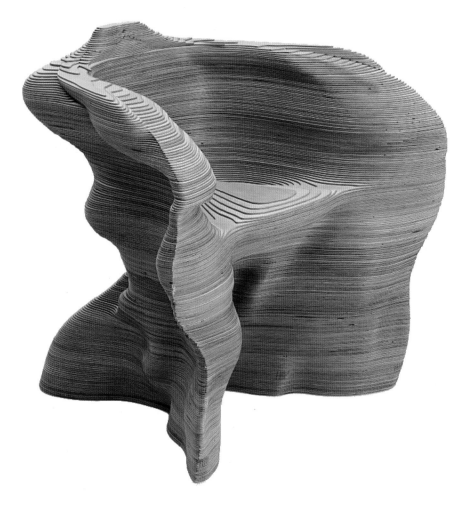

Right 25   This product photo of
the Moulinex Robot Marie Hand
Mixer, 2004, demonstrates how
George Sowden managed to
achieve an aesthetic and tactile
form from an unpromising
schematic.

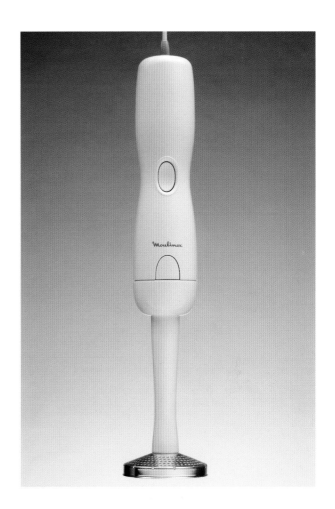

Below 24   Milan-based George
Sowden's concept sketch for the
Moulinex Robot Marie Hand
Mixer, 2004, is a good example
of a package-constrained
schematic drawing. Pre-sourced
components such as a motor and
a gearbox have to be squeezed
into the design before styling
the external skin of the product.
(*See also* Fig. 2.24)

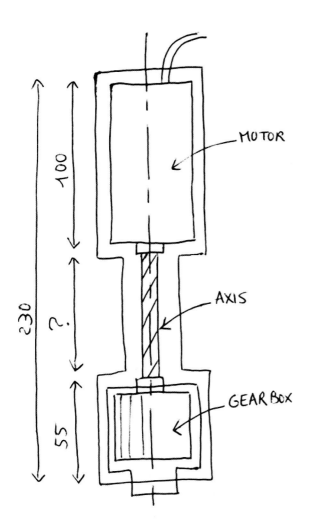

An average product, if there is such a thing, will be a synthesis of proprietary items bought-in from catalogues, such as electric motors, springs, nuts and bolts, combined with known parts, available parts and parts that have to be specifically tailored to the particular product being designed. The design will be constrained by the suitability and properties of the raw materials—sheet steel, for example, comes in standard thicknesses—and by the manufacturing techniques to be employed—a plastic object, for example, will need a taper if it is to be released easily from its mould. Batch size too has implications for the design. For capital goods, produced in, say, batches of ten, it may not be economic to invest in the kind of expensive tooling necessary for mass-produced consumer goods.

Conclusion

The chapters that follow divide the design and drawing process into these four distinct phases. But before that are some introductory chapters on all the tools and techniques, both manual and computer, that you will need to be able to fulfil your role as a product/industrial designer.

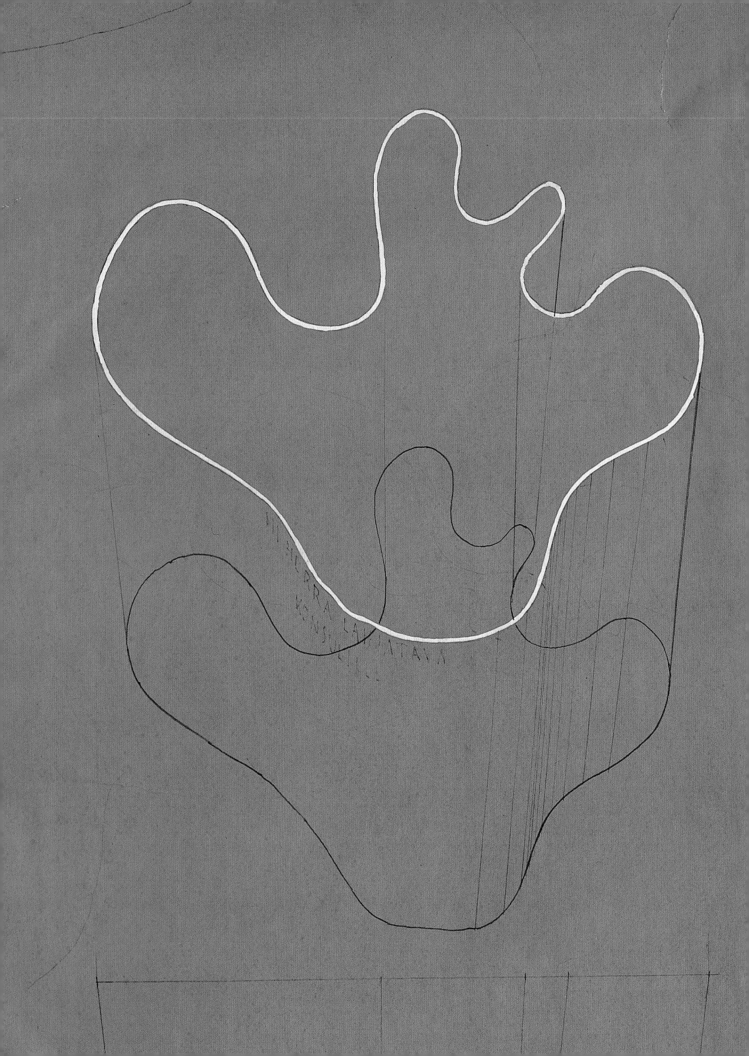

"Thought changes our life and our behavior. I also believe that drawing works in the same way. I am a great advocate of drawing, not in order to become an illustrator, but because I believe drawing changes the brain in the same way as the search to create the right note changes the brain of a violinist. Drawing also makes you attentive. It makes you pay attention to what you are looking at, which is not so easy."
Milton Glaser

1

A brief history of designers' drawings

Opposite Alvar Aalto, Glass vases, 1936. Crayon and cardboard collage. The artist made these concept drawings for Iittala Glassworks, Finland, for the 1937 Paris World's Fair. These vases were the precursors of Aalto's Savoy vases and were inspired by Eskimoerinden Skinnbuxa (the leather trousers of an Eskimo woman). Courtesy Iittala Group, Helsinki, Finland. (*See also* figs. 13, 5.20, 5.21)

Designers and makers have been drawing since the beginning of civilization. The first link between drawing and manufacture can be traced to the time when, according to Greek legend, Dibutades traced round the shadow (a projection) of her lover, which her father then cut out and made into a sculpture. Symbolic or schematic drawings have been in evidence since the Bronze Age—there is a plan view of an ox-drawn plough dated to 1500 BC at Fontanalba —and similar schemes can be seen in Egyptian paintings.

Right 1.1   Paolo Uccello (1395–1475), Chalice, c.1430–40. Pen and ink on paper. This perspective study of a chalice bears an uncanny resemblance to a CAD wireframe drawing. Courtesy Bridgeman Art Library, London.

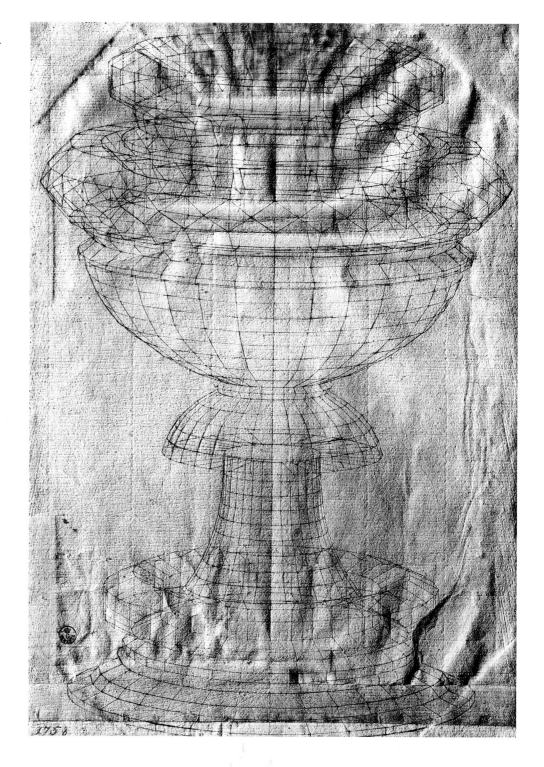

Above 1.2   Matthew Boulton
and James Watt, General view
of a steam engine, 1795. Pen and
ink, washed and shaded with
watercolour, 11⅝ x 16½ in
(29.5 x 41.8 cm). Courtesy
Institution of Mechanical Engineers,
London.

The ancient Greeks laid down the foundations of geometry and the methods of Euclid were taught almost exclusively until the end of the nineteenth century. Greek astronomers, notably Apollonius of Perga (c.262–190 BC) around 250 BC, conceived the notion of projections and understood both orthographic (also known as parallel) and stereographic (or conical) projections in their flattened maps of the semi-spherical heavens. A great number of Greek writings have been lost over the centuries, so it is perfectly possible they knew of perspective, especially considering that stereographic projection is a special form of generalized perspective.

Both the Renaissance artist Paolo Uccello (1397–1475) (Fig. 1.1) and architect Filippo Brunelleschi (1377–1446) are credited with inventing the principles of perspective from around 1420. This is not to say that in drawings the third dimension did not exist prior to the Renaissance, for various kinds of non-converging oblique projections can be seen in drawings from all cultures from the earliest times.

In the Middle Ages, drawings—it appears to our modern eyes—gave more emphasis to the mechanical

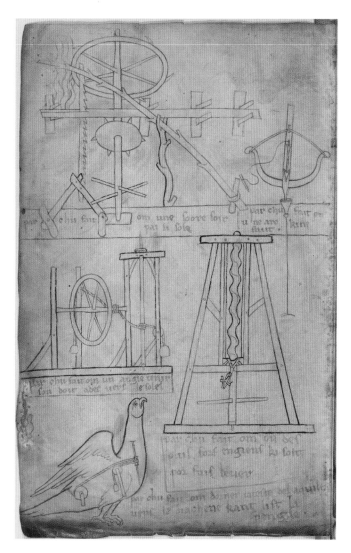

Above 1.3 Villard de Honnecourt, Machines, c.1220–1235. Leadpoint on parchment with a sepia wash. These machines, drawn by the medieval mason (or clerk) Villard de Honnecourt (fl.1190–1235), look naive by current standards, due to his diagrammatic approach to the third dimension. However, they served as an aide mémoire and hardcopy record for master craftsmen and inspired the nineteenth-century gothic revival. Courtesy Bibliothèque Nationale de France, Paris.

features and attributes of a machine than to depicting physical reality. The Abbess Herrad of Landsberg (c.1130–1195), in her *Hortus Deliciarum* (Garden of Delights) of 1160, for example—a compendium of all the sciences and crafts studied at that time—sacrificed geometrical truths and comparative sizes and positions of components in favour of describing, in the conventions of the time, how the undershot mill (or whatever the subject matter in question) actually worked. Her empirically produced drawings are as inscrutable and difficult to "read" as an engineer's orthographic (plan and elevation) drawings are to the layperson of today.

The influence of art and architecture

The many types of drawing currently used by designers evolved independently of each other in different disciplines during the Middle Ages in Europe. The "one object, one drawing" school of thought can be traced down from the perspectivists; the multi-view (plan and elevations) approach came mainly from the architects.

The earliest documented plan of a building is carved on a statue of Gudea from Ur (a city in southern Mesopotamia, in present-day Iraq)—and now in the Louvre—and is dated to 2130 BC. It depicts a drawing of a ziggurat—a temple with stepped sides—carved onto a drawing board, with accompanying drawing instruments. A plan view appeared to be sufficient for master stonemasons to build cathedrals for many centuries. Amédée-François Frézier (1682–1773) is reputedly the first architect to have shown plans and elevations drawn together, to scale and projectionally linked by means of construction lines, in 1738.

The architectural method, being a mature methodology, crossed over into mechanical engineering at the start of the Industrial Revolution—the late-eighteenth-century steam engine drawings of Matthew Boulton and James Watt (Fig. 1.2) are reminiscent of architectural drawings of the time, finished as they are in watercolour washes, with shading and added shadows to heighten the realism.

The history of design drawing goes hand in hand with the development of drawing instruments. Euclidean geometry demands only compasses and a straight edge. Protractors and set squares were invented much later and were derived from master masons' tools, such as those in the c.1220–1235 sketchbooks of Villard de Honnecourt (Fig. 1.3).

In Napoleonic times, Gaspard Monge (1746–1818) revolutionized design thinking in 1795 with his theories of "descriptive" geometry. By 1868, Englishman A. W. Cunningham was writing that in continental Europe there were "elegant drawing methods through which all manner of three-dimensional problems could be tackled on paper". Craftspeople did undoubtedly make drawings, even though they were probably scratched on slate, chalked on a blackboard or inscribed *in situ* on the material to be worked on. But Cunningham wanted to see systematic drawing education replace custom and practice.

Obscurity almost befell Sir William Farish (1759–1837), another pioneer of drawing methods, whose 1820 work on isometrics (*see* Chapter 2) languished for many years in an academic journal.

Early in the nineteenth century, almost all design drawings were produced directly by engineers and craftspeople, but the sheer volume of work consequently meant that less-skilled draughtsmen and copiers had to be employed. This led William Binns, in 1857, to develop the three-view orthographic or solid geometry drawing method (Monge's geometry only demanded two plane views) so that a highly finished drawing could be created from a designer's rough.

The influence of shipbuilding

The methods for representing complex "sculptured" surfaces—often curving simultaneously in two dimensions—derive mainly from the shipbuilding trades (Fig. 1.5). During the late sixteenth century, ship designs were conventionally drawn in three views: sheerplan (side view), draught (front view) and bodyplan (plan).

By the end of the seventeenth century, drawings had become more stylized. Rib sections were simplified by depicting only the outside curves, and because the ribs were symmetrical about a line running down the center of the ship, only half of each was drawn, stern to amidships shown on the left of a centreline, bow to amidships to the right (Fig. 1.4).

Various waterlines were also drawn, to show how the ship would sit in the water under various loads. These were abstracted into imaginary planes, which could themselves be used to define the shape of the hull: as curves in the plan view; straight lines in the elevations. A set of these "contours" could be used to define a solid streamlined body. More usually, however, they would be treated as an additional method, as a series of sections accompanying a conventional three-view drawing.

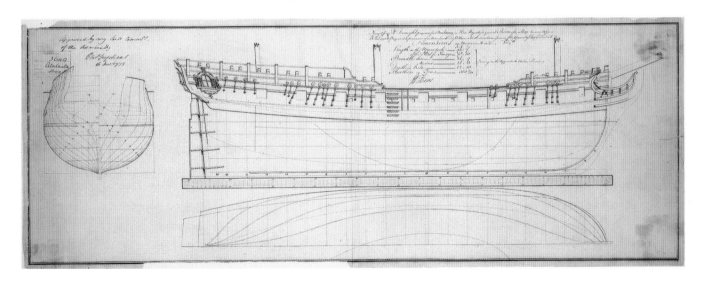

Above 1.4 The sloop *Atlanta*, 1775. Ink and watercolour drawing. This sketch is more like a twentieth-century engineering drawing, with its arrangement of half-plan (a ship is symmetrical), front and side elevation. Conventions were already being implemented: the contours of the ribs on the front elevation are depicted stern to amidships on the left, bow to amidships on the right. Courtesy National Maritime Museum, London.

Right 1.5   A sixteenth-century ship, c.1586, from Matthew Baker's *Fragments of Ancient English Shipwrightery*. Watercolour drawing with a schematic layout of the sails and rigging. This precursor to the presentation drawing was probably undertaken as a showpiece to record the external details of the ship. Courtesy Pepys Library, Magdalene College, Cambridge, England.

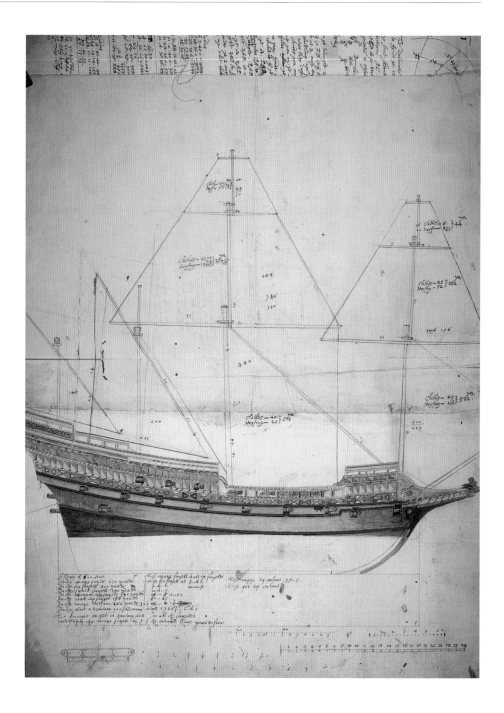

Mass production

When all products were handmade by a single workshop, drawings were not really necessary, but when mass production became commonplace they were much more important, especially if components were to be made at different locations and were then expected to fit together.

In 1815, the US military decided to manufacture standard muskets with interchangeable parts. The aim was that muskets could be stripped down, the parts thrown in a heap, mixed with parts from other armouries, reassembled randomly and always work first time.

Initially, "perfect" muskets were sent out to be copied. In 1852, Ferdinand Redtenbacher (1809–1863), a German engineer, thought of a better method. As a drawing is easier to handle than lumps of metal, it could be considered an instrument for design, imitating real objects on paper so that they can be assessed, any failings judged and incompatibilities smoothed out before an expensive prototype is fabricated. The use of a drawing as a symbolic representation of a product meant that the process of design could be separated from production, and the rate of production could be stepped up, with small, mass produced and standard component parts of the product being manufactured simultaneously.

This was arguably the beginning of the product design profession as it is recognized today (Fig. 1.6). A designer with a drawing was capable of a greater perceptual span than the craftsperson who came before; it soon became customary to send a tracing in ink, rather than the original, to the workshop. The First World War and the coming of reprographic methods of copying meant the end of colour codes, which had to be replaced by more legible mechanical tints or forms of cross-hatching in black and white.

Since 1927, engineering drawing practice has been the subject of national and international standards. In the UK, the appropriate code is British Standards Institution

Below 1.6 Charles Rennie Mackintosh, Chairs for the Ladies' Room at Miss Cranston's tea rooms in Glasgow, 1903. Pencil and watercolour on woven paper, 13 x 20 in (32.8 x 50.6 cm). These delicate wash studies use a simple elevation for overall dimensions and proportions, supplemented by a more deliberate perspective, placing the chair into its contextual environment. Photo © Hunterian Museum and Art Gallery, University of Glasgow. Mackintosh Collection.

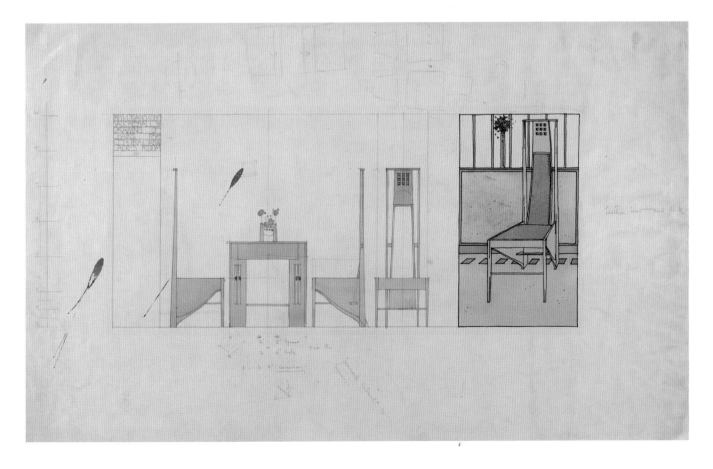

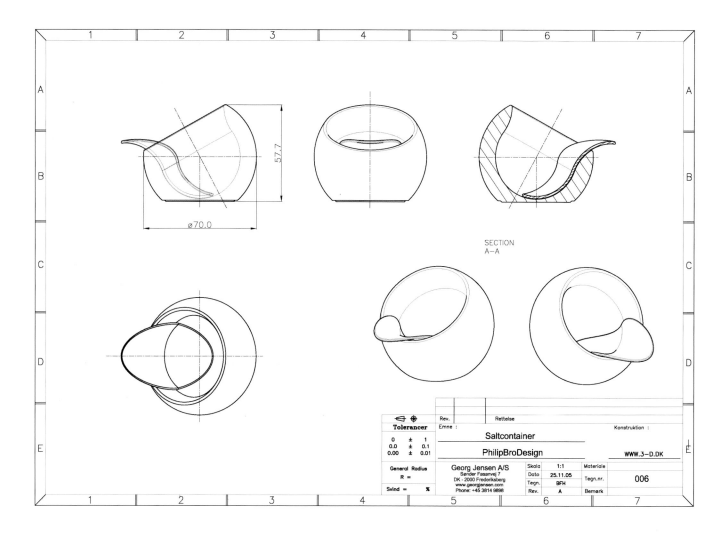

	Rev.		Rettelse			Konstruktion :
Tolerancer	Emne :					
0 ± 1			Saltcontainer			
0.0 ± 0.1			**PhilipBroDesign**			WWW.3–D.DK
0.00 ± 0.01						
General Radius	Georg Jensen A/S	Skala	1:1	Materiale		
R =	Sønder Fasanvej 7	Dato	25.11.05			
	DK - 2000 Frederiksberg	Tegn.	BFH	Tegn.nr.		006
Svind = %	www.georgjensen.com Phone: +45 3814 9898	Rev.	A	Bemærk		

SECTION
A–A

Above 1.7   *Philip Bro Ludvigsen for Georg Jensen, Pro/E CAD drawing of* Twist *salt container. Courtesy Georg Jensen, Denmark.*

BS8888 (replacing BS308); the US standard is ASME (American Society of Mechanical Engineers) Y14.5M. These standards include size formats, line types, lettering, dimensioning, the way sectioning should be carried out and such details as the symbols for representing screw threads. European countries have their own standards —in Germany, for example, set by DIN (Deutsches Institut für Normung)—and there is also an international standard, ISO 128. Designers, however, often take a pragmatic approach, using conventions with which they feel most comfortable. The standards issue is exacerbated by large companies having their own internal standards, and design practices can be forced under contract to conform to the client's "house style".

The presentation drawing is a relatively recent invention, whose development runs parallel with the growth of the design groups and their relationship with industry. The perspective "realism" of the presentation drawing has been challenged by design groups such as Memphis, who have used axonometric and oblique projections to communicate different truths about a product's form and function. Designers such as Aldo Rossi and companies such as Alessi go further, publishing philosophical "concept" sketches and contextual paintings to help sell the products they design.

The origins of computer-aided design

Today, CAD (computer-aided design) has the potential to return designers to the workshop days in which they take full responsibility for realizing their original concepts without compromise or interpretation by others on the factory floor.

The principles of automatic repeatability and programability in machines have their origins in the punched-card operated looms of Falcon (1728) and Jacquard (1800). Most present-day CAD systems derive from a computer program called Sketchpad, developed in 1963 and based on the PhD thesis of Ivan Sutherland at the Massachusetts Institute of Technology. Sketchpad had many of the features found in modern 2D drafting systems. For example, it was interactive: the designer could communicate instantaneously with the computer, whereas previously jobs would be processed in batches, sent away to a central computer, and the results received perhaps the next day. Furthermore, commonly used elements could be stored in "libraries" and called up when needed in new drawings. It should never be necessary, Sutherland insisted, to do the same thing twice.

Using CAD, drawings can be created full size at a scale of 1:1 (remember, the computer screen is just a window into the computer's database) and output later at all the different scale factors—1:20, 1:100, etc.—required by the various contractors and allied trades in a multi-disciplinary project (Fig. 1.7).

CAD can speed up the design-to-production process, getting better products out to market faster. It can unify the various stages in the design cycle, smoothing the transition between the once distinct phases of concept design, to visuals, to model, to parts drawings, into a seamless transmission of a single idea. With cleaner, legible and more precise drawings and 3D models, CAD eliminates ambiguity from designs, and allows better communication between engineers, designers, management and sales staff.

It is debatable whether CAD stifles creativity or not, but in expert hands it can give the designer the time to try alternative "what if?" solutions. CAD can be integrated with analysis, simulation and evaluation programs—to test a

design for strength and to check that it meets performance expectations—so that potential design failures are caught and eliminated on the screen, rather than later on the shop floor. And as legislation on product liability and safety becomes increasingly important to the manufacturing industry, CAD can help designers avoid errors, predict potential pitfalls and prevent them occurring, and control the escalating amount of complex data.

With CAD it is also easier to work out exactly how much a product will cost to make, and so the factory can reduce the amount of stock and work-in-progress on the shop floor.

Manually produced engineering drawings used to take up a great deal of physical space. Storing this information in a computer database not only makes it more accessible and more likely to be consulted, but liberates office space. Systems built around personal computers are now affordable by even one- or two-person companies, making them able to compete on equal terms with the largest multinationals. Like it or loathe it, CAD, like word processing, is here to stay. A designer may still use a pencil and paper right at the beginning of a project, but a computer will be used for the remainder of the process.

How drawing is taught

Can drawing be taught? Or is it simply a matter of unlearning? Is it a natural skill built into our genes? "Everyone can draw, until told they can't," is a quotation attributed to John Lennon, amongst others. Certainly, practice helps. The formal training many contemporary students receive may only be an hour's life drawing a week—and that's not compulsory. But it was not always so. The way drawing has been taught in the past, and the importance attached by a society to a drawing education, has had a fundamental bearing on how we regard drawing today.

In the mid-fifteenth century, the commentaries of Lorenzo Ghiberti and the systematic treatises of Leon Battista Alberti extended the basic theory and practice of drawing as the common unifying principle of the visual arts. For Leonardo da Vinci (Fig. 1.8), drawing had become "not only a science but a deity", permitting the precise exploration of areas where language is powerless. He saw painting as a science of knowledge but drawing as a method of enquiry. Drawing, he said, is the tangible form of the idea, the inventive act that

Right 1.8   Leonardo da Vinci, Flying machine. Ink drawing. This fanciful *macchina volante* (flying machine) is a pictorial concept sketch with notes. Leonardo often used exploded and cutaway drawings to help explain the inner workings of his inventions, and he almost invented orthographic projection by showing multiple views of the same object but always with an added third dimension. Courtesy Bibliothèque de l'Institut de France, Paris, France. Lauros/Giraudon/ Bridgeman Art Library.

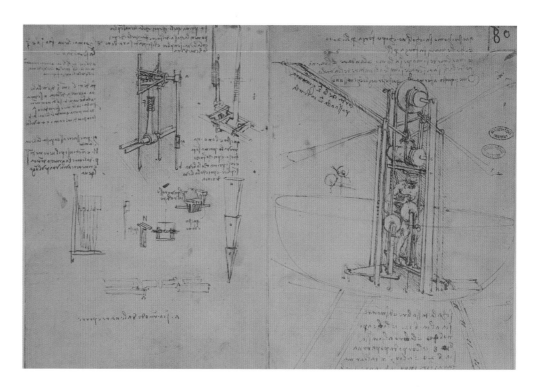

produces a work of art. This is echoed by Giorgio Vasari (1511–1574), who said: "Drawing is nothing else but a visible expression of the concept we have in our mind."

A drawing is thus a means of externalizing a concept, but it is also a very personal statement; it is something much more than just an arrangement of marks on paper. A drawing is an analogue of the real thing: a stylized collection of symbols, assumptions and learned shorthand that can be read, or misinterpreted, just like writing. David Hockney, in a preface to Jeffrey Camp's book *Draw: How to Master the Art*, says: "If you can draw, even a little bit, you can express all kinds of ideas that might otherwise be lost—delights, frustrations, whatever torments you or pleases you. Drawing helps you put your thoughts in order. It can make you think in different ways."

The codification of drawing

Drawing is a language that has been codified and formalized over the years and the way we draw influences the way we see. Form and harmony are not intuitive absolutes, but are the result of systematic drawing methods.

The codification of drawing began in the Renaissance but was perfected in the textbooks of the nineteenth century, in which axioms were presented to analyse design problems. Most of these textbooks taught drawing in a dry, linear style. This was true not only for mechanical design, but for the decorative arts as well, for example textile design, in which design was being constrained by the technology of the increasingly mechanized means of production.

An example of the dogmatism can be seen in William Robson's *Grammigraphia* (1799) which states: "Lines are four; perpendicular, horizontal, oblique and curve. All the variety of appearance in nature is presented by a combination of these four lines placed agreeably to proportion and position. A line is the continuation of a point. A point can proceed in four ways only and from these we can derive a mathematical account of all the common figures: angle, square, circle, ellipse, oval, pyramid, serpentine, weaving and spiral. Use line as distinct and as determinate as possible." Drawing based on empirical observation began to take a back seat.

In a period of national resurgence following the Napoleonic wars, the German states, especially Prussia, adopted the ideas of the Swiss educationalist Johann Heinrich Pestalozzi (1746–1827) in kindergarten schools. This *pedagogische Zeichnen* was quite distinct from expressionistic or *Kunstzeichnen* drawing and was based on an "alphabet" of simple geometric figures. The activity of drawing, according to Pestalozzi and his followers, begins with exercises that enlarge and develop a child's existing understanding of space and form.

Engineer and member of the Edinburgh Aesthetic Club, James Nasmyth, writing in 1883, said: "Viewing the abstract forms of the various details of which every machine is composed, we shall find that they consist of certain combinations of six primitive or elementary geometrical figures, namely: the line, the plane, the circle, the cylinder, the cone, and the sphere." This was not just a statement of fact and the practical problems of precision machining, it was also a statement of aesthetic intention. He was developing a visual grammar appropriate to the technology.

This pedagogical form of drawing became known as "conventional art" by the mid-nineteenth century. The expected manner of execution was hard, clear, unshaded pencil work. The designer Christopher Dresser (1834–1904) wrote in 1858 that: "drawing for decorative purposes should coincide with an architect's plans of a building. A series of drawings, which shall convey a perfect knowledge of every part."

Geometric versus naturalistic drawing

Dissent came from art critic John Ruskin (1819–1900) who, also in 1858, spoke of the savagery of geometric drawing. In its promotion of tonal and impressionistic drawing, his *The Elements of Drawing* was anti-linear and anti-geometric. Pedagogic drawing pointed towards an industrial future and the cult of the machine, so

naturalistic drawing (Fig. 1.9) pointed towards the handcrafted past and the cult of the vernacular. Despite the protests of Ruskin, pedagogic drawing was adopted by schools of design almost universally. It was factual, positive and modern.

By the end of the nineteenth century, art was being considered as a spontaneous creative impulse. Paul Cézanne (1839–1906) argued that: "conception cannot precede execution since expressions can never be the translations of clear thought. Drawings and paintings are no longer different factors: as one paints, one draws. The more harmony there is in the colours, the more precise the drawing becomes." Drawing had merged with the act of painting. And in the world of the artist, drawing is increasingly seen as a branch of art separate from painting.

Form follows drawing method

An attempt to teach art and design together was made at the Bauhaus (Fig. 1.10). This German movement had many sources, which included the "education through art" teachings of the Italian doctor Maria Montessori. The Bauhaus was preceded and influenced by the

Right 1.9   Søren Georg Jensen (1917–1982), Sterling silver candlestick no.1085, 1960. No matter their scale, the weight and density of his forms are held in a delicate balance with the spaces in between, enlivening their Modernist formality with a light, lyrical touch. The uncompromisingly simple pair of columns are given relief by the semi-hollowed outer edge. The design was revived, in stainless steel, in 2006. Courtesy Georg Jensen, Denmark.

Deutscher Werkbund of 1903, a movement in which
Lothar von Kunowski (1866–?) encouraged students
to "reveal the essence rather than the appearance of nature
and materials in order to achieve true expression". Peter
Behrens (1868–1940) trained as a painter and taught at
Nuremberg before he was appointed "artistic adviser"
to the electrical company AEG where he designed light
fittings, posters and the first Modernist building. He wrote
in 1907 that "inner laws determine form in architecture,
industrial design, and craft". His students were encouraged
to consider the intellectual principles of all form-creating
work and to attempt to discover and reconcile the laws
of art with those of technique and material.

In 1919, Walter Gropius (1883–1969) issued the founding
manifesto for the Bauhaus. He believed that art could not
be taught, but that craftsmanship could, so it stated that
six categories of craft training would be offered: sculpture,
metalwork, cabinet-making, painting and decorating,
printing and weaving. Drawing was listed separately and
would include landscape, still life, composition, freehand
sketching from memory and imagination, and "design
of furniture and practical articles".

At Weimar, drawing was taught by Johannes Itten
(1888–1967), who encouraged self-expression amongst the
students. He rejected "dead conventions" and also taught
that the laws of form and colour could be interpreted and
understood both intuitively and objectively. Before drawing
a circle, students had to experience a circle eurhythmically
by swinging their arms in the air. The three basic forms—
the square, triangle and circle—were experienced through
gesture, modelled in clay, and then represented graphically
on a 2D plane. Students were made to absorb the qualities
of materials by touching, handling and drawing from
memory, and to create new textures by montage and
collage. This would provide a sensuous appreciation of the
quality of materials that would lead to an understanding
on both an intellectual and emotional level of their
potential for design purposes.

Drawing in the early Bauhaus years, however, had
little to do with designing. In 1923, László Moholy-Nagy
(1895–1946) was instrumental in turning the crafts-based
workshops into "laboratories for evolving new type-forms
and norms for mass production". The concern was with
creating prototypes that would serve as guides to craftsmen
and industry, rather than drawings.

At Dessau in 1925, analytical drawing was taught by
the artist Wassily Kandinsky (1866–1944) as "an education
in looking, precise observation and the precise
representation not of the external appearance of an

Below 1.10 Herbert Bayer,
Magazine cover, 1928. As this
image shows, the Bauhaus taught
that the forms of products can be
assembled from simple "primitive"
geometrical shapes—the cone,
sphere, cube and so on. Computer-
aided solid modeling systems use
the same principles today.

object, but of constructive elements, the laws that govern the forces (= tensions) that can be discovered in given objects, and of their logical construction. An education in clearly observing and clearly reproducing relationships, where 2D phenomena are an introductory step leading to the three-dimensional."

Modernist design

The painter as a form giver was fundamental to early twentieth-century design theory. In the Dutch De Stijl movement, abstract painting demonstrated the universal laws of form. The rumbling car (baby wagon) of Gerrit Rietveld (1888–1964) was a demonstration that an object of beauty could be manufactured from mostly straight-machined parts (Fig. 1.11).

Gropius had hoped that the skill and vision of the painter could be directly applied to industrial production. But the activities of art and design proved too fundamentally different to mix successfully as Georg Muche (1895–1986) admitted in 1926 when he wrote: "The forms of industrial products, in contrast to the forms of art, are super-individual, in that they come

about as a result of an objective investigation into a problem … The limits of technology are determined by reality, but art can only attain heights if it sets its aims in the realm of the ideal."

The subject of drawing in design was given scant attention during the twentieth century, its role relegated to a necessary but relatively unimportant component of the design process. Modernism and its fundamental tenet of "form ever follows function" (an aphorism attributed to the American architect Louis Sullivan, 1856–1924) led to design being systematized through the 1960s, with an emphasis on word-game problem-solving skills. Drawing seemed too intuitive and obvious to be of any real help. Designers' drawings became invisible; they were always there, but not made public.

The joy of drawing

Post-Modernism, with its sometimes irreverent clash of art and design, again makes a show of the designer's drawing. Drawing is rarely discussed in the manifestos of groups such as Memphis, the Milan-based group led by Ettore Sottsass (1917–) (Fig. 1.12), but they are there to see, in

Right 1.11   Gerrit Rietveld, Baby wagon ("Rumbling car"), 1923. These sketches show a form developed from the same straight, machined lengths of wood used in the famous red/blue chair. The drawing uses an isometric projection, with details in elevation; architectural drawings from the De Stijl movement were rendered mainly in axonometric projection. Courtesy Rietveld Shröder Archive, Utrecht.

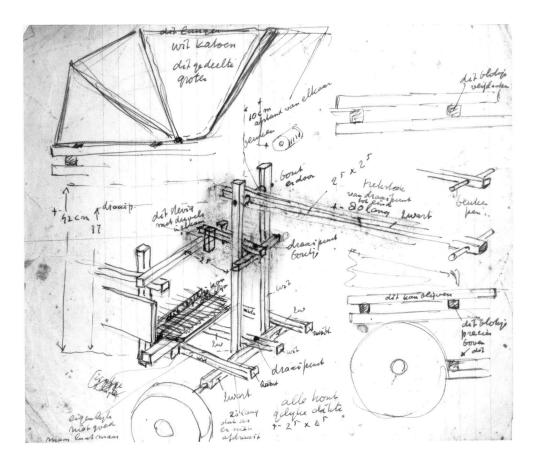

Below 1.12 Ettore Sottsass, Casablanca sideboard, 1981. Oblique drawing, ink and gouache. This was a key piece in the Memphis Group's first collection. The sideboard is veneered with brightly coloured and patterned laminates designed by Sottsass for the firm Abet Laminati. Courtesy Sottsass Associati EEIG, Milan.

Opposite 1.13 Henry Dreyfuss (1904–1972), Tractor, 1959. Drawing on yellow tracing paper. This drawing is a dramatic perspective study for the John Deere company. Courtesy Cooper-Hewitt, National Design Museum, Smithsonian Institution.

glorious technicolour, amongst the product photographs in the group's catalogues and publicity material.

Sottsass, and fellow designers such as Michele de Lucchi and George Sowden, were inspired to set up Memphis in 1981 by a line in a Bob Dylan song entitled *Stuck inside of Mobile with the Memphis blues again*: "Oh but your debutante just knows what you need, but I know what you want." Design is never the solution to a problem, says Sottsass, because no problem in the age of fashion and consumerism is a motionless event that can be isolated and grasped. Memphis designs endeavour not to convince, but to seduce, inventing functions and creating demands.

In a way, this echoes the stance made by the American "anti-Modernist" industrial designers of the 1940s, such as Harold Van Doren (1895–1957) and Walter Dorwin Teague (1883–1960), who, faced with the difficulty of finding an "honest" or "natural" form for new consumer products such as the vacuum cleaner, enclosed them in sleek, streamlined and visually simple shells, deliberately intended to appeal directly to the consumer and hence increase sales (Fig. 1.13).

At the very least, the achievement of Memphis, and of the other Post-Modernist groups, has been to reintroduce colour, pattern and ornament into design. Design today is not only solving functional needs, but creating fun, excitement and anticipation.

It could be argued that in the past objects were rectilinear because boxy shapes were easy to draw and represent in orthographic projection. CAD systems make repetitive features such as arrays of fine parallel lines easy to incorporate, and so they are. Now 3D modeling systems make it possible to design and manufacture organic freeform curvilinear shapes.

Memphis designers overhauled conventional means of representing three-dimensionality by using unexpected axonometric and oblique projections (which are also an indicator of their architectural training), and often prefer flat, cartoon-like colour to "realistic" rendering in order to stimulate an emotional reaction in the potential user of the products, who has been taught to equate "design" with "good taste".

Conclusion

Over the past two decades, the biggest influence on drawing has been the computer. Not only is the computer used routinely to finish off and enhance drawings started manually and then scanned into the computer for further manipulation in programs such as Adobe Photoshop, but the look of computer-rendered images has had an influence on the handmade drawing. The ubiquitous drop shadow of graphic design and the embossed and shaded logos so easy to achieve on the computer have made an appearance in hand-rendered pencil and marker drawings.

New York designer Tucker Viemeister believes that the designer's media of choice has a great and direct influence on the shapes and forms of the products created. "It is analogous to the role words play in the development of ideas. The Inuit have something like 137 different words for snow. Pantone dictates the number of colours we can use. Magic Marker technique suggests sharp shapes; pastels, smooth forms; Fome-Cor, crisp boxes; CAD, tricky intersections and repetitious vents and textures. You can see an obvious parallel between modern styles and design media."

Sottsass asserted that design should be "a real-time activity". Only the act of drawing, as opposed to modelmaking, can deliver the spontaneity to keep up with such a prolific and fertile creative mind. Sottsass, in his preface to Penny Sparke's 1982 monograph, laments about real life: "the daily grind, the anxiety, the confusion, the excuses of a headache or the radio that would not let you work in peace, the thousands of cards covered in sketches that seemed so brilliant because you never risked finishing them …" Despite this (ironic) melancholy, with designers such as Sottsass and the New American designers, the future of the design drawing is assured.

"Oh! che dolce cosa è questa prospettiva!"
"Oh! What a sweet thing perspective is!"
Paolo Uccello

2

Basic drawing skills

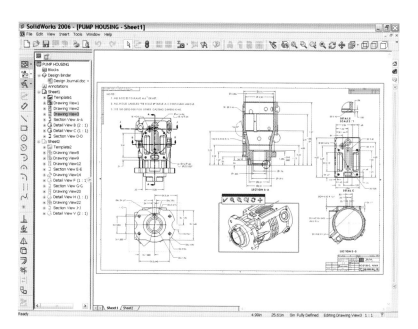

Right 2.1   Screenshot showing a
3D pictorial drawing (an isometric)
of a pump housing alongside the
2D orthographic drawings, 2006.
Courtesy SolidWorks Corporation.

Below 2.2   A shipwright's office,
from Matthew Baker's *Fragments
of Ancient English Shipwrightery*,
1586. This shows designers at work
on the plan of a ship. The drawing
is depicted as a true plan in this
"naive" watercolour and not, in
keeping with the rest of the picture,
in perspective. Courtesy Pepys
Library, Magdalene College,
Cambridge, England.

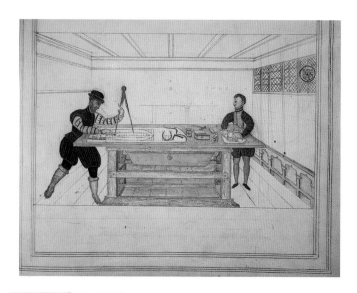

Most people, and that means most designers too, will draw
intuitively, albeit unconsciously, informed by the history
of art. They draw "by eye", in much the same way that a
self-taught musician will play "by ear". Any formal drawing
at school or college will be through life drawing, or maybe
learning to draw a still life by analysing the geometric
forms the objects approximate. You may also have been
shown the rules of perspective, drawing rows of telegraph
poles or trees by the side of a straight railway track or road
diminishing to infinity, all joined together by invisible lines
converging towards a theoretical vanishing point.

At the initial concept stage, your jottings are meant
for your eyes only and scant attention will be paid to any
formal means of representation; the main point is getting
the fleeting idea down on paper before it disappears. Later
in the design process, you will need to present those more
refined concepts to the client or co-workers, and the
drawing will have to look a little more realistic. Finally, to
communicate the detailed design to those manufacturing
the product requires precision to create a drawing that is
clear and full of information.

The aim of the product designer's drawing is to make
a representation of a real or imagined 3D object in marks
on 2D paper or pixels on a 2D computer screen (Fig. 2.1).
If the designer's intentions are to be communicated
faithfully to others in the design team and to those
responsible for manufacture, this drawing must be
a complete and unambiguous representation of the
designed object, and various conventions have grown
up over the years to expedite this process (Fig. 2.2). While
a pictorial sketch may be adequate at the earlier stages

Right 2.3 Erno Goldfinger, Metal chair with a spring seat, 1925. A classic set of orthographic drawings on architects' yellow tracing paper. Note that, as the chair is symmetrical, he has only drawn half of it in the plan view. Courtesy RIBA Library Drawings and Archives Collections, London.

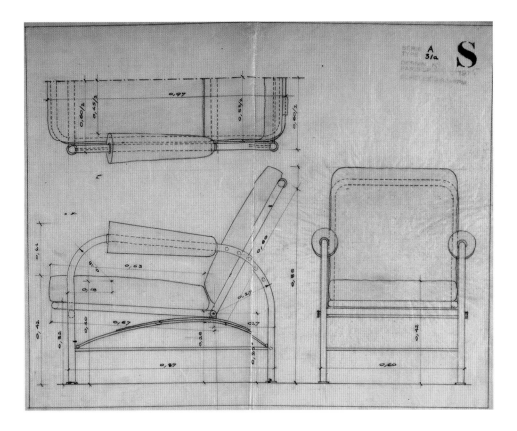

of design development, the 2D orthographic projection —a plan and two elevations (*see* Chapter 8)—is the conventional way of communicating the form and geometry of the product from design to production (Fig. 2.3).

But a set of orthographic drawings may not be sufficient to explain a complex 3D detail, and auxiliary views may be necessary. Orthographic drawings are also difficult for the layperson to visualize, to "read". So when a designer presents proposals to a client or manager it is now expected to be in the form of a 3D pictorial representation, usually a perspective drawing. Perspectives are so ingrained in the collective consciousness that most designers can draw them unconsciously. Here, for the more rigorous designer, a formal but simplified method has been included. Other non-perspective projections, used mostly by designers from an architectural background but gaining popularity amongst all designers, the metric projections of isometric, axonometric and so on—also known as paraline—are also described.

Perspectives

Practical perspective is a way of introducing systematic distortions into drawings to represent reality. Objects appear to diminish and their sides converge as their distance from the viewer increases. Lines drawn between the object and the observer will intersect the picture plane (or the sheet of drawing paper, which here is assumed to be held vertically in front of the viewer, normal to the line of sight) at various points (Fig. 2.4). A perspective drawing is made by plotting these points and connecting them together. The horizon is assumed to be infinitely distant so parallel lines will eventually meet at what are termed *vanishing points*.

A perspective, it should be remembered, is a simulation of reality—in real life there will be many changing vanishing points as the designer's (two) eyes and head move and wander around the scene.

It is likely that the rules of perspective were understood by the ancient Greeks or Romans, but it became a science during the Renaissance, with artists and architects such as Piero della Francesca, Leonardo da Vinci and Albrecht Dürer writing treatises and devising elaborate set pieces to show off their skills in constructing scientifically accurate views of the built environment.

Perspective aids (the descendants of the *camera obscura*) began to appear in the eighteenth century, notably James Watt's perspective apparatus, Cornelius Varley's graphic telescope, Peter Nicholson's perspective delineator (an instrument for drawing lines to inaccessible vanishing

Right 2.4   Alan Pipes. Perspective lines drawn between the object and the observer will intersect an imaginary window known as the picture plane (or the sheet of drawing paper, which here is assumed to be held vertically in front of the viewer), normal to the line of sight, 2003.

points) and William Hyde Wollaston's *camera lucida* (similar prism-based models are still available today). Most 3D computer modeling programs commonly contain interactive perspective routines.

Perspective drawings convey more or less the actual physical appearance of an object, so have considerable value in enabling the layperson, client or end user to appreciate the designer's vision. The underlying theories of perspective are complex, and second-hand shops are full of books, ancient and modern, outlining systems and methods for setting up perspectives, usually from orthographic projections which, from a design point of view, is putting the cart before the horse, and are of more use to the technical illustrator, who begins work when the design is finalized.

A designer will, more often than not, be generating a more finished perspective from a rough freehand sketch. The only time a designer might be working from 2D drawings would be in the case where a series of design proposals are constrained to enclose pre-sourced components.

Constructing a perspective

The art of constructing a credible perspective is in choosing the viewpoint, and hence the position of the horizon and the vanishing points. A well chosen viewpoint will give an impression of size and scale, will show off the object to the best advantage, and bring to the fore its most important features. Small objects, such as mobile phones, are usually viewed from above. A long thin object, such as a railway locomotive, might need an accentuated amount of perspective to give it length as it recedes. The vanishing point will be near to the object. A short squat object, such

as a washing machine, will be closer to the isometric, with almost parallel edges and infinitely distant vanishing points.

Consider too the composition of the drawing, and the positioning of the object on the paper. In most industrial design applications it is an advantage to render perspectives at or near full size. This is obviously not always possible for furniture and large-scale machinery, and automobile designers are usually content with just a full-size elevation on the wall. Before computers, full-size templates for parts of ships, for example, were drawn out in vast lofts, often above the workshops where the parts would be fabricated.

Designers will mainly use two-point perspective, that is, with two vanishing points. One-point perspective—with one vanishing point towards which all lines except those normal (at right angles) to the viewer's sight line will recede and converge—is fine for drawing railway lines or long, straight roads with telegraph poles either side, but not much use for the average product. It is more appropriate for drawing interiors or vistas, though it can be used to show the layout of components inside, say, a computer or piece of electrical equipment. (The height of the pole, incidentally, can be deduced by the proportion of it between the horizon and the ground, which corresponds to the height of the viewer's one eye above sea level; see below.)

The imaginary lines that join horizontal lines of a building, say, to the vanishing point, are called sight lines, guide lines or orthogonals—receding parallel lines at right angles to the field of vision. A vertical axis through the vanishing point is called the viewer's location point. One-point perspective assumes that the viewer is at a fixed point looking with one eye through the "window" of the paper into the 3D world beyond, and artists such as Dürer

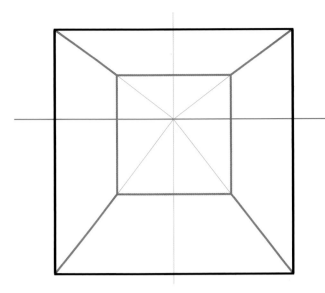

Above 2.5 One-point perspective, with one vanishing point towards which all lines except those normal (at right angles) to the viewer's sight line will recede and converge, is fine for drawing railway lines or interiors, but not much use for the average product.

Below 2.6 Two-point perspective has two vanishing points, placed on the horizon to the left and right of the object. A vertical axis through the vanishing point is called the viewer's location point.

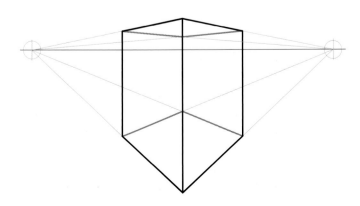

have used devices and grids to peer through as an aid to creating perspectives from a fixed point (Fig 2.5).

The cube as a basic perspective unit

Two-point perspective has two vanishing points, placed on the horizon to the left and right of the object (Fig. 2.6). The closer the vanishing points are, the more distorted and exaggerated the perspective. Verticals, however, will remain parallel. The visual field of our eyes is around 60 degrees, with some awareness for a further 30 degrees. Within these limits, two-point perspective works well. Traditional systems for setting up a perspective can be inaccurate, complicated and time-consuming, but, more importantly, the methods are prescriptive, in that you need a plan and elevations before you can construct the perspective.

Jay Doblin's 1956 system is a simplified method tuned to the needs of designers. It uses a cube as a basic perspective unit to measure height, depth and width concurrently. If you can construct a cube in perspective, it can then be multiplied and subdivided to build up a framework for describing any shape of object.

Doblin's system imagines the viewer standing on an infinite tiled floor, comprising perfectly square tiles (Fig. 2.7). If the line of sight is 45 degrees to the sides of the tiles, along a diagonal, it will meet the horizon at the *diagonal vanishing point* (DVP). Lines projecting from the sides of the tiles will meet the horizon at the left and right vanishing points, which will be equidistant from the DVP. The side-to-side diagonal will be horizontal and parallel to the horizon. It will experience no convergence and so provides a constant unit of measurement. Using this grid, a cube of any rotation can be constructed, which, with the proviso that it is placed in a position between the centre and around halfway to the vanishing points and that its nearest angle is greater than 90 degrees, will look suitably undistorted.

This cube can be subdivided by first intersecting the diagonals to find the midpoint. A circle within a true square will have its centre at the intersection of the diagonals and will be tangent at the midpoints of the sides of the square. A circle in perspective is, in fact, an ellipse, although it appears to be asymmetrical—the half nearer the viewer is obviously less foreshortened and looks fatter. This is not an anomaly. What has happened is that the major axis of the ellipse (the line that divides the ellipse into two equal halves along the longest dimension) is tilted from the vertical. Concentric circles in perspective, as you

Step by step 1:
Constructing a 30°/60° Doblin perspective
by James Wright

SS 1.1   James Wright first draws a Doblin cube. This is particularly important as the object that he is drawing is predominantly a cubic shape.

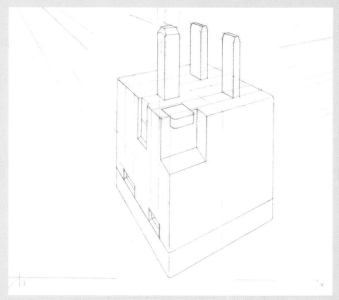

SS 1.2   He accurately draws in the parts and details using the actual object as a guide, if possible. He pays attention to scale, proportion and perspective. He puts in more perspective lines to help. He corrects the drawing as he goes along. He has to be as accurate as possible; this will mean fewer adjustments later.

SS 1.3   Once correct, James traces the drawing onto a clean sheet. He decides how he wants the object to look, where the lightest areas will be, where the shadows will be, etcetera. Then he uses pencils to create the surfaces he wants. He tries to be realistic with shadows and light according to the object, but he manipulates the object slightly if need be to create the drawing he wants, as long as it still looks realistic.

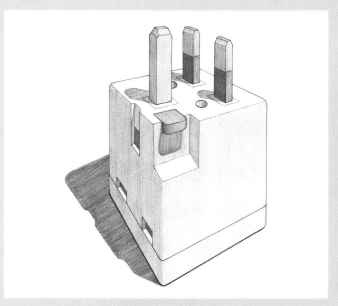

SS 1.4   He uses technical drawing pens of different line widths and a ballpoint pen to draw around the edges to strengthen the image, paying attention to line weight. He adjusts areas of light and dark until the image has the impact that he wants. He finally tidies up the image.

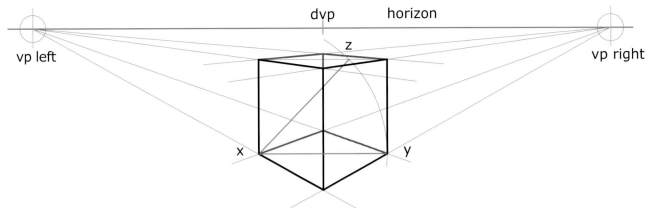

Above 2.7   A cube drawn using Doblin's 45°
method. Draw a horizon and place vanishing points
(vp) left and right. Bisect the horizon between them
to locate the diagonal vanishing point (dvp).
A vertical dropped from here will be a diagonal on
a horizontal perspective square; the other diagonal
will be a horizontal line. Draw lines from the
vanishing points to intersect these diagonals.
Complete the cube by rotating line *xy* by 45°
upwards and drawing a horizontal line through point
z to intersect the verticals from the corners at *x* and *y*.
The other sides can be completed by drawing
perspective lines through the intersections to the
vanishing points.

would find when drawing an automobile wheel for
example, would have displaced major axes. The minor axis
(the line that divides the ellipse into two equal halves along
its shortest dimension) will, however, coincide with a line
drawn perpendicular to the perspective circle (the axle
of the wheel). The major axis, and therefore the longest
dimension of the ellipses, should therefore run at right
angles to your axle line. An ellipse guide or template can
be used to draw a circle in perspective if it is tangent at the
midpoints of all four sides of a perspective square and if
its minor axis coincides with the perspective perpendicular
(*see* Hot tip, p. 65).

From the cube and the circle/ellipse, it is possible
to construct other "primitive" geometrical shapes:
cylinders, cones and spheres (the sphere is unique in
perspective as in outline it always remains a circle!). This
45-degree oblique view is useful for drawing objects with
two interesting sides, but could look dull and monotonous
if the sides are of similar dimensions, as in a refrigerator
for example. A similar set-up using a 30/60-degree
orientation (and with one vanishing point twice as far
from the DVP as the other) would result in a more pleasing
asymmetrical composition (Fig. 2.8).

Below 2.8   A cube drawn using the more
convincing 30°/60° Doblin perspective. Draw a
horizon and place vanishing points (vp) left and
right. Bisect the horizon between them to locate
mid point (mp) *y*. Bisect the distance between vp left
and mp *y* to locate *a*. Bisect *a* and vp left to give
mp *x*. Draw a vertical at *a* and mark near angle of
the cube *n* where desired. Draw a horizontal line
through *n* and draw perspective lines to locate two
edges. Draw the vertical *nz* then rotate the line to
locate *x* and *y*. Draw a line from mp *y* to *y* to locate
point *1* at the intersection. Repeat for mp *z* and *z*
to locate point *2*. Draw perspective lines though *1*
and *2* to complete the horizontal square. Draw
verticals at each corner, then perspective lines to
z to complete the cube.

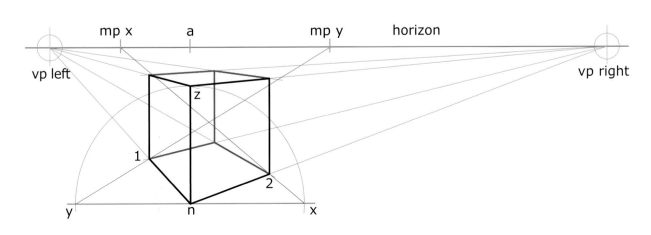

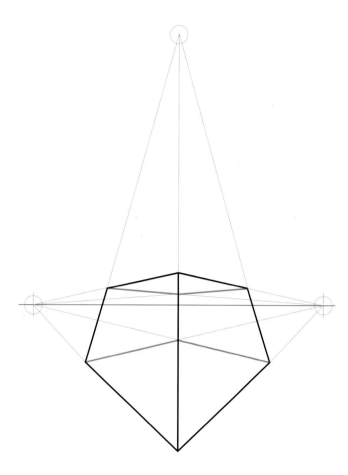

Three-point perspective

Two-point perspective is a special case of three-point perspective, in which the vertical lines are parallel to the picture plane. A better representation, although some designers prefer the purity of two-point perspective, would have the vertical lines of a small object (situated below eye level) converging towards some third vanishing point directly below the object. The sides of a large object, such as an office block viewed from the ground, would similarly converge upwards to some vanishing point in the sky (Fig. 2.9).

Three-point perspective assumes three horizons, forming the sides of an acute triangle. Simplifications to the construction can be contrived when the cube is symmetrical, with the front and rear corners coinciding with the line of sight and, for a less monotonous composition, with the faces inclined 45 degrees to one horizon, 30/60 degrees to the others. Most designers will use their judgment to introduce convergence to vertical lines (Fig. 2.10). The foreshortening of vertical distance for small objects near eye level is roughly proportional to the amount of convergence.

Some books on perspective insist that three-point perspective is unnecessary, as the drawing is subject to the same laws of optics as the object. If a tall object is drawn with parallel verticals and viewed from the same stationary point as the original object, the lines on the drawing representing the verticals on the object should converge in the same manner and by the same degree. Remember, however, perspective is not necessarily the whole truth—it is a convention with many assumptions and not an

Above 2.9   Three-point perspective has the vertical lines of an object converging towards a third vanishing point directly below it—or in the case of a large object, above it.

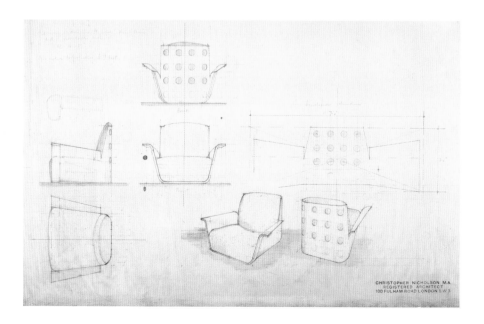

Right 2.10   Christopher Nicholson, Plywood armchair, 1937. The preliminary design for Isokon includes a couple of perspectives, front and rear views, alongside the 2D orthographic representation. Courtesy RIBA Library Drawings and Archives Collections, London.

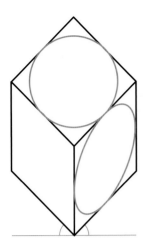

Above left 2.11   An axonometric projection contains a true plan with planes going off at 45° angles. Circles on a plan remain true circles, but circles in elevation become ellipses.

Above right 2.12   George Sowden, Acapulco clock, 1981. The Post-Modern Memphis Group revived the use of paraline projections, as in this axonometric drawing. This was a convention common in architecture but, until the Memphis Group, rare in product design presentation drawings.

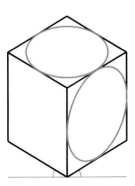

Above 2.13   An isometric projection produces a less extreme and "unrealistic" drawing than an axonometric one. Elevations are constructed using a 30° grid and, as a result, the "plan" is distorted. Circles appear as ellipses in both plan and elevational views.

explicit means of representing the way a person perceives the real world.

Metric projections

The metric projections—isometric, axonometric and so on—are simple pictorial methods of drawing objects so as to give an impression of three-dimensionality. They are often dismissed by designers as being cheap substitutes for "true" perspectives, although they were used successfully by the De Stijl group in the 1920s and in the work of the Memphis designers of the 1980s, amongst others. They can be set up from orthographic projections and drawn to various scales on proprietary pads preprinted with grids, and are thus a useful addition to the designer's toolkit. They have another important advantage over perspectives: length, breadth and height dimensions are retained in measurable form on metric projections.

Axonometric projections contain a true plan and are the simplest to set up from existing drawings (Fig. 2.11). As a means of representation, they are most often associated with interior design and architecture (Fig. 2.12). Drawings are usually made with the aid of a T-square and a 45-degree set square, although as long as the plan remains true, the angle at which it is tilted to the horizontal can be varied to produce the best effect. Circles on plan remain true circles in an axonometric projection, but circles in elevation become ellipses.

There is some contention between architects and engineers over this term. Axonometric is a word that has been used by architects for hundreds of years for what engineers now often call planometric. Engineers use the word axonometric as a generic term to include isometric, dimetric and trimetric drawings. A compromise would be a new word, axometric, to help try stamp out the confusion, but so far this has not caught on. Another name for non-perspective projections is paraline.

Isometric projections (Fig. 2.13) were developed by Sir William Farish in 1820 as a form and derivative of orthographic projection. Isometry means "equal measures", because the same scale is used for height, width and depth. An isometric projection produces a less extreme and "unrealistic" drawing than an axonometric projection. Elevations are constructed using a 30-degree set square and, as a result, the "plan" is distorted. Circles appear as ellipses in both plan and elevational views. Verticals have true depth; measurements along the isometric axes can be taken off the drawing using an isometric scale

Right 2.14   A screenshot from
SolidWorks, showing an isometric
drawing of a part alongside
orthographic representations, 2005.
Courtesy SolidWorks Corporation.

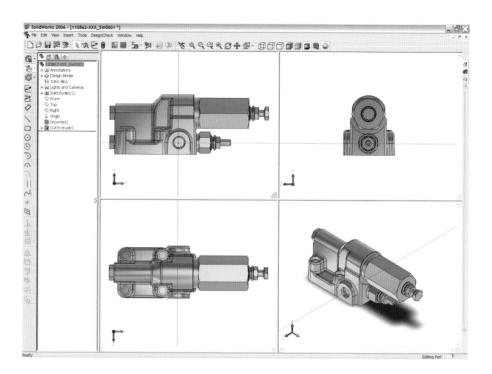

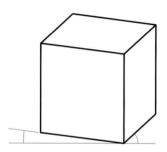

Above 2.15   Trimetric projections require the
use of scales or templates for each axis; the
dimetric is a special case in which the scales
of two of the axes are the same. Dimetric
projections use "idealized" angles of 7° and 42°
to the horizontal for the x and y axes.

Below 2.16   Oblique projections are used
where the front elevation of the object is of
particular importance. The oblique angle is
usually 45° and the oblique lines can be any
length. In a cavalier projection (below left) they
are true lengths; in a cabinet projection (below
right) they are half the true length.

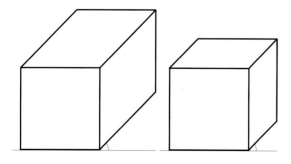

(measurements along the isometric axes are 0.816 true
size) (Fig. 2.14).

Two "pictorial" systems popular during the Second
World War, based on isometrics, are the more generalized
trimetric and dimetric projections. Trimetric projections
require the use of scales or templates for each axis
(Fig. 2.15); the dimetric is a special case in which the scales
of two of the axes are the same. Dimetric projections
use "idealized" angles of 7 degrees and 42 degrees
to the horizontal for the x and y axes. Conventional
approximations are used for manual drafting, but precise
angles and scales can be built into a CAD system.

To recap in general terms: the types of pictorial
projection isometric, dimetric and trimetric require the
application of one, two and three scales, respectively.
Exploded views (*see* Chapter 8) are almost always executed
in isometric or perspective.

Oblique projections (Fig. 2.16) are used where the
front elevation of the object is of particular importance,
in furniture design for example (Fig. 2.17); the side and top
views of an object are tacked onto the edges of the front
face. To make the side and top faces join, they are distorted
and the line representing the common edge runs at an
oblique angle across the picture surface. The lines
representing the top and side faces are usually parallel,
although they can converge to give an inverted perspective
effect, or they can converge to give a normal perspective.
Oblique projections are the precursors of perspective and,
despite being logically impossible, are found on Greek vase

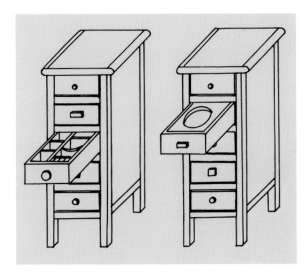

Above 2.17   George Sowden, Commode, 1992. This drawing for Artifort (for Murphy's Mental Room, a tribute to Samuel Beckett) uses an oblique cavalier projection.

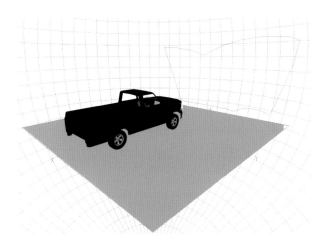

Above 2.18   This spherical projection generated by Loughborough University's SAMMIE (System for Aiding Man-Machine Interaction Evaluation) ergonomics program shows the projected vision path through a dirty windscreen (the area cleaned by the wipers), which is important for safety checks, 2006.

Right 2.19   A Catia V screenshot from Dassault Systèmes, in which DMU (digital mock up) allows development teams to create digitally a product—a manikin user and its environment— then analyse it, in this case to study visibility through a windscreen, 2006.

decorations from the fourth century BC and were used in Chinese paintings until the eighteenth century AD.

The oblique lines emerging from the elevation can be any length: in a cavalier projection they are true lengths; in a cabinet projection they are half the true length.

The oblique angle is usually 45 degrees. The horizontal oblique projection, in which only the front and side of the object are visible, and the vertical oblique projection, in which only the front and top of the object are visible, are special cases where this angle is 0 degrees and 90 degrees respectively. In oblique projection, upright cylindrical objects always look distorted.

Any shadow projected onto a flat plane is an oblique projection; incorporating shadows onto a drawing, as was common practice in the nineteenth century to add realism (and called sciagraphy in architecture), is effectively superimposing an oblique projection onto an orthographic projection.

Spherical projections

Spherical projections, more recognizable in maps of the world, are sometimes encountered by designers. They are an aid to designers of, say, truck or bus cabs subject to visibility safety regulations (Fig. 2.18). European Union regulations, for example, stipulate the driver's ground plan visibility from the windscreen and through rear-view mirrors (Fig. 2.19). In Australia, a cab's B post must not be within 130 degrees of the driver's field of view. (The pieces of metal that hold up the roof of the cab are called posts or, in the US, pillars. The one at the front

is designated the A post/pillar, the next one back is the B post/pillar, and so on.)

A Mercator projection, in which a 360-degree spherical field of vision is mapped onto a cylinder and then opened out flat, can verify that legislation is being conformed to, but would be tedious to perform manually. Ergonomic modeling programs can—once a 3D scene has been input—generate views in different projections through the "eyes" of a driver direct through the windscreen and windows or via convex, concave or plane mirrors, and can visualize any distracting internal reflections. Elliptical Aitoff projections are used for aircraft cockpit visibility analysis.

Orthographic projections: plan and elevations

Of all the many ways of representing on paper a three-dimensional object, the orthographic projection of a plan, elevations and sections is the most abstract and the most commonplace. Its rigidity has probably been responsible for the way many products look today—boxy and, in effect, only two-and-a half-dimensional, the simple extrusion of a 2D profile with maybe a few rounded edges and details added as a finishing touch. More "organic" shapes are almost impossible to communicate orthographically, and traditional designers of doubly curved surfaces (shapes that are smoothly curved in two dimensions, such as turbine blades and automobile bodies) have the tortuous task of having to draw a series of 2D sections, with the interpolation between them left to the toolmaker.

The method of orthographic projection, perfected by William Binns in 1857 and based on Dürer's method of 1525, is notoriously ambiguous, and hundreds of conventions have grown up (BS8888 and ASME Y14.5M, for example) to try to make sense of it—describing what should be seen, and what is hidden but must be indicated, say, by a dotted line. It needs a degree of expertise to be able to read them, so the layperson, the client or the ultimate end user of the product are at a severe disadvantage.

A designer might have a shape in mind that could be described parametrically—for example, a cylinder of a certain height and diameter manufactured in brass—but the production department would still expect to receive a fully dimensioned set of "engineering" drawings. Except for the simplest shapes, it is often necessary to accompany the set of orthographics with an "auxiliary" isometric or perspective sketch to complete the description. Fortunately, CAD, and 3D solid modeling in particular, is eliminating the need for a "blueprint" (the name still used for a set of plans), providing all the information needed for manufacture in a single coherent computer model.

The principle of orthographic projection is to float the designed object inside an imaginary box comprising planes at right angles, or orthogonally, to one another (Fig. 2.20). If the sides of this box are thought of as being windows and are peered through in turn, then the silhouette or projection of the designed object onto the bottom horizontal window is called the plan view, the projection of the same object onto the front vertical window is called elevation 1 (or front elevation), and onto an adjacent side vertical window, end elevation 2 (or side elevation). Now imagine the box to be hinged. The

Right 2.20 The orthographic projection of a plan, elevations and sections is the most abstract representation of an object, but also the most commonplace. The designed object is floated inside an imaginary box comprising planes at right angles, in other words, orthogonally, to one another. If the sides of this box are thought of as being windows and are peered through in turn, then the silhouette, or projection, of the designed object onto the bottom horizontal window is called the plan view; the projection of the same object onto the front vertical window is called elevation 1 (or front elevation); and onto an adjacent side vertical window, end elevation 2 (or side elevation).

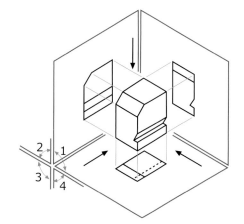
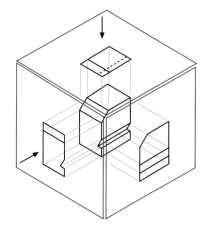

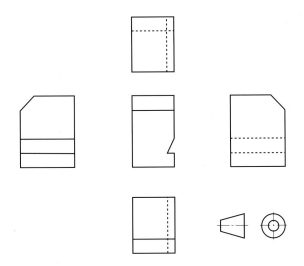

Above 2.21   For first-angle projection, imagine the object placed on a surface. From the face (front) view, centre, it is rolled to the right to reveal its left side, rolled to the left to show its right side, rolled up on its back to show its bottom, or rolled face down to show its top.

Below 2.22   For third-angle projection, consider the object to be a box to be unfolded, as if it were behind a glass surface. The left image shows its left side and the right image shows its right side; above shows the top and below shows the bottom view.

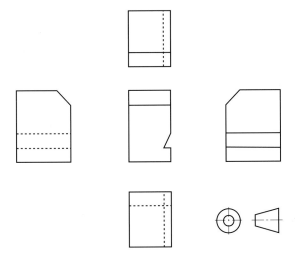

horizontal plane (the plan) is swung down through 90 degrees and end elevation 2 (or side elevation) is also swung round through 90 degrees, so that all three projections now lie on the same plane of the paper. Remove the object and an orthographic projection of a plan and two elevations remains.

In practice, the plan would be drawn first, then the elevation of the front face drawn immediately above it and the end elevation to the right, all lined up and in scale so that common dimensions can be taken off. This arrangement is known as first-angle projection (Fig. 2.21). Third-angle projection (Fig. 2.22) has the views arranged such that elevation 1 is placed below the plan, with end elevation 2 to the left of elevation 1. This has the advantage of placing the features of adjacent views in juxtaposition, making it easier to project one view from another when drawing, and to associate these features when dimensioning or reading the drawing. The term "third-angle" is used because, compared to "first-angle" projection, the directions of projection are rotated through two right angles about the object. Second-angle and fourth-angle projections are also possible, but do not result in useful images.

For first-angle projection, imagine the object placed on a surface. From the face (front) view, centre, it is rolled to the right to reveal its left side, rolled to the left to show its right side, rolled up on its back to show its bottom, or rolled face down to show its top.

For third-angle projection, consider the object to be a box to be unfolded, as if it were behind a glass surface. The left image shows its left side and the right side shows its right side, above shows the top, and below shows the bottom view.

A combination of the two systems, termed mixed projection, has the plan placed below the elevation— the position of salient features on the object will often determine the type or hybrid of arrangement used, although UK and European practice favours first-angle and US practice favours third-angle projections.

The European penchant for the first-angle projection is said to derive from the conventions embodied in Gaspard Monge's descriptive geometry of 1795; US practice broke with tradition towards the end of the nineteenth century as American draughtsmen tended to be college-trained and hence more influenced by educationalists who postulated the idea of drawing as a graphics language.

By 1953, the UK drafting standard BS308 (precursor to BS8888) had put both first- and third-angle projections

onto equal footing. The third-angle projection is now
commonly used both in the USA and the UK, although
first-angle projection is still the preferred method
in continental Europe. Designers tend to use the form
of projection most appropriate to the application. For
drawing a long thin object, such as a train, a third-angle
projection would be easier to read: the front elevation,
for example, would be placed on the sheet of paper to
the right of the side elevation and adjacent to it.

Sections and scrap views

A section is a slice through the object, projected orthogonally,
to show internal details or changes in profile for complex
shapes (Fig. 2.23). The cut solid is shown cross-hatched, and
the point at which the section is taken is indicated on one of
the views according to the national or international standard
being conformed to. Unlike a real section, sections on an
orthographic drawing will often show, by convention, details
impossible to see with the naked eye.

Sometimes, the three conventional orthogonal views
will not be sufficient to show an interesting detail on the
product to its best advantage (Fig. 2.24). An auxiliary
projection is a view taken from an odd angle, not at right
angles to the object (and hence not orthogonal to it),
which may be added to the set of orthogonal projections
to make an understanding of the form a little clearer.
A scrap view is an enlarged portion of the object, perhaps
drawn from a slightly different viewpoint, to highlight an
important detail or possible problem area.

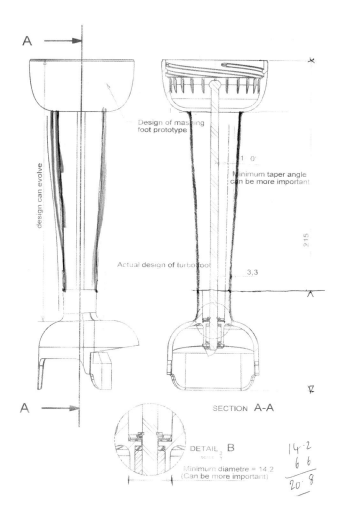

Above 2.24   George Sowden, Robot Marie Hand Mixer,
2004. This printout of the drawing for the Robot Marie
hand mixer for Moulinex has been amended by hand as
part of the design development cycle. (*See also* fig. 25.)
Note the section and detail. There is no plan view.

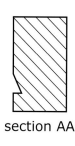

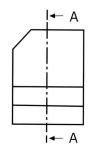

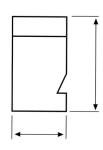

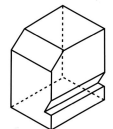

Right 2.23   A section is a slice through
an object, projected orthogonally, to show
internal details or changes in profile for
complex shapes. The cut solid is usually
shown cross-hatched.

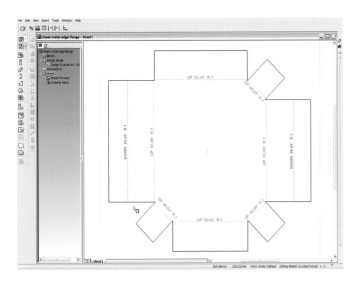

Above 2.25 Flat pattern development
takes a 3D form, such as a cardboard
box or sheet-metal object, and unfolds
it into 2D so it can be cut from a sheet
and fabricated. Courtesy SolidWorks
Corporation.

logo position

Above 2.26 Ron Arad, MT Series chair, 2005.
Doubly curved surfaces, such as this side section
view for Driade, are notoriously difficult to
explain in 2D drawings; 3D computer models
such as this one using Autodesk Maya are so
much clearer.

Surface or flat-pattern developments are used when it is necessary for manufacture to "unfold" an object, if it is to be made, say, from sheet metal or cardboard (Fig. 2.25). The techniques for opening out a surface graphically onto one plane are similar to those used in orthographic projection.

3D surface and solid modeling

Drawing, for designers, is the means to an end. Designing is not just about making pretty pictures: the aim is to produce a physical product that can be manufactured. Being able to work in three dimensions has obvious advantages over making marks in two. Traditionally, if a designer wanted to work in three dimensions, the only way was through modelmaking—in clay, cardboard or polystyrene foam. With computers, however, the designer can now "draw" in the virtual world of 3D.

It is ludicrous to suppose that designers of products containing complex doubly-curved shapes, as found in automobile bodies and turbine blades, could even hope—without assuming some degree of telepathy—to retain control of their designs from concept through to production with just a plan, an elevation, a couple of sections and perhaps a sketched isometric to define the part completely and unambiguously. A cylinder, for example, curves only in one direction and a doubly-curved surface bends in two directions simultaneously (Fig. 2.26). It is no exaggeration to say that most cars, pre-computer, were really "designed" by the patternmakers and panel beaters and were not always perfectly symmetrical.

With computer aids, however, there is no excuse. But tried and tested methods die hard and despite there having been 3D systems since the earliest days of CAD, 2D drafting systems—which only emulate traditional drawing methods—retain a dominant position in the market (Fig. 2.27). A 3D solid modeling system does require more computer power and memory, but the biggest obstacle has been a fundamental one—being able to put aside hundreds of years of "tradition" and get back to the basics, learning to carve and sculpt "solid", albeit computer simulated, objects (Fig. 2.28).

A solid modeler is a kind of virtual reality machine that creates computer models which think they are real physical objects in 3D space. The best-known applications are in computer animation for movies and games, but they also have a serious side in product design and manufacture. There are two distinct kinds of 3D modeler

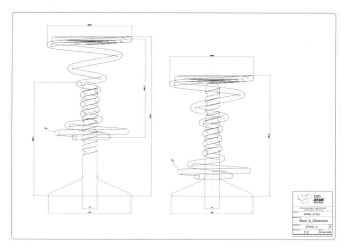

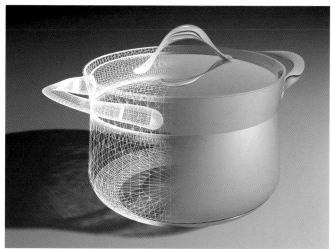

Above left 2.27 Ron Arad, Screw stool, 2006. A traditional 2D orthographic drawing for Driade, 2006, was created using Bentley's MicroStation 2D drafting software.

Above right 2.28 Mario and Claudio Bellini, My Lady steel cooking pot, 2003. This is a wireframe, part rendering in Rhinoceros for Barazzoni SpA.

Below left 2.29 Raysan Al-Kubaisi, Glass, 2006. Objects that are rotationally symmetrical about an axis can be created by sweeping a 2D profile around that axis, as demonstrated by this glass created in 3D Studio Max. The profile is shown on the left, with a wireframe centre and the rendered object on the right. This operation is also known as lathe, after the workshop tool.

Below right 2.30 Héctor Serrano, Waterproof lamp, 2003. The designer used the sweep/lathe command in Cinema 4D to create this shape for Metalarte.

in CADCAM (computer-aided design and manufacture): surface modelers and true solid modelers (also known as volumetric or geometric modelers). Surface modelers were developed specifically to satisfy the needs of the aerospace and automotive industries with their freeform "fair" shapes. Solid modelers have been more successful with chunky regular shapes, made up from building blocks, although the two are converging. It has been the aspiration of vendors to introduce the functionality of surface modelers and their ability to drive NC (numerically controlled) machine tools, such as milling machines, into their more generalized solid modelers.

Most modelers can "sweep" a complex 2D profile through space (Figs. 2.29, 2.30), either extruded in one

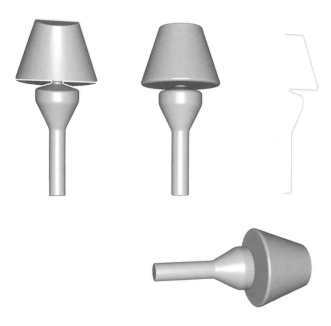

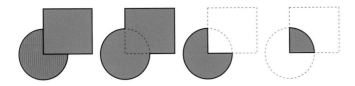

Above 2.31 The Boolean operations of union, difference and intersection can be used to create complex shapes from simple geometric primitives, such as spheres, cubes and cylinders. This is a simple explanation in 2D.

dimension or rotated about an axis, and the resulting solid can be further manipulated using the Boolean operations of union, difference and intersection (Figs. 2.31–2.35). This is analogous to the manufacturing processes of extrusion, milling and shaping on a lathe. Others achieve integration by adopting a common mathematical representation, such as NURBS (non-uniform rational B-spline), for both types of modeler.

The most rudimentary type of 3D representation is the 2D (x,y) profile extruded simply and linearly into the z-axis, the kind of shape that can be manufactured by a router or milling machine with a straight up-and-down motion and no undercuts. This is referred to as a 2½D model. It is possible for a skilled draughtsperson to construct 3D-looking paraline projections using a supposedly 2D-only system.

For both types of solid modeler, a 3D wireframe model is created first (Fig. 2.36). Edges and vertices, constructed from lines of zero thickness, form a pattern of polygons on the model's surface. Although each vertex and line exists in 3D space, a wireframe picture can be confusing and ambiguous to the viewer. Depth cueing—making the

Top left 2.32 Raysan Al-Kubaisi, Two geometrical primitives, 2006. The designer demonstrates Boolean operations in 3D using 3D Studio Max. First he places a cube and sphere in different colours (for clarity) in 3D space so that they overlap each other. Courtesy Raysan Al-Kubaisi.

Top right 2.33 Raysan Al-Kubaisi, Boolean union, 2006. Here the Boolean operation of union is applied. The image doesn't look much different, but the two primitives are now joined and "fused" together, and a blend could be applied between them to smooth the transition. Courtesy Raysan Al-Kubaisi.

Bottom left 2.34 Raysan Al-Kubaisi, Boolean difference, 2006. Here the Boolean operation of difference is applied to subtract the sphere from the cube. For clarity the rest of the removed sphere has been left in wireframe. Courtesy Raysan Al-Kubaisi.

Bottom right 2.35 Raysan Al-Kubaisi, Boolean intersection, 2006. Here the Boolean operation of intersection is used to retain only those portions of the two primitives that were overlapping. Again, for clarity the removed portions of the cube and sphere are shown in wireframe. Courtesy Raysan Al-Kubaisi.

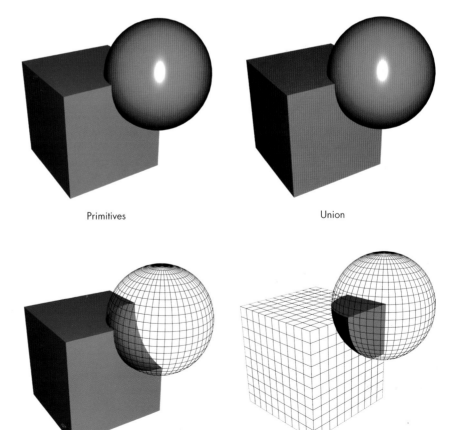

Primitives

Union

Difference

Intersection

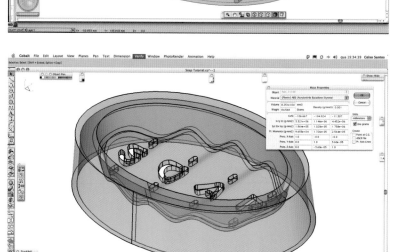

Above 2.36   Stuart Lawson, Patio chair, 2003.
This is a wireframe of a chair designed for
Marks & Spencer using FormZ software.

Right 2.38 and 2.39   Celso Santos, Soap
dish, 2004. Rio21 Design used Boolean
operations to model this soap dish in Ashlar-
Vellum's Cobalt. The lettering had been extruded
then subtracted from the dish using Boolean
difference to punch holes in the shape of the
letters through the wavy surface.

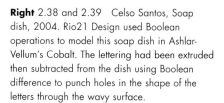

Below 2.37   This 2006 ghosted illustration
of a Jaguar XK revealing its inner details is
a computer 3D rendering using Lightwave 3D.
Courtesy Jaguar cars, Coventry, England.

parts of the picture closest to the user brighter and/or
thicker—can help, but for hidden-line images to be
generated, faces must be "attached" to those polygons.

A surface model can be shaded (and hence look solid
enough) and can be used to generate toolpaths for NC
machine tools, but a solid modeler has an in-built sense
of identity. The model knows its inside from its outside—
what is solid and what is not—a hole, for example. Solid
modeling promises the designer a simulation that thinks
it is a real prototype.

The model can be viewed from any angle in photo-
real colour, the outside can even be rendered transparent
(*see* Chapter 8) so that complicated innards are revealed
(Fig. 2.37), assemblies can be exploded into component
parts, sections cut, and the object can be dematerialized
and turned inside out—making holes, voids, risers and
feeders (for plastic mouldmaking applications, for example)
visibly solid, whilst the material they were milled and
bored from is rendered as empty space (Figs. 2.38, 2.39).

A solid model can be weighed, knows its volume, centre of gravity and moments of inertia, and can detect clashes and interference with other components, clamps or machine tools. The model can be used to produce the meshes needed for stress analysis, it can be used to verify delicate toolpaths before machining and it can be used to provide diagrams for technical manuals. It can come up with the data for process planning and for automated computer-aided inspection, testing and quality control.

Types of solid modeler

There are two main types of solid modeler: CSG (constructive solid geometry) and B-rep (boundary representation). Most solid modelers date back to one of two research efforts from the mid-1960s: the Build system at Cambridge University in the UK; and the Padl project at Rochester University in the USA. Most commercial programs incorporate a standard third-party "engine" called a kernel, such as ACIS (Alan, Charles and Ian's System), a B-rep program based on Shape Data's Romulus now owned by Dassault Systèmes Spatial, which is used in TurboCAD. Parasolid, another B-rep kernel from UGS (formerly Unigraphics) is used in SolidWorks. Note that these use different file formats for importing and exporting data, which can be a problem. ISO 10303, also known as STEP (Standard for the Exchange of Product model data) is an international standard all modelers aspire to (more on this in Chapter 7).

Solid modelers are classified by the way they store the description of the shape's geometry. In a CSG system, the final shape is described and maintained internally by a tree structure of the building-block primitives (simple shapes such as cubes, cylinders and spheres) (Fig. 2.40) plus the Boolean operations (union, difference and intersection) used on them to arrive at the model—a step-by-step history of the design process. Imagine a set of children's building blocks—not only cubes but also cylinders, cones, pyramids, etc. Because they are virtual, you can not only stack them in different combinations, but you can also merge them together or subtract one shape from another, removing a cylinder from a cube to make a hole, for example.

A B-rep modeler keeps a list of all the faces, edges and vertices of the model, together with the Euler topological and adjacency relationships between them (so as to prevent any Escher-like impossible objects from being created). B-rep models are constructed either by converting existing wireframe or surface models by

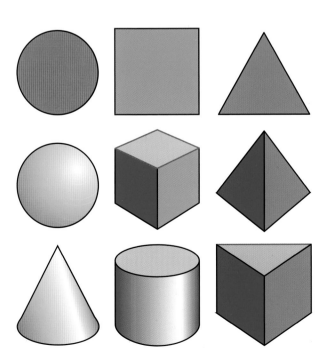

Below 2.40   Geometric primitives are the basic building blocks of form and include such shapes as cubes, spheres, cones and cylinders, which can be combined using Boolean operations to create more complex shapes.

Step by step 2:
Modeling a gamer's mouse
by Thomas Parel

In this sequence, Thomas Parel shows how to model and render a gamer's mouse using a 3D solid modeler program, SolidWorks, and 2D "paint" programs Corel Painter and Photoshop.

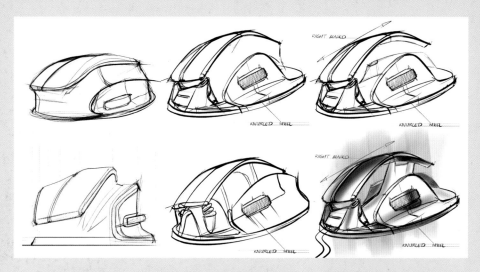

SS 2.1   He begins by quickly generating concepts in Corel Painter using the Thick'n'Thin Brush 5 on an 11 x 17-inch document, 150 dpi. These are typically loose drawings that depend on rough lines and quick underlays to inspire new forms. Thomas sketches on a 10 x 12-inch Wacom Intuos 2.

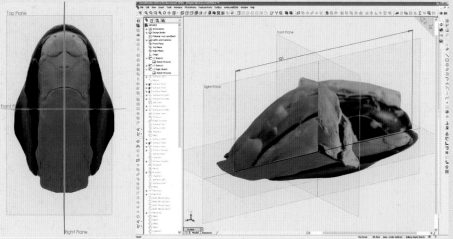

SS 2.2   In order quickly to evaluate some of the newer ideas and pinpoint ergonomic areas, Thomas makes a rough clay model. He photographs the digital photos and crops them to their envelope. He deletes their backgrounds using Photoshop, then he saves them as bitmaps to use as underlays in SolidWorks.

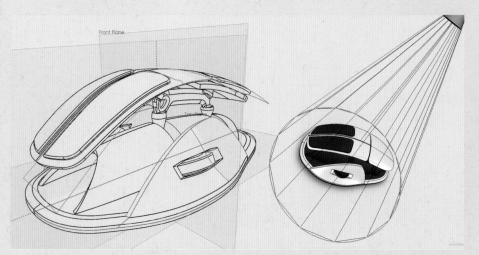

SS 2.3   By using orthographic views, he can trace over the images so as to create 3D curves in space. These curves then create rough 3D CAD surfaces. He adds details to images in 2D. Solid modelers excel at mechanical component creation such as scroll wheels and internal components. Thomas can save time by tracing over screen captures later in the design process so as to create accurate concepts.

SS 2.4 Product design renderings are best with simple light setups. Thomas uses a spotlight in this rendering and a plane as a diffuse light. He turns on indirect illumination to create subtle bounce light interactions between the floor and the mouse. He sets the inner faces of the mouse to a constant shader that is coloured greenish blue. This brings out some internal details.

SS 2.5 Using a large brush in Photoshop, Thomas airbrushes the background to black. He lengthens the highlights on the metallic portions to emulate real-life highlights. He paints on a new layer and then uses the Magic Wand to erase the overspray on the mouse. Then he paints two broad strokes on the new layer to re-sculpt the scroll wheel area in 2D. He uses the Digital Airbrush to create large soft strokes and Eraser to erase soft borders.

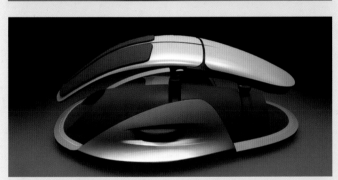

SS 2.6 Large strokes usually indicate a smooth surface transition, while a small brush stroke usually indicates a more abrupt surface change. Thomas uses this technique to create incisions around the side scroll wheel. Small strokes of white indicate small fillets that are facing the light source. Similarly, dark strokes indicate fillets that are facing down. He uses the Thick'n'Thin pen to create sharp strokes and the Rectangular Eraser 20 to create sharp borders.

SS 2.7 Thomas draws a large red light pipe along the side of the mouse using a Square Conte 8. To enhance the atmosphere, he adds a glow to the shadows on the floor. The overmould on the mouse buttons is blending with the background, so he adds a little rim lighting with a small stroke around the edge. He adds a subtle dark airbrush stroke to the shadow on top of the mouse to accentuate the contrast. He can now stroke in the little details such as the dial on the internal sliding components.

SS 2.8 Thomas adds text in Photoshop. He uses Free Transform to distort and shear the text so that it looks correct in perspective. The green glow looked fine but he decides to change the inner glow to red so that the colour plan of the mouse is cohesive. He does this by selecting a colour range (Select>Color Range), and then shifting the hue and saturation (Ctrl+U). Finally, when the values of the rendering look right, he adds extra sparkle by shifting the levels (Ctrl+L) to increase the contrast between shadows and highlights.

adding faces, or by sweeping 2D outlines along linear or circular paths to enclose a solid object. These can then be further combined or subtracted with other intermediate shapes using Boolean operations. This is analogous to the manufacturing processes of injection moulding, casting, forging and thermo-forming. B-rep modelers are also useful for flat-pattern development in sheet-metalwork.

Many modern modelers use a hybrid approach: starting with CSG, then converting the working model to a B-rep definition and storing both. The CSG model might then be used for mass-property calculations, such as moment of inertia and the surface area, and the B-rep file's edge data downloaded to another program to produce tooling data and the 2D engineering drawings that most manufacturers still insist on.

Another type of modeler is termed a faceted modeler, more commonly used for reproducing human faces in CGI (computer-generated imagery) movies or reverse engineering physical models, in which all the difficult-to-compute curved surfaces are approximated and replaced by small planar facets, usually triangles, like the surface of a gemstone. The larger the facets, the faster the processing, but the smaller the facets, the closer the approximation is to smooth reality. Apart from speed, another attraction is that faceted modelers can reproduce very complex surfaces. Subdivision is used to create smoothish surfaces out of arbitrary meshes, rather like a carpenter making a smooth rounded curve from a square piece of wood by first sawing a 45-degree chunk off a corner, then repeatedly cutting away at the sharp edges until the corner is relatively smooth.

Parametric modelers

Most solid modelers are now parametric, using features and constraints to define the model, giving dimensions labels rather than fixed numbers. If a parameter is later modified, the model can then adapt to reflect the update. This suits the designer at the concept stage (*see* Chapter 5) because no firm decisions may yet have been made about precise dimensions, and the designer, for now, would like to keep things "fuzzy". Parametric modeling does, however, require more care in model creation. An injection-moulded part may have thousands of features, and modifying an early feature could perhaps cause later features to fail.

As an example, consider a shaft created by extruding a circle by 100mm. A hub can be assembled to the end of the shaft. Later, if the shaft is modified to a length of 200mm, then the hub will relocate to the end of the shaft, and the engineering drawings and mass properties will all reflect the changes automatically. Pro/Engineer (or Pro/E for short) and SolidWorks are examples of interactive feature-based parametric solid modelers (Fig. 2.41).

Parametric modeling also lends itself to re-use of data. A whole family of similar parts can be contained within one model, for example. An example of parametric modeling is in the creation of characters in CGI movies or computer games. A character is described by parameters that locate key body positions. The model is then built from these locations and when the parameters are modified, the model is rebuilt, creating frames for the animation.

Automated manufacture, with no manual intervention, is the most tantalizing promise of solid modeling, but restricts choice and could make parts more expensive to produce. Nevertheless, there are rays of hope.

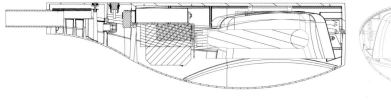
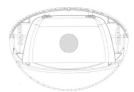

Right 2.41   Pearson Lloyd, Millennium street furniture light head, 2004. The designers used Pro/E (along with Cobalt, Photoshop and Cinema 4D) to develop the CAD visualization for the City of Westminster, London.

Opposite 2.42   Drawing a wheel in perspective: the short axis of the ellipse should align with the car's axle, as in the drawing on the right.

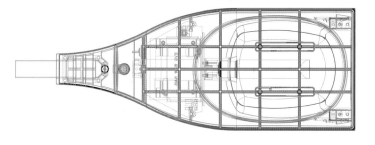

Machining blanks, on screen, by subtracting the volume swept out by the cutter tool will verify the efficacy of the toolpath and check interference with any clamps and fixtures. Furthermore, new software techniques, such as OOP (object-oriented programming) will bring along so-called expert systems for "easy" applications, such as sheet-metal development and plastics injection-mould design, a few steps closer to practical reality.

Photo-real rendering and lighting effects (described more fully in Chapter 6) and automatic generation of perspectives (or any other kind of metric projection) from solid modelers strive to produce "models" that to the viewer's eye and brain are indistinguishable from a real physical prototype. If a perspective drawing is only a *visual* simulation of reality, a computer solid model is a drawing that exists in three dimensions (and hence can be rotated and translated in 3D space) that also possesses almost as many physically measurable attributes as the real thing.

Conclusion

In the near future, the fully computerized designer may no longer be required to construct accurate perspectives and paraline projections using manual methods, but at least should be able to distinguish between, say, two-point and three-point perspective, and recognize the names of all the exotic projections there are to choose from to communicate effectively, by means of intuitive sketches, the design intent to others in the team and in manufacture. Constructing a 3D computer solid model may seem daunting at first but, like learning any new piece of software, it will become second nature with practice, and the advantages of encapsulating the prospective product's geometry and other attributes within a single document will pay dividends down the line. And with the skills learnt here, if the computer rendering doesn't quite look as it should, you'll know what went wrong!

Hot tip:
How to draw automobile wheels in perspective

A wheel comprises several concentric circles and when a circle is viewed at an angle we see an ellipse. This viewing angle is called the degree of the ellipse. A perfect circle is at 90 degrees; a zero degree ellipse is a straight line. An ellipse has two axes: the minor axis and the major axis. The minor axis divides the ellipse into two equal halves across its narrowest dimension and the major axis divides the ellipse across its long dimension. The minor and major axes cross each other at 90 degrees. In perspective, the minor axis goes through the centre of a square enclosing it, but the major axis does not (Fig. 2.42).

When putting wheels on cars, the minor axis is always aligned in the same direction as the axle. Unless the front wheels are turned or the wheels have extreme camber, this axle is also perpendicular to the centerline of the car. Assuming the minor axis of your ellipse is drawn correctly, but looks wrong, its degree may need adjusting. Draw a box around the ellipse following your lines of perspective. If your ellipse does not touch in the middle of each side of the box, then the degree is wrong. Adjust the degree of your ellipse by making it wider or narrower until you can draw a box around it that touches exactly in the middle of each side.

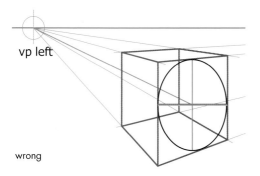

wrong

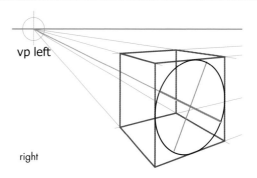

right

Case Study 1: Seymourpowell

Seymourpowell was founded in 1984 by Richard Seymour and Dick Powell, both passionate proponents of drawing. Royal College of Art graduates, they met whilst teaching at St Albans School of Art. Dick Powell is also the author of the influential Presentation Techniques *(Little Brown, 1990) and insists on all their job applicants taking a drawing test. The company, based in west London, is run by a six-strong team of directors, with around forty-five staff in total.*

Its client list includes Ford, Nokia, Jaguar, BMW, Minolta, Yamaha, Tefal, Hewlett-Packard and Casio. SPF (Seymourpowell Foresight) provides product-related research for clients, either as part of new product development or as an independent service.

Seymourpowell believes that design is the integrating element that defines a product, rather than simply the external styling of a product. Design is rather the evolution and innovation of the architecture of a product according to its function, usage, appeal, engineering and build quality—as well as its look, which of course remains a key component. The company believes that design has a vital role to play in the whole lifecycle of a product, including its marketing and positioning, as well as its strategic implications for the client company. The designed product is the final embodiment of this process.

The Calor Aquaspeed Iron

"Innovation requires a consummately well-articulated vision of what you are trying to achieve—one that all parties, from the engineers to the eventual consumer, can believe in," says Dick Powell. "Innovation requires at least one person who fully understands all the ramifications of that vision and is armed with the authority and means to make it happen."

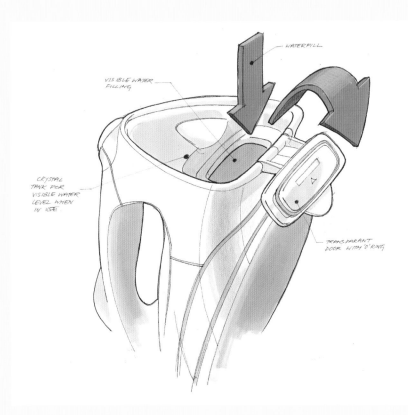

Right CS 1.1 An early sketch exploring the iron's rear trap door, but married to a more classic heel. This is a typical Seymourpowell sketch and is the way in which they work when speed is important. It is executed with a 0.1 Fineliner fibretip pen and then shaded using Pale Blue and Federation Blue markers. Restricting the colour palette makes for speed and economy, but is also effective at communicating intent.

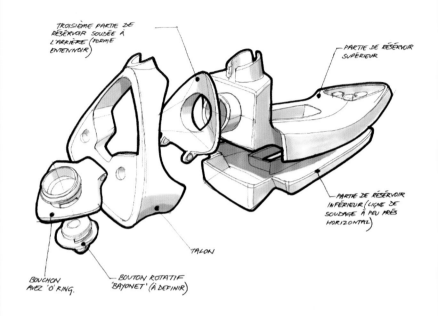

Seymourpowell has designed trains, cars, digital watches and laptops, but the hardest product to design, according to Powell, has to be the steam iron. Why? Because the complexity of a steam iron's internal workings is wholly inseparable from its external form, which in turn is determined by its ergonomics on the one hand, and its functionality on the other. Factor in the need for ease of manufacture, low cost and reasonable investment, as well as on-shelf differentiation in a market in which products are more alike than different, and you can begin to understand why the word styling (and by that Powell means external design) is a wholly inappropriate word.

Calor is a French company and brand that belongs, along with Tefal, Rowenta and Moulinex, to the SEB Group. Seymourpowell's relationship with the SEB companies goes back to 1985, when it designed the world's first cordless kettle, the Freeline, for Tefal.

Calor irons already have a unique differentiation point: their enamelled soleplates. Other irons are typically stainless steel or anodized aluminium. These enamelled soleplates give them a finish that makes them very durable and resistant to scratching or discolouration. Printing two different colours of enamel—one as a base colour and the second overprinted as a series of lines and details—allows the iron to float on the ridges created by the two-colour surface, decreasing friction and increasing its glide and hence the speed of ironing. Calor designers made the most of this by aiming for a streamlined, dynamic, *fast* look. Enter Seymourpowell Foresight asking the key question: does *fast* still work as a core value? The conclusion was that it did indeed work as a basic identity for Calor/Tefal, communicating efficiency and contemporaneity.

In parallel with the research, the creative team began to generate concepts around specific ironing problems (Fig. CS 1.1). Two immediate problem areas were identified: filling an iron with water through a hole the size of a postage stamp, and stability—to combat the iron's annoying tendency to topple off the ironing board. The solutions are obvious: as large a filling hole as possible, and a huge heel for stability.

Right top CS 1.3   Quite early in the design process, and certainly at concept development, designers need to be precise about clearances, form and construction. This is done orthographically (side, top and back views) in 2D CAD using Vellum/Graphite, because it's much faster than using Alias, more flexible, and easier to change. This work is usually accompanied by handmade foam models. These models can be split on their major axis to help perfect the 2D silhouette. Once happy with the 2D CAD, the lines are exported as EPS and brought into Illustrator or FreeHand as paths. The paths are then added to and new paths created to act as masks for rendering in Photoshop. Photoshop rendering is no different from manual airbrush rendering—the designer needs to understand how light and colour work on a complex form—but is in every respect much easier and faster.

Right below CS 1.4   Defining the 3D form using Alias, the preferred software for resolving complex forms. The designers go through several iterations with surfaces, starting with "quick surfaces" in order to machine foam models and discuss the concepts with the client, and to provide the technical team with initial data with which to work. Early surfaces are sometimes used to output photo-realistic renderings as backup to early foam or "grey" hard models. Grey models are made of a hard material but sprayed in a single colour. They are made to check form, and for user research into their handleability. Shown here are final production surfaces, which demand great skill to produce, especially in the control of draught, moulding intent and surface continuity.

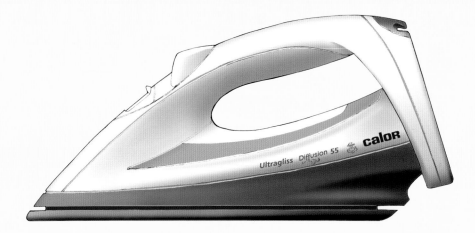

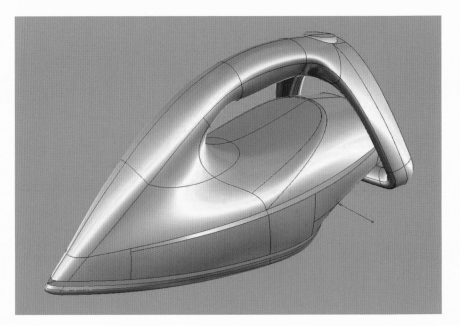

Powell's experience of working with talented creative engineers is that they are rarely at their best trying to resolve an abstract problem. But give them the same challenge where they can understand exactly what is needed and in what form, and they will examine an array of potential solutions methodically and analytically until they find one that works (Fig. CS 1.2).

For this project, they were able to articulate a concept at the very beginning of the process, initially as a series of sketches from the creative workshop (Fig. CS 1.3) and quickly thereafter as foam models, which the development team of the company, as well as its senior management and marketing, could immediately get behind.

The concept put in place was for an open-back iron, in which the heel is a large loop on which the iron could sit for enhanced stability, but without adding bulk and weight (Fig. CS 1.4). Inside this loop, at the back of the iron, was a large trapdoor through which the reservoir might be filled more quickly and conveniently (Fig. CS 1.5).

Not surprisingly, most of the problems revolved around the innovation of filling the iron from the rear and had to do with sealing, air pockets, venting and with keeping water safely away from the electrical components.

The new iron was eventually named the Aquaspeed. It was launched in January 2004, and since then sales have more than met expectations, because its design effectively communicates its benefits—speedy, fuss-free filling and improved heel stability without weight (Fig. CS 1.6). The Calor culture understands that innovation is the best, perhaps the only, way to maintain a strong brand in the face of low-cost me-too products from the Far East. As a manufacturer of consumer products, Calor understands the fundamental role of design as a creator of attractive products. But, much more importantly, they value design at a strategic level and as a creative catalyst for innovation … and that's why Calor is Seymourpowell's favourite client!

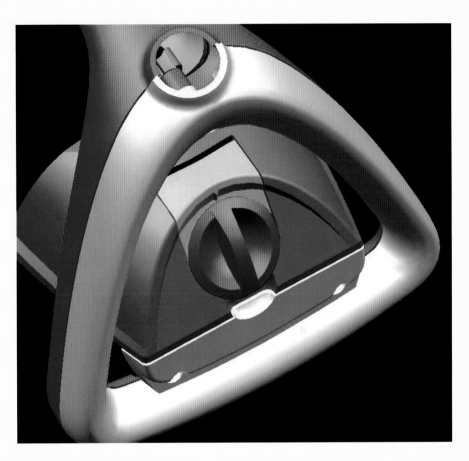

Right above CS 1.5 Detailed resolution of the trapdoor. Many different solutions had to be explored. Details such as this are often detached from the whole and studied piecemeal. Here, the designer is working in Pro/E and looking at the implications of hinging lower in the iron.

Right below CS 1.6 Aquaspeed, the finished product. If you compared this with the finished model, in all ways other than colour you wouldn't be able to spot the difference: a blink-test would say they are the same; a closer inspection would reveal some less obvious changes.

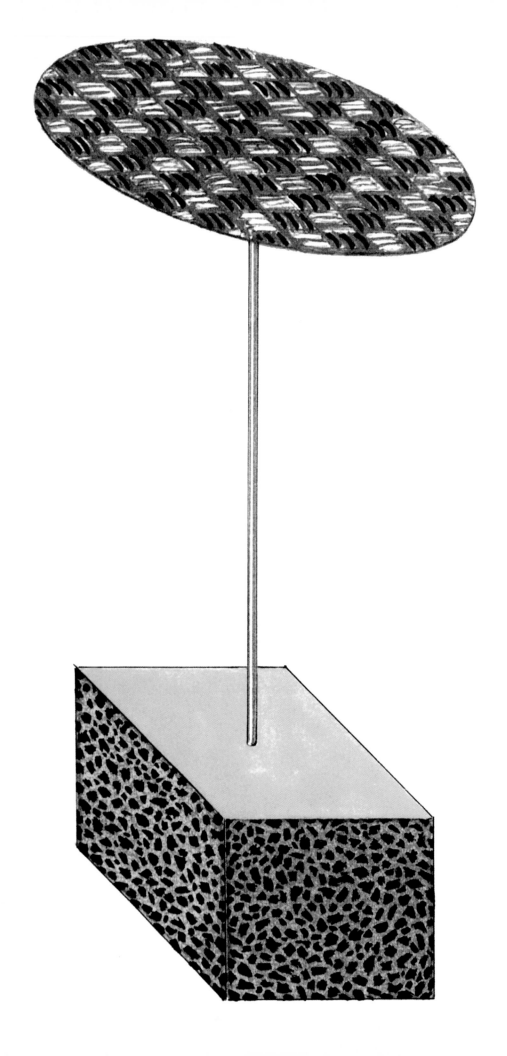

3

Tools and materials

Opposite Ettore Sottsass, Tea table, 1979. Indian ink and coloured pencil. The designer rendered an oblique drawing for Alchymia, the precursor to Memphis. Courtesy Sottsass Associati EEIG, Milan.

Every designer now has a computer, maybe more than one, but there is still a vital role for the more humble manual tools of the trade. These can be crucially important to some designers, superstitiously clinging to particular brands of pencil or ballpoint pen; others may find unfamiliar media exciting, stimulating or dangerous. Yet others find the choice of medium irrelevant, choosing to put their skills as a problem-solver above mere questions of technique. Designer or not, most people will be familiar with the instruments of writing and drawing by hand— they are effectively the same, both being used for making marks and communicating ideas. And anyone fascinated by the contents of stationery shops or graphics supply stores will be aware of the amazing variety and diversity of the products on sale there.

Each has its place in the designer's toolkit and the purpose of this chapter is to shed light on these products, identifying them according to their most appropriate place in the design process; the following chapter is intended to help clarify and perhaps demystify the components that make up a CAD (computer-aided design) system.

Pencils

Soft pencils are used mainly at the concept sketch stages of design; harder pencils, with the point cut into a chisel shape, for outlining the presentation drawing and for producing engineering drawings. The pencil is the original disposable drawing instrument, being economical and efficient (Fig. 3.1). Pencils are controllable and versatile— producing a wide tonal range (Fig. 3.2) that is both permanent yet adjustable—and black graphite ones, at least, are easy to erase. Before pencils were invented, thin rods of silver, zinc or lead were used for drawing. These are collectively known as silverpoint.

The "lead" in a pencil is a misnomer—graphite (pure black carbon) was once called "black lead" or plumbago (that which acts like lead)—and the association has stuck ever since. The word *pencillus* meaning "little tail" refers to the brush used by the Romans to write on papyrus.

We take the humble pencil for granted, but once it was worth its weight in gold. Graphite was first discovered at Borrowdale in Cumbria in 1564, and this mine was the only deposit ever found containing graphite of such purity. It was only worked for six weeks of the year, shipments to London were protected by armed guards and until 1860 the English Guild of Pencilmakers held the world monopoly on the sale of the thin square sticks.

Top 3.1   The pencil is the most economical and eco-friendly drawing implement, capable of creating a wide range of marks, which can easily be erased. Woodless graphite pencils have wider leads for more expressive work.

Bottom 3.2   Graphite pencils come in different grades, from the hardest and greyest 9H (top left) to the softest and blackest 9B (bottom right). The mid-range F and HB are in the center.

In 1662, the German carpenter Friedrich Staedtler used sulphur and antimony to bind crushed graphite into usable sticks. Pencil "lead" today is composed of less pure graphite—mostly from Mexico—and Bavarian clay, fired like porcelain in a kiln. This process was devised in 1795 by a French chemist called Nicholas Jacques Conté, an officer in Napoleon's army, when war cut off supplies of the English and German products. Now, for the first time, pencils could be graded from hard to soft by varying the relative proportions of graphite and clay.

Caspar Faber started up his own pencil manufacturing business near Nuremberg in 1761, and by 1840 the company was producing the familiar hexagonal pencil in its standard size and grades of hardness. A classification of the time had HH for engineers, H for architects, F for sketching and B for shading. George William Monroe, a cabinet-maker in Concord, Massachusetts, made the first American wood pencils in 1812 and, in 1856, Alfred Berol founded the Eagle Pencil Co.

The more clay there is in a pencil lead, the harder it is. The midpoint for hardness (or degree) and the most general-purpose of pencils is HB, standing for hard and black. Softer and blacker pencils of degree B to 6B are favoured by artists and designers for freehand sketching and rendering—2B is the degree of hardness most favoured for general-purpose work around the designer's studio (Fig. 3.3).

On the other end of the scale, pencils of degree H to 9H are used mainly for technical and engineering drafting—the very hard ones being used by stonemasons and steel workers. Odd grades include F (for firm), between HB and H, developed for shorthand writers, and the extremely soft EB and EE.

The traditional wooden pencil has the lead, which also now contains some wax for smoothness, bonded into a sandwich of mature Californian incense cedar slats. Despite there being 2 billion pencils produced each year, there is apparently no threat to the environment as the

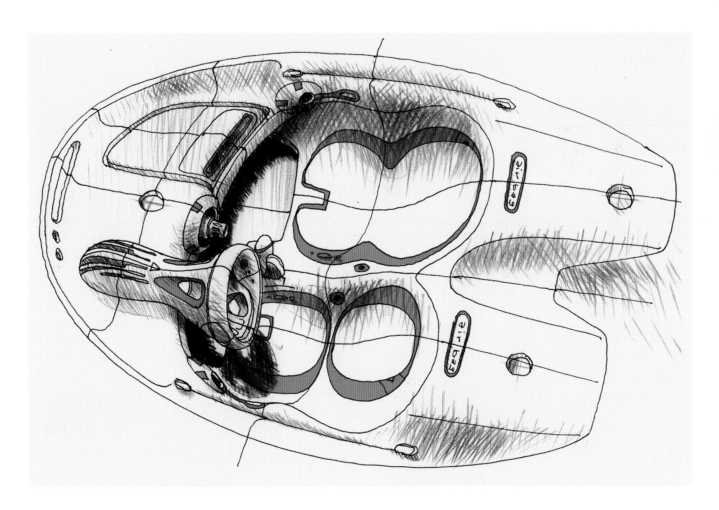

Above 3.3   Etienne Salomé, Car interior, 2005.
The artist used black pencil, with Photoshop for
the red.

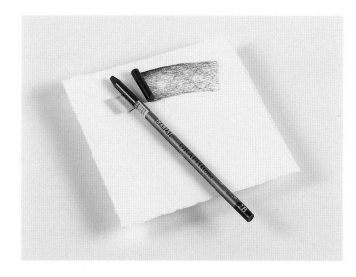

annual logging in the Pacific Northwest does not exceed the growth rate. ForestChoice pencils are manufactured from Forest Stewardship Council (FSC) certified incense cedar.

A good quality pencil has a bonded lead, usually etched with acid, that will not shatter inside the wood if the pencil is dropped, nor slide out in use. The sometimes seen six-sided cross-section of a pencil is an ingenious way of preventing it from rolling off a tilted drawing board.

Pure graphite pencils—sticks of graphite encased in a thin plastic shell, are available in hardnesses HB to 9B, and are good for sketching where contrast is important and large areas are to be covered (Fig. 3.4).

Water-soluble graphite pencils, such as Berol's Karisma Graphite Aquarelle and Rexel's Derwent Sketching, come in three grades—light (HB), medium (4B) and dark (8B)—and can produce a line-and-wash effect when the pencil marks and areas of shading are dampened using a wet brush. It should be remembered, however, that too much water can make paper cockle and it should be stretched beforehand, and that the effect is irreversible.

Polymer-based leads for drafting on translucent film, Mylar or drafting vellum were first introduced in the 1960s by Faber-Castell. The clay binder of the traditional pencil is replaced by a combination of oil and a polymer resin.

Top 3.4   Derwent's Graphitone is a large-diameter woodless pencil made of graphite mixed with clay. It can be used as a conventional pencil for fine details, or unfolded into smaller implements, or applied on its side to create broad strokes. It is available in many grades.

Above 3.5   Coloured pencils are less easy to erase than graphite pencils. They are also available in a water-soluble form, so that a deft application of water by brush can produce a watercolour effect to a blend. Crayons are a blunter instrument but with vibrant colours.

Right 3.6   James Wright, Car interior, 2005. The artist used coloured pencils in this sketch.

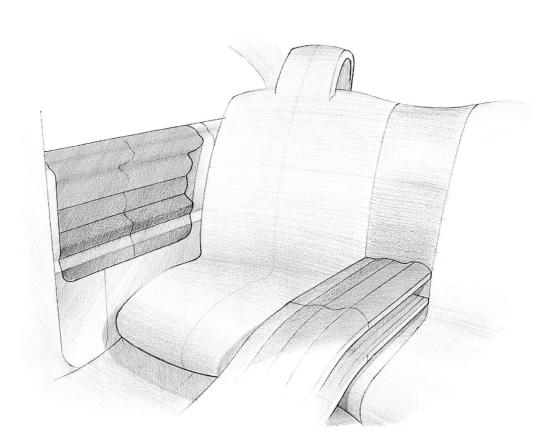

This produces a lead that is stronger, denser and harder wearing than conventional lead, but a special solvent-based eraser is required, however, to correct any mistakes.

Coloured pencils (Figs. 3.5–3.8) are manufactured in a similar way—from a mixture of white kaolin, waxes, pigments and adhesive binders—but are not fired. The range of colours (most suppliers have around 80) can include metallics, and both warm and cool greys. Some types, such as Berol's Verithin, are hard and thin; others, such as the Prismacolor line (called Karisma in the UK), are soft, flat and blendable with the finish of dry gouache. The Swiss-made Caran d'Ache Prismalo "watercolour" pencils are water-soluble, like the graphite pencils mentioned earlier.

Other useful pencils include a non-reproducible blue for "invisibly" marking artwork, and a greasy Chinagraph that will draw on anything, including glossy photographs.

Automatic pencils

The main drawback of the traditional wooden pencil is that it needs to be sharpened every now and again. Clutch pencils first appeared in the 1900s, using leads originally produced by Faber for use in compasses. These have spring-loaded jaws, activated by a push button that also houses a sharpener. The lead can be withdrawn into the barrel for protection when the pencil is not in use. London designer Glen Tutssel once said he would never flee from a flame-engulfed studio without his battered 15-year-old Faber-Castell clutch pencil.

Push-button mechanical pencils from firms such as Pentel and Pilot are now replacing the clutch pencil (Fig. 3.7). These come with leads fine enough not to need sharpening, in different lead thicknesses (0.3–0.9 mm) for consistent weights of line, and look sufficiently hi-tech. They are inexpensive and lightweight, and the round ones can be revolved between the fingers on long stretches of line to achieve an even finish. The removable button usually reveals an eraser and a cleaning wire. Top-of-the-line ones have auto-lead feed for non-stop drawing and adjustable lead protector sleeves.

Pastels

Pastels are used for subtle shading and rendering rather than line drawing and are used for presentation drawings. Soft pastels are made from powdered pigment bound in gum tragacanth or methyl cellulose, and usually contain a fungicide. There are over 550 shades, but for most purposes between 50 and 100 will suffice (Figs. 3.9, 3.10).

Weakly bound pigment has been used to colour drawings from the fifteenth century, and was revived by the nineteenth-century Impressionist Edgar Degas. Soft pastel is used by designers as a quicker substitute for the blending effects produced by airbrush. The medium is extremely fragile and vulnerable and the drawing needs to be protected with PVA fixative as soon as it is completed. The act of fixing the pastels, however, can make the colours darker, a fact that should be remembered and taken into consideration at the outset.

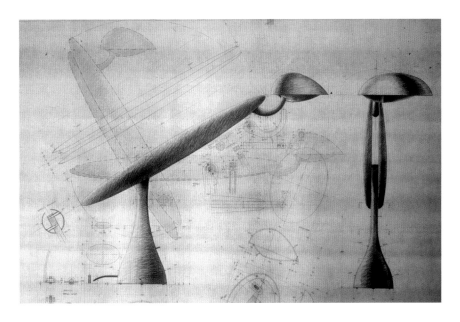

Left 3.7 A mechanical pencil such as The Shaker from Pilot (shake twice and it's ready to write) requires no sharpening and can be refilled with lead. Other mechanical pencils are available with leads of different thicknesses, and plastic leads can be used to give an ink-like weight to engineering drawings on polyester film.

Above 3.8 Isao Hosoe, Heron desk lamp, 1994. The artist used coloured pencils directly over a "blueprint" elevation in this engineering drawing for Luxit SpA.

Above 3.9 Pastels are the subtlest medium, being made from pure pigment in a binder. They can be used directly, or scraped into powder using a scalpel and applied with absorbent cotton. Their images can then be manipulated and blended using a finger or a paper stump.

Pastels can be used directly, or scraped into powder using a scalpel and applied with cotton wool. They can then be manipulated and blended using the finger or a proprietary rolled paper stump (known to artists as a tortillon). An eraser can be used to create the effect of highlights. Pastel dust can also be dissolved in solvent and applied in broad "streaky" strokes like a marker—with the added bonus of being erasable when dry.

Oil pastels are more flexible versions of hard crayons, being made from pigments, hydrocarbon waxes and fats. Heat melts them (hot hands make them harder to control), and white spirit can be used to dissolve them. Background effects and textures can be achieved by combining oil pastels, perhaps distressed by scalpel scratches, with washes of watercolour or acrylics, making use of their wax-resistant properties to create a fully toned drawing quickly. Watercolour will not soak into the paper where there is a layer of oil pastel, but will blob and break up, producing interesting textures.

A boxed set of pastels is a beautiful object in its own right and should last for decades—but designers should ensure that the chosen brand sells single-stick replacements for commonly used colours. Unwrapped pastels with a square cross-section such as Faber-Castell's Polychromos range (120 colours) are more versatile than the round

Right 3.10 King and Miranda Design, Pepa lamp, 1990. The artist used pastels and chalk on tinted paper in this expressionistic concept drawing for Arteluce Flos.

Right 3.11 Mathias Bengtsson, Slice chair, 2000. The artist used red conté for this concept drawing.

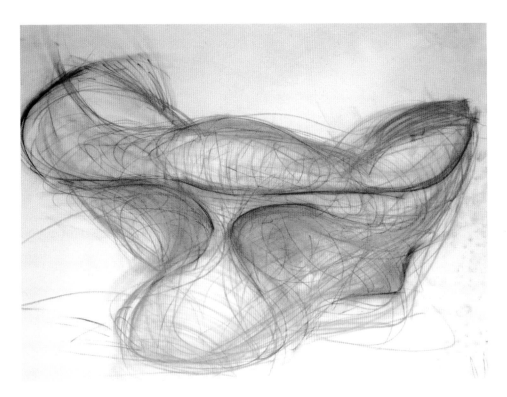

Above 3.12 Charcoal is the most primal medium, and the messiest, but it can also be bought encased in wood.

paper-wrapped types because they can be applied quickly using the long edge and do not roll off the drawing board.

Using chalk and so-called conté crayons (in the "traditional" colours of sanguine, sepia and bistre, as well as black and white) on mid-to-dark toned paper is also a time-honoured method of producing an effective "fully-toned" image directly and economically (Fig. 3.11). The white chalk creates highlights of great luminosity and the dense rich pigment that characterizes conté can be made to look soft and smoky when manipulated with a paper stump. Charcoal (Fig. 3.12), made in sticks from fired willow, is a fast, expressive and responsive drawing medium favoured by artists for initial sketches or drawings in their own right, but is probably considered too messy for most designers.

Pens

Ballpoints and fibretips are used at the concept sketch stages of design (Fig. 3.13); technical pens are used for engineering drawings, though some designers prefer to use these at all stages of the design process. And whilst a cult fountain pen such as a Lamy Safari, Parker Duofold or Montblanc Meisterstück may be useful for signing autographs, contracts or cheques, fine-lined water-based fibretips from Edding or Sakura are more likely to be

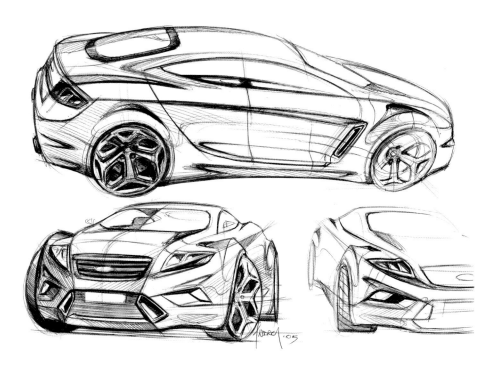

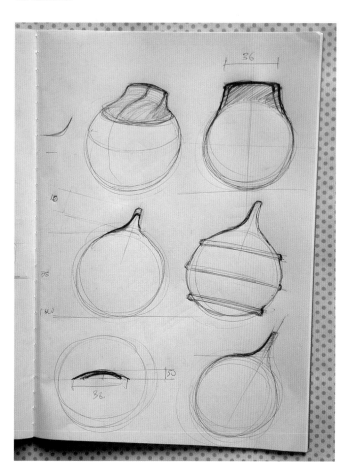

found in the designer's studio as general-purpose
sketching pens.

The common ballpoint—invented in 1938 by Hungarian
emigré Laszlo Biró, and popularized by Frenchman Marcel
Bich—can be used to create crisp edges on presentation
drawings (Fig. 3.14). Daring designers enjoy the thrill of
not being able to erase ballpoint lines. Pentagram designer
Angus Hyland says: "It's not the easiest media to use. It's
sticky and you can't really modulate the line width. But it
has speed. Cross-hatching is possible and you can get a
halftone out of it by altering the pressure." The London
studios of Pentagram once even hosted an exhibition
entirely devoted to ballpoint drawings by designers and
artists.

For freehand drawing it is difficult to find better
than an old-fashioned dip pen tipped with a Gillott 303
or Brause 361 nib—with which the line width varies
responsively according to hand pressure—using non-
waterproof Indian ink for its flow qualities. A dip pen
(Fig. 3.15) does not have its own supply of ink, so must
be dipped into an inkbottle periodically. Dip pens,
however, can cause problems for left-handed designers,
who tend to push the nib point first, making it prone
to dig into the paper and cause ink spattering.

Some designers swear by the brush pen (Fig. 3.16),
with its flexible nylon brush-like nib and its own reservoir
of ink or replaceable cartridges, which in the hand of
an expert is very responsive to pressure, producing fine
black lines of variable width.

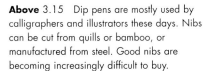

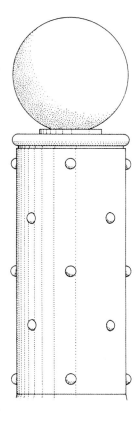

Above 3.15   Dip pens are mostly used by calligraphers and illustrators these days. Nibs can be cut from quills or bamboo, or manufactured from steel. Good nibs are becoming increasingly difficult to buy.

Top right 3.16   A brush pen such as this one from Tombow provides the line of a brush—it broadens with pressure—with the convenience of a felt-tip pen or marker. It has two tips— a flexible brush tip at one end and a hard nylon tip at the other—both fed from the same waterbased ink reservoir.

Bottom right 3.17   The Rotring Rapidograph is the archetypical technical pen. It gives a precise consistent black ink line in various line widths but it is notoriously difficult to clean.

Right 3.18   Michael Graves, Pepper mill, 1993. The designer used a stippled technique for this pen drawing of a pepper mill for Alessi.

Technical pens for drafting lines of consistent width in Indian ink on tracing paper or film have been in use since the 1930s, notably Pelikan Graphos, with a nib similar to that of a conventional fountain pen. Before that, engineers used ruling pens that look like adjustable forceps, the drop of ink kept in its place by surface tension. The Rotring Rapidograph (Fig. 3.17) was introduced in 1952, a pen with a cylindrical tubular nib available in different diameters producing lines of consistent widths from 0.13mm to 2.0mm. The ink flow from the ink reservoir or disposable cartridge is regulated by a fine wire filament running through the middle of the cylindrical nib. The aim of all developments of the technical pen has been to ameliorate the big problems of blobbing and of the Indian ink drying and clogging the nib, and to obviate the irritating need to keep stopping and shaking the pen (and hence moving the wire filament) in order to keep the ink flowing evenly.

All manner of inventions have been tried, from damp and hermetically sealed caps, ultrasonic cleaners and standby humidifiers, to disposable capillary cartridges— and completely disposable pens. Pens are available with tungsten carbide (most makes) or ceramic tips—all proprietary solutions to the same problem of wear. Technical pens are also useful for stippling (Fig. 3.18) and freehand hatching, and can be used for stencilling ellipses and lettering, using plastic guides. Unlike other pens, the stepped tubular nib can go right up to the ruler or stencil without the ink coming into contact with the straight edge, thereby avoiding blotting and ruining the drawing.

CAD systems and their once ubiquitous pen plotters made even greater demands on the technical pen for high-speed precision and reliability. Plastic-tipped points (for drawing on glossy film), pressurized ballpoints and rolling-ball cartridges were tried, but as inkjet printers have taken over, the need for technical nibs has diminished.

Erasers

Of course, in theory, a good craftsperson never needs an eraser. But the person who never made a mistake never made anything—and an eraser can be a creative tool too (as pointed out in the previous section on pastels). The grubby eraser that was only good for smearing meticulously prepared artwork is now a thing of the past, thanks to the modern-day plastic version. These can be cut and shaped to make a sharp clean edge. Putty or kneadable erasers that can be moulded to a point are useful for picking out highlights on presentation drawings.

Markers

The stock in trade of the graffiti artist and the scourge of the subway manager, the marker pen (Fig. 3.19) replaced the airbrush as the *de rigueur* medium for design presentations (Fig. 3.20). The specialized technique of marker rendering, which is akin to watercolour painting, has been the subject of many books over the years, but

Above 3.19   Markers were the drawing tool of choice for designers, before computers took over.

Right 3.20   Alexander Åhnebrink, Mountaineer watch, 2000. The designer used a Pantone black marker pen and Stabilo Boss pink highlighter to draw this concept sketch.

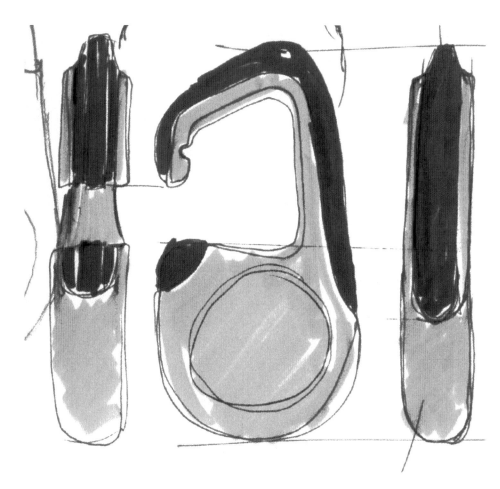

now it has itself been largely superseded by the computer (*see* Chapter 4).

Spirit-based felt-tipped markers are quick and convenient to use, although the result is often ephemeral—marker colours can be very fugitive and fade fast under the influence of daylight and ultraviolet light. They are available in various shapes and sizes, with nibs from hard ultrafine to broad chisel-shaped. Letraset's Pantone Tria (three nibs in one) range has 293 colours, including 11 warm and 11 cool greys, with a set of 24 colours specifically for product designers. Acrylic fibre and polyester is now used in place of felt (so the term felt-tip pen really no longer applies), with polyacetal for fine points. Healthier xylene-free inks have also been introduced—the smell of the old-style inks could be quite addictive.

The original marker was the Magic Marker, invented in 1952 by Sidney Rosenthal, who put a wool felt wick and writing tip into a fat, squat glass bottle full of ink. He named his device Magic Marker because it could make a mark on almost any surface. In 1970, he sold the rights to the name, making millions. In 1989, Binney & Smith, manufacturer of Crayola crayons, entered into an exclusive licensing agreement for rights to the brand and in 2002 launched their inkTank range of permanent markers, highlighters and whiteboard pens.

Paint and ink

Before markers, designers coloured their drawings using washes of watercolour (aquarelle) (Figs. 3.21, 3.22), the

Below 3.21   Greg Vedena of co-lab*,
Arch De Valise (suitcase bus shelter).
Pen and watercolour on trace paper.
Photo: Tim Thager.

Right 3.22   Shin Azumi, Trace armchair, 2004. The designer chose free watercolour applied wet on wet for this evocative, ghost-like drawing for the Italian firm Desalto.

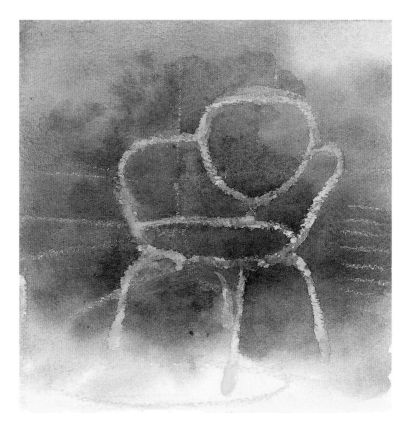

Below 3.23   John Fox, F117 Nighthawk box artwork, 2005. The illustrator used gouache, applied both by brush and airbrush, to create the background for this artwork for Airfix. The aircraft itself was drawn in pencil, then scanned, and colour was added using a Wacom Intuos tablet and Photoshop.

more opaque gouache (body colour) (Fig. 3.23), or a combination of both. These traditional media have been joined by acrylic and PVA-based paints that can be used thick or thin and hence have the characteristics of both watercolour and gouache. They have strong adhesion to all kinds of surface and are waterproof when dry.

Gouache (often called Designers' Gouache) and specialist paints such as process white are used by designers for adding highlights to marker drawings, and for brushing-in fine details and lettering. It is still considered good advice to buy the finest quality Kolinsky red sable brushes (a good selection comprises sizes 00, 1 and 3), although very good synthetic brushes are also available, and to look after them—they should be washed and rinsed straight after use (they must never be left point down in a jar of water) and stored with the points upwards.

Transparent drawing inks come in beautiful bottles, but usually contain shellac for water-resistance when dry, so brushes should always be cleaned with methylated spirit or proprietary solvent. Some dye-based inks (as opposed to pigment-based inks) are bright and intense when new but can be fugitive and fade quickly, especially in sunlight. Make sure you buy lightfast inks if they are available.

Airbrush

The airbrush, once the supreme instrument for photo-realistic technical illustration, is all but obsolete, replaced by computer graphics software such as Adobe Photoshop and Corel Painter. Air compressors lie idle in the corners of designers' studios all over the world. So why bother with a section on airbrush? As with letterpress printing,

once thought extinct, there are still enthusiasts out there who like to do things by hand, and the airbrush may yet see a revival.

There is evidence that 3500 years ago, Aurignacians—the earliest group of humans in Europe—used air painting, blowing pigments through the hollow leg bone of a deer, using hands as stencils, to decorate their caves. The airbrush, as used by pre-computer designers and illustrators, was invented in 1879 by Abner Peeler, although the first practical device was introduced in 1893 by Charles Burdick as a quick and efficient way of applying paint to a surface. Initially, it was taken up mainly by photographic retouchers and championed by Herbert Bayer at the Bauhaus (where it was used to produce the geometric shapes on the famous 1928 Bauhaus journal cover illustration, for example) who was attracted by its modern combination of art and technology (*see* Fig. 1.10).

Airbrush was and still is used mostly in technical illustration because of its capacity to make soft gradations of tone that subtly model 3D forms and give a much smoother finish than ordinary brushwork. Its mechanical "untouched by human hand" finish is also ideal for the technological nature of the objects being depicted (Fig. 3.24).

As a technique, however, it is labour-intensive to the extreme. The areas not being painted must be masked

Right 3.24 Jan Frohm, *Lola* racing car, 1998. This technical illustrator used traditional airbrush for this ghosted image. He painted the livery on acetate overlays so that he didn't need to repaint the basic car each time.

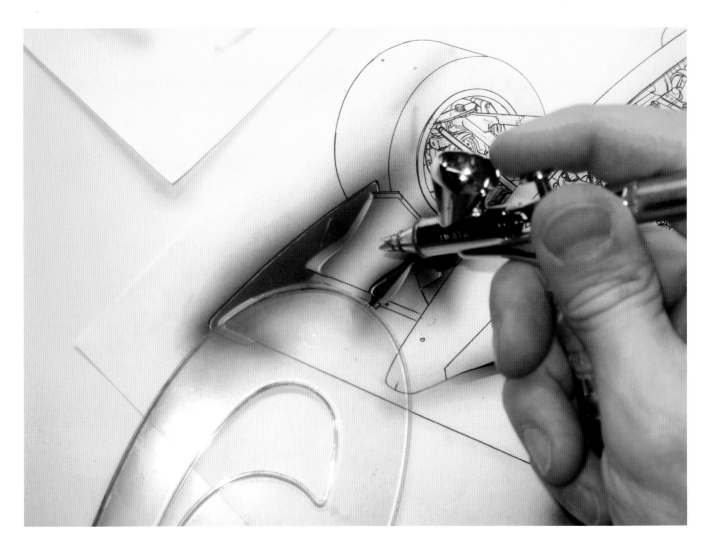

off and the instrument must be cleaned thoroughly every
time the colour is changed. There is a great deal of
methodical thought needed before all the stencils and
masks are cut (Fig. 3.25). Many designers might use an
airbrush at some time or other—if not for complete
illustrations, to put reflections or extra shine on a marker
drawing of a car body, for example, or for spraying models
to make them look more "solid".

The basic principle underlying the operation of
an airbrush is that when a stream of gas, for example
compressed air, is forced through a narrow orifice, its
pressure drops. If a tube feeding from a reservoir of
liquid—paint, ink or dye—is positioned where the gas
flow is at its fastest, then the pressure drop will cause the
liquid to be drawn into the stream of gas and atomized
into a uniform fine spray.

The cheaper airbrushes used by modelmakers work
by external atomization, with the gas blown across the
liquid feed at the very tip of the airbrush. This results in
an incomplete mix and a less than perfect spray. Airbrushes

intended for illustration use internal atomization to mix the liquid and gas under more controlled conditions. The quantity of paint, ink or dye mixing with the gas is controlled by the position of a tapered needle that fits snugly into the nozzle through which the spray emerges.

There are three basic types of airbrush: the single-action, the fixed double-action and the independent double-action. The single-action airbrush has a control button that is pressed to allow gas to flow. The ratio of paint to gas cannot be controlled, nor can the spray create a pattern. All the designer can do is to move the airbrush closer to or further from the paper. A fixed double-action airbrush has a lever that controls the flow of both the paint and the gas but not the ratio of one to the other. The first fraction of travel opens the gas valve, the rest retracts the needle allowing paint to flow into the gas stream. Thus a designer can begin spraying gradually and finish off by reducing the paint flow to nothing.

An independent double-action airbrush gives the designer the greatest amount of control. The lever is pressed down for the gas flow; pulled back to vary the paint supply. Thus a designer is able to spray pure air at full speed and then feed in the paint in small controllable quantities, to achieve delicate effects. This type of airbrush is easier to keep clean, as an occasional blast of air can be used to clear any obstructions in the nozzle.

The type of paint feed also varies from model to model. To cover large areas, a suction feed connected to a jar underneath the airbrush is used. Most designers use a gravity feed—from a bowl, cup or recess on the top of the airbrush. This takes a smaller quantity of paint, but makes the airbrush lighter and more manoeuvrable. Proprietary liquid inks and watercolours for airbrushes come in bottles with droppers in their caps for filling the cup or recess. The gas supply can come from cans of butane or freon gas, from carbon dioxide cylinders (as used for beer pumps) or from air compressors powered by an electric motor.

The technique of airbrushing revolves around the application and arrangement of stencils and masks to shield the areas of the drawing that the designer doesn't want painted. Loose masks of paper or clear acetate film cut into shapes used with weights give a slightly blurred edge. It is more common to use a combination of masking film and tape. Low-tack self-adhesive film, such as Frisk film, is cut in position on the drawing using a scalpel. The two sets of masks thus produced (one a negative of the other) are therefore guaranteed to fit together exactly.

For large areas it is more economical to mask most of the area with plain paper, reserving the film for critical edges. Masking tape is used for straight edges and smooth sweeping curves. An inexpensive and disposable alternative for spatter effects is an old toothbrush, dipped in paint and flicked with the back of a ruler. Letraset sell an attachment to a marker, the LetraJet (Fig. 3.26), which gives an airbrush effect by blowing gas across the

Right 3.26 The LetraJet air marker attaches to a standard marker pen. The trigger controls the flow of air over the nib, forcing the colour off the nib and onto the page and resulting in an airbrush effect.

Above 3.27 Alvar Aalto at his desk in the 1940s. Note the drawing instruments he has around him, including the set square (triangle) and a French curve. Photo by Eino Mäkinen. Courtesy Iittala Group, Finland.

nib of a marker. A spray diffuser is a low-tech device comprising two narrow tubes, hinged and angled at 90 degrees with a small gap between them. One end is placed in a container of paint and if the other end is blown down, the blast of air will draw paint up the other tube forming an aerosol of fine droplets which fall on the paper, giving a spatter effect.

Computer airbrushes (*see* Chapter 4), first found on Quantel's Paintbox 2D "paint" system, never have trouble matching colours for retouching and can do things that a conventional airbrush artist would find impossible to do mechanically—make masks and stencils with a soft vignetted edge, for example.

Drawing instruments

Whilst concept sketches will be drawn freehand, for more precise drawings later in the design process, designers may need the aid of drawing instruments. The most familiar will be the traditional geometry set of compasses, dividers, rulers, protractors and set squares (Fig. 3.27). In the past, fascinating devices were invented for generating ellipses and variable curves, for enlarging and reducing, and for aiding the production of perspectives—all collectors' items now and commanding high prices at auction.

Designers still use sets of stencil templates for ellipses, and French curves or bendy splines for more complex shapes. Computer-generated curves, however, are more accurate and controllable.

Conventional drawing boards include built-in straight edges with parallel motion, and some may have combination protractor/set square devices (called drafting machines) with convenient clickstops at the most commonly used angles of 15, 30, 60 and 90 degrees.

Papers and boards

Paper is a natural organic product, plant fibres held together by their own molecular forces (Figs. 3.28, 3.29). The surface texture and absorbency of the paper are a function of the amount of filler (usually china clay) added and the degree of pressing through rollers. Thin layout paper or thicker cartridge paper can be used for concept sketches. HP (hot pressed) is the smoothest and best for presentation line work; rough and the so-called Not (meaning not hot pressed, in other words, cold pressed) are more suited to watercolour painting. For engineering

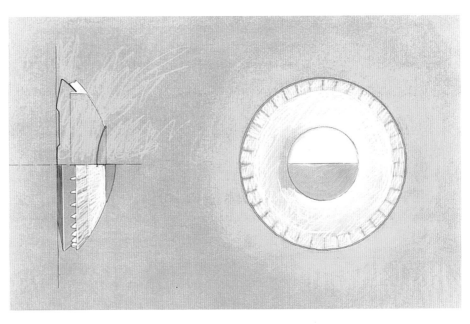

Above 3.28   King and Miranda
Design, Symbol lamp, 1997. The
designers chose mid-toned tinted
paper to use white chalk and yellow
pastels effectively, as in this
rendered set of orthogonals of the
Symbol lamp for Marlin Lighting.

Left 3.29   El Ultimo Grito
(Roberto Feo and Rosario Hurtado),
Micos inspiration drawing, 2005.
This front-of-envelope sketch,
incorporating collage and
Photoshop lines, was drawn
using a mouse.

drawings, designers use vellum, not the skin of a calf but
dense smooth transparent paper, usually shiny on one
side and matte on the other, to take the ink. It is difficult
to tear and so strong that mistakes and ink lines can
be scraped off using a scalpel.

Paper that is to take watercolour or gouache should be
stretched first by immersing in water and attaching it to
a slightly absorbent surface, such as an unprimed wooden
drawing board, using gummed paper tape. To avoid having
to stretch paper, sheets of watercolour paper can also be
bought in blocks, with several sheets glued around all sides
to prevent cockling when wet. For marker work, bleed-
resistant and bleed-proof layout pads are necessary.

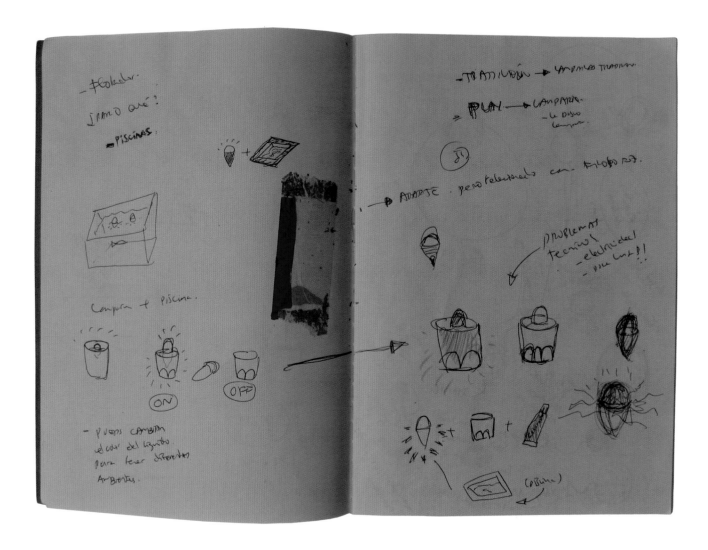

Above 3.30   Héctor Serrano, Waterproof
swimming pool lamp, 2003. The designer used
a sketchbook to jot down spontaneous ideas
for his project.

Most designers find it easier to use ready-made
cardboard-backed paper that does not cockle. Traditional
boards, such as Bristol board, have been superseded by the
lighter weight, polystyrene foam-based boards, for example
Fome-Cor, which is available in different thicknesses.

The weight of paper (or basis weight in the USA)
is measured in g/m^2 or gsm (grams per square metre)
in Europe and lb (pounds) per ream (500 sheets of the
specified size) in the USA. Layout paper is graded at
50–70 gsm; cartridge paper for sketching at 96–150 gsm;
watercolor paper at 285–535 gsm. The sizes of paper have
been standardized everywhere except the USA to the DIN
standards A0, A1, A2 and so on, each having half the area
of the preceding size. The sides of all sheets are in the ratio
1:√2. A0 is nominally 1 square metre in area and forms the
basis of the series. Designers will mostly encounter A4
(210mm × 297mm) for sketching and the larger A1 (594mm
× 841mm) and A0 (841mm × 1189mm) for production
drawings. Paper sizes in the USA are measured in inches
and the equivalent to A4 is US Letter (8½ × 11 in).

At the concept stage, designers may use a great deal of layout paper. This comes in metric A4-size pads and its translucency helps in developing successive designs from embryonic ones by tracing over the previous design or using it as a guide. This quality of layout paper also allows underlay drawings to be used when building up perspectives.

Colored cover paper, sugar paper, black art paper or Ingres (paper with ingrained fibers of contrasting colours) can be used with pastels for presentation quality drawings. Only the most expensive papers are pigmented at the pulp stage with lightfast pigments; most are coloured with dyes that fade sooner or later.

Many designers keep a sketchbook (Fig. 3.30)—a habit encouraged at art school—especially when they are away from the computer in a café or coffee shop. These range from the handy pocket-sized Moleskine (90mm × 140mm, 3½ in x 5½ in), ideal as an ideas book, to larger ring-bound or stitched cartridge paper pads with more space for doodling and trying out different designs.

Other equipment

The drawing board has become synonymous with the iterative nature of the design process, as when the exasperated designer sighs with resignation: "Back to the drawing board!" The plain rectangular drawing board with tee-square has been in existence since the 1700s, though the forerunner of today's model was introduced by engineer Marc Isambard Brunel, the father of the more famous engineer, Isambard Kingdom Brunel, in the mid-nineteenth century.

Even in studios with CAD, drawing boards can still be seen—they are good places at which to sit, think and sketch, and are ideal as a base to spread around lots of scraps of paper.

A surgical scalpel and a heavier duty craft knife are useful for cutting masks, paper and board. And to stick things back together and for mounting paper onto board, rubber solution can be spread thinly with an applicator or spatula. Surplus gum can be removed cleanly when dry using a homemade "rubber" of dried-up gum. Some designers prefer glue sticks or aerosol adhesive, for wrinkle-free mounting. Adequate ventilation is essential before using spray glue. The hobby of scrapbooking has introduced "glue dots" dispensed from rolls, ready to be applied to surfaces needing to be stuck together.

Other accessories include pencil sharpeners, low-tack masking tape and matte frosted "magic" tape for mending, a large soft brush for removing debris from the work in progress, talcum powder for de-greasing and "lubricating" surfaces, a cutting mat with a "self-healing" surface and lighter fuel to stop it getting sticky, plus rolls and rolls of soft tissue or paper towels to mop up accidents and generally keep things clean and tidy.

Conclusion

The manual tools that designers use for making marks listed above may seem obvious and self-evident—after all everyone knows what a pencil looks like. But anyone fascinated by the range of products available in a stationery shop or a graphic arts supply store may wonder what they are all used for. It is only by experimenting with different pens, pencils and types of paper that designers will find the tools they are comfortable using, and will best facilitate the conversion of pure thought and hand action into physical drawings understandable by other members of the design team.

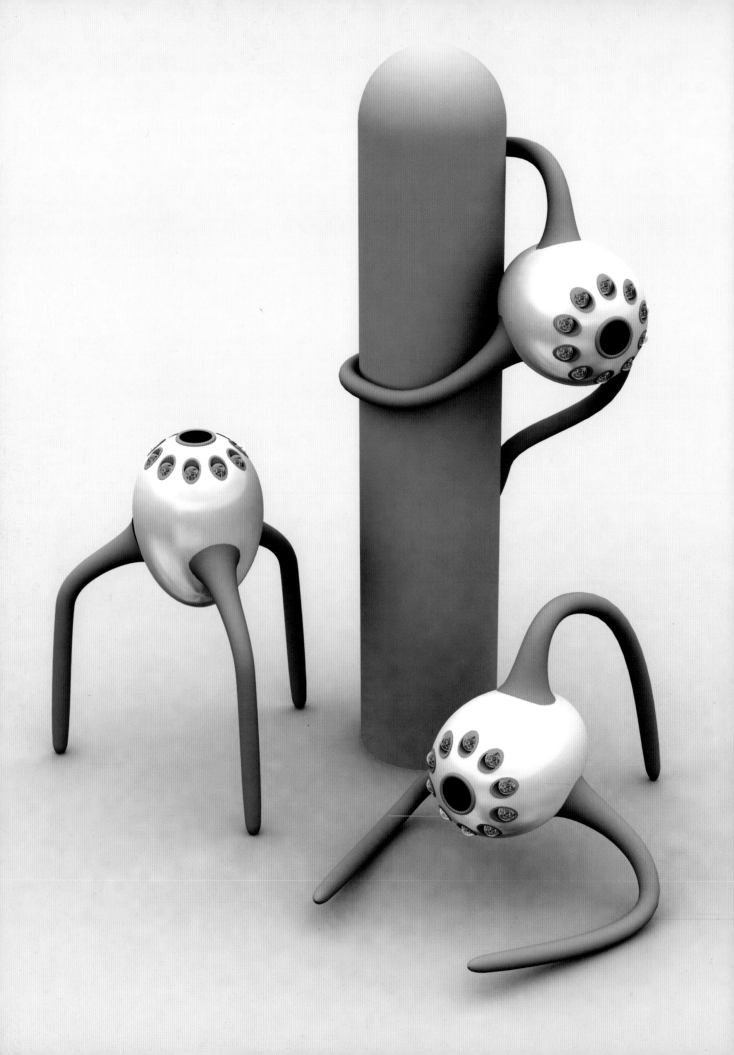

4

Computer systems

Opposite Thomas Gardner, Video baby monitor, 2005. This photo-real rendering— a wireless camera that transmits to a handheld computer screen, allowing the parent to supervise their child from another room— was created in 3D Studio Max.

Today, the computer system is just another tool, like those described in the previous chapter, but such an important and misunderstood one that it deserves a chapter of its own. Computer systems have two main components, each equally important: hardware and software. This chapter will deal mostly with the equipment you can see and feel—the hardware. Software, that part of a system which supplements the brainpower and experience of the designer and makes the hardware come alive, will be addressed as it is encountered in the chapters that follow, which track the various stages of the design-to-production process.

There is a lot of perhaps unfamiliar jargon used in specifying a computer system. What on earth is a 2.7GHz CPU with 1Gbyte of RAM, 512Mbytes of frame buffer, and a 1680 × 1050 32-bit LCD display? This chapter aims to make sense of the numbers and acronyms. And how exactly can a computer help you draw? Well, it is not actually much help with sketching, at present, but it does have an Undo button and you won't ever have to buy ink (except for the printer) or paint again. When it comes to precision drawing, the computer cannot be surpassed— straight lines will always be mathematically straight and right angles perfectly square. Just as the word processor— which superseded the typewriter—always produces clean copy, no matter how many times the design is revised, the printouts will always be pristine.

The take-up of CAD (computer-aided design) systems started first in the more downstream activities, in 2D drafting applications; in fact, CAD stood for computer-aided drafting. In the early days, the cost of a CAD system was far beyond the means of an individual designer and only affordable by large corporations in the automotive and aerospace industries. Since then both the hardware and software have become cheaper and more powerful, and CAD systems can be used in all stages of design, though currently not so much at the concept stage where the pencil still rules. In addition to pure CAD systems, there are also 2D illustration and "paint" systems such as Adobe Photoshop, originally developed for retouching photographs, and vector programs such as Adobe Illustrator for technical illustration, plus 3D surface and solid modeling and rendering systems, perhaps more familiar in CGI (computer-generated imagery) applications for animated movies, for example. All of these find a place in the designer's toolbox, either used independently or integrated together.

Not so long ago, a designer's studio would contain rows of drawing boards. Today the landscape has changed completely, with almost everything the designer needs contained within the casing of a computer. The computer brings control and flexibility to the designer's desktop. It won't do the designing for you, of course. A computer is merely a tireless tool, to be put to work as and when necessary, alongside the pencil and layout pad.

In the past few years much of the equipment described in this chapter has become commonplace; you may even have most of the hardware described here at home. Some technologies have already become obsolete. However, it is important to know how it works, what it is capable of, what its limitations are and what trade-offs in working practice you will be expected to make.

Simply having a computer does not make you into a better designer. But a good designer, armed with a computer, can do wondrous things. The main advantage is the almost total control of your design, from initial concept to finished product. There is a disadvantage to this, though; you will also have to take responsibility for all your design decisions—and their impact downstream in manufacture.

Early CAD systems came in the form of *turnkey* systems—packaged and integrated assemblies of all the hardware, software and support, all from one vendor. You turned the theoretical key and off you went. Turnkey suppliers bought-in components from third parties and re-packaged or "badge engineered" them, perhaps adding some proprietary go-faster boards as well as their own software, before passing on the thoroughly tested value-added system to the end user.

There were turnkeys for 2D "paint", such as Quantel's Paintbox, and turnkeys for CAD from suppliers such as Computervision, Intergraph, Applicon and Calma, from the late 1960s—expensive systems based on minicomputers. But with the introduction of the IBM PC in 1981 and the launch of AutoCAD software a year later, everything changed. CAD became affordable by the smallest practice or individual designer. And nowadays, all kinds of software are available to run on off-the-shelf computers.

The computer processor

The word "system" is used a lot in computer talk. It is a catch-all term, and usually means "everything"—the hardware and software together. The software that looks after the internal workings of the computer is called the operating system. And an item of software can be referred to as a program, a package or, again, a system.

Right 4.1 A PC computer system, such as this Hewlett Packard HP xw4300 Workstation, is usually built around an Intel Pentium 4 microprocessor and a Microsoft Windows XP operating system.

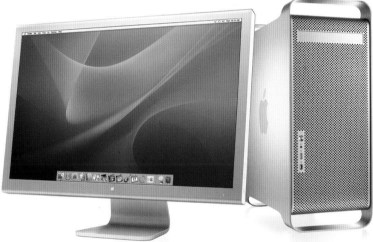

Below 4.2 An Apple Mac G5 with a 23-inch screen. Macs used to be based on Motorola and IBM chips but have now opted for Intel chips. The operating system, however, remains their own, designated by a number, for example, OS 10.5.

Most people recognize a computer from the name it has on the front: it may be an IBM PC (or more likely, a PC-compatible clone) or an Apple Macintosh. These are all personal computers—a self-contained system that is powerful enough to do the job you have in mind.

The next grade up is a computer called a workstation, from a supplier such as Sun or Silicon Graphics. These are much more powerful than personal computers, but they take up more space and are more expensive. As PCs have become more powerful, the distinction between PC and workstation has begun to blur.

Although the abbreviation PC stands for personal computer, it refers to a specific class of personal computer, namely the original IBM PC and compatible computers from suppliers such as Hewlett-Packard (Fig. 4.1). IBM-compatible PCs mostly use the Microsoft Windows operating system, and contain an Intel or AMD processor.

The Apple Macintosh is a personal computer, but not a PC (Fig. 4.2). Programs designed for the PC will not work on a Macintosh, and vice versa, although versions of a program such as Photoshop are available for both kinds of computer, will operate in similar ways and be able to share files. It is possible to emulate PC software on a Mac, and generally a Mac can read PC files but not vice versa. Apple has begun to use Intel chips recently, rather than the Motorola or IBM chips it has used until now, so the differences may well become less obvious.

System software

As stated above, specific software "applications" will be discussed later in the chapters on various stages of the design process. There are many levels of software inside the computer, however, which are mainly invisible to the user. At the lowest level, you need a program built into the machine that loads (or boots, as in "pull yourself up by the bootstraps") all the other programs.

At the next level is the operating system. This looks after the computer's internal workings, particularly the operation of the hard disk memory. It is often specific to the make of computer: PCs use Microsoft Windows or Linux, a public-domain operating system. The Macintosh's operating system is just a number, such as OS X (ten). Workstations mostly use versions of AT&T's Unix. The operating system usually comes with the computer when you buy it, and upgrades can be bought

on CDs or DVDs and installed on the hard disk. You see evidence of the operating system at work when you switch on the computer. It checks that everything is in working order, then it awaits your instructions.

Software is written in a programming language. Computers "think" in binary code (using the numbers in base 2, namely 0 or 1, on or off), but this is too cumbersome for humans to get to grips with. Thankfully, the average designer will not have to learn programming, but higher-level languages are sometimes available—so-called scripting languages—so that users can customize (adapt) the applications software to their own preferred ways of working.

Today's operating systems contain an "intuitive" GUI (graphical user interface) that simplifies communication between the human and the computer.

The central processing unit

At the heart of the computer is the CPU (central processing unit), comprising a microprocessor silicon chip or set of chips (chipset). Raw speed in computer terms is measured by the internal clock speed, measured in MHz (megahertz, or millions of cycles per second) or GHz (gigahertz, or billions of cycles per second). For example, an Apple G5 runs at 2.5GHz.

At every cycle of the clock, the CPU processes an instruction, or part of one. These are not the instructions

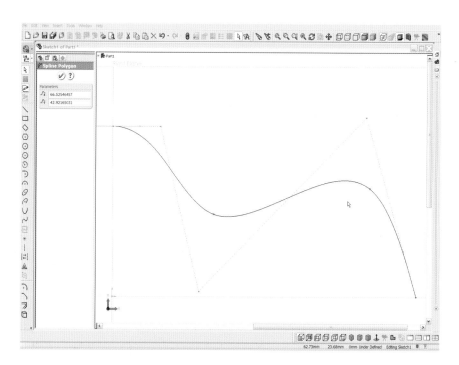

Right 4.3   A SolidWorks screenshot from a PC with a screen resolution of 1600 x 1200 pixels showing a freeform spline curve and its associated polygon. Once it was only possible to draw controllable curves using piano wire or bendy plywood strips.

you key into the computer, though. The computer breaks down your complicated instructions into millions of simple ones, which it calculates very quickly.

Computers for graphics applications have special requirements. Pictures take up enormous amounts of memory compared with text and, to move them around, the CPUs on these systems require some help. They are therefore augmented with various speed-increasing subsystems, or cards, to control the colour graphics on the screen (Fig. 4.3).

All this, however, is pure speed and, like the top figure on an automobile's speedometer, is an abstract quantity. Some computers may be able to redraw the screen after a tricky manipulation more quickly than others. But how quickly a designer actually completes a given job ultimately depends both on the efficacy of the software and on the proficiency of the operator.

Memory: ROM and RAM

Data is stored permanently on the computer's hard disk drive. Computers also have two sorts of chip-based memory. Firstly, ROM (read-only memory) chips have instructions manufactured into them—some of the computer's operating system—and they cannot be altered. These instructions remain on the chip even when the computer is switched off.

Secondly, local memory, containing the immediate job in hand, is in the form of RAM (random access memory) chips that are wiped clean each time the power is switched off. The amount of RAM a computer has available is measured in bytes, each equal to 8 bits (bit is short for binary digit). A kbyte, k or kilobyte is not a thousand bytes as you may expect, but 1024 bytes, which is equal to 2^{10} (2 to the power of 10, or $2 \times 2 \times 2 \times 2 \times 2 \times 2 \times 2 \times 2 \times 2 \times 2$). A megabyte, written 1 Mbyte, is more than a million bytes. A gigabyte, or Gbyte, is more than 1000 Mbytes.

There is a reason for the strange number 1024. Computers count in binary numbers, 0s and 1s. Thus, to a computer, "round numbers" are always powers of 2 (such as 4, 8, 16, 32, 64, 128, 256, 512 and 1024), and that is why you will often see these particular numbers associated with computers. Saved data is stored in a hard disk drive. It is always advisable to back-up important data to CDs, DVDs or an external hard drive, in case your computer crashes.

Computers also commonly have "cache memory". This is a portion of RAM that holds the most recently used data from the hard disk ready for further action, thus increasing the apparent speed of access to the user.

Frame buffers

A frame buffer is a short-term memory store between the processor and the display screen.

The frame buffer or VRAM (video read-only memory) contains the current image in the form of a bitmap of pixels (picture elements). It comprises several layers or planes, with one bit (a 1 or a 0) stored for each pixel on each plane. The number of planes, and hence the number of bits allocated to each pixel, determines how many colours or greyscale shades the displayed pixel can be.

A mono screen, without greyscales, has 1 bit per pixel. An 8-plane system can handle 2^8 (256) different colours or greyscales. A 24-plane system can display 16·8 million, a number sufficient to produce realistic-looking images. A 32-bit system has 24 bits allocated to colour, the rest for other things—on a Mac, for example, the extra 8 bits are called the "alpha channel" and are available for animation effects.

Displays

The computer's display is the window into the system (Fig. 4.4). CAD was once, unbelievably, done without a screen—the very first systems output direct to a pen plotter—but nowadays a screen is essential. The first computer displays appeared in the 1950s and were called vector refresh or calligraphic displays because the electron beam drew the picture onto the phosphor in random vectors, lines and arcs, like an Etch-A-Sketch. Although the images were superbly crisp, they were expensive and were prone to flicker as the drawing became progressively complicated.

Displays became reasonably affordable when Tektronix invented the direct-view storage tube towards the end of the 1960s. This type of screen did not require continuous refreshing—an electron gun wrote the picture onto the screen in a similar way to the vector refresh display and a low-voltage flood gun kept it there until the altered drawing became so cluttered it had to be repainted. Tektronix needed a phosphor that was bright, had long persistence, and that could hold a stored charge. The only one that would fit the bill happened to be green. The popularity of the green-screened 4014 display all through

Above 4.4 A flat LaCie 120 LCD (liquid crystal display) monitor has a resolution of 1600 x 1200 pixels and viewing angles of 170° horizontally/vertically. Bulky flickering CRT (cathode ray tube) displays are almost a thing of the past.

the 1970s gave the colour a new meaning—green became the colour associated with high technology.

The storage tube is now a museum piece, as too will be the CRT before long. Computer displays based on the cathode ray tube (CRT) are being replaced by flat liquid crystal display (LCD) monitors. Because CRTs require depth between the beam projection device at the back and the screen, these monitors are very bulky and heavy. LCD technologies make it possible to have much thinner monitors, commonly known as flat-panel displays. LCDs work by blocking light rather than creating it, while light-emitting diode (LED) and gas plasma work by lighting up display screen positions based on the voltages at different grid intersections. LCDs are flicker-free and require less energy than CRTs and are currently the primary technology for laptop computers. They have a crisper image, and produce less heat and radiation.

What make a CRT work are substances called phosphors: electrically active materials that luminesce when bombarded by electrons. Computer and television screens are called raster displays, from the Latin *rastrum*, or rake. The electron gun at the back of a CRT scans the whole screen in horizontal lines, top to bottom, usually 60 times a second (60Hz).

Each scan line is chopped into chunks called pixels (picture elements). Each pixel on the screen is described by one or more bits in the frame buffer. The resolution (fineness) of a raster display is measured by the number of pixels horizontally by the number of scan lines vertically—1280 × 1024, for example.

So-called active-matrix LCDs depend on thin film transistors (TFT). Basically, TFTs are tiny switching transistors and capacitors. They are arranged in a matrix on a glass substrate. Liquid crystal materials emit no light of their own and most computer displays are lit with built-in fluorescent tubes above, beside and sometimes behind the LCD. A white diffusion panel behind the LCD redirects and scatters the light evenly to ensure a uniform display.

To address a particular pixel, the proper row is switched on, and then a charge is sent down the correct column. Since all of the other rows that the column intersects are turned off, only the capacitor at the designated pixel receives a charge. The capacitor is able to hold the charge until the next refresh cycle. And if the amount of voltage supplied to a crystal is carefully controlled, we can make it untwist enough to allow some light through. By doing this in very exact and very small increments, LCDs can create 256 levels of brightness per pixel.

A colour LCD has three subpixels with red, green and blue colour filters to create each colour pixel. By control and variation of the voltage applied, the intensity of each subpixel can range over 256 shades. Combining the subpixels produces a possible palette of 16.8 million colours (256 shades of red × 256 shades of green × 256 shades of blue). Colour displays use an enormous number of transistors. For example, a computer with a resolution of 1024 × 768 needs 2,359,296 transistors etched onto the glass! If there is a problem with any of these transistors, it creates a "bad pixel" on the display, showing as a tiny dot.

Software optical illusions such as anti-aliasing are used to improve further the perceived resolution of screens, smoothing out the staircase effect seen on diagonal lines near the horizontal. It does so by colouring the pixels around the diagonals that actually define the line or edge in subtle shades of the current foreground and background colours.

Input devices

What makes a designer's computer system different from a home or office system is the device that allows designers to draw—the stylus and digitizing tablet of the input device. Computer graphics users have long augmented the computer keyboard and mouse with other methods for manipulating on-screen cursors and entering shape descriptions. There have been light pens and touch screens, rolling balls, joysticks, thumbwheels and the digitizing tablet (Fig. 4.5), with a pen-like stylus or a puck with buttons, depending on preference. Also included in the category of input device are scanners that can be used to input existing pictures or small 3D objects ready for computer processing.

Digitizing tablets such as the Wacom Intuos or Graphire perform a dual role: they can be used to point and pick software commands from a menu, or to draw pictures. The Cintiq has a built-in display (Fig. 4.6) so the designer can draw directly onto the screen (Fig. 4.7). To simulate the action of the traditional marker, input device vendor Wacom has an "Art Marker" stylus (Fig. 4.8) for use with its Intuos and Cintiq tablets. It not only uses the Intuos's features of pressure and tilt, but also rotation sensing technology. With its chisel-shaped nib, it enables designers to create virtually any type of brush effect or marker stroke. An airbrush stylus is also available (Fig. 4.9).

A digitizing tablet with a cordless pressure-sensitive stylus can be used with some draw (vector) and paint

Above 4.5 Graphics tablets are even more precise than rolling balls. This Wacom Intuos 2 oversize A4 is aimed at CAD applications with its cross-hair puck/mouse, but it can also be used with a pen-like stylus.

Right 4.6 The Wacom Cintiq is a tablet with a 21-inch (533 mm) 1600 x 1200 LCD screen, so you can draw directly onto what you can see using a pen stylus with 1024 levels of tip and eraser pressure sensitivity.

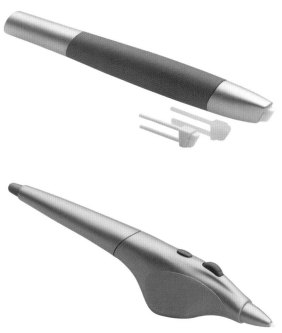

Above 4.7   Ron Arad, Ripple chair, 2005. The designer used a Cintiq with Corel's Painter software to draw this sketch of a chair for Moroso.

Top right 4.8   The Art Marker stylus has, like its traditional counterpart, a broad, angled pen-tip, made of either plastic or real felt. It is rotation-sensitive, so you can change the width of your stroke by turning the pen-barrel, just as you would with a real felt marker.

Bottom right 4.9   The Wacom Intuos airbrush realistically simulates ink application, spray distance and tilt angle. The finger wheel has 1024 levels of fine graduations and when you release it, it remains in that position, unlike a conventional airbrush, ensuring that digital ink is applied constantly.

(bitmap) programs (*see* Chapter 6) to create images more naturally and intuitively than using a mouse and keyboard. Larger format models can also be used to digitize (or trace) existing drawings, or more usually maps.

The conventional mouse (Fig. 4.10) works in relative coordinates rather than absolute ones, so it can get lost in space. It is fine for menu picking, but little use for drawing. Turn the mouse upside down, however, and you have the rolling ball (Fig. 4.11)—a device that has been used in air-traffic control for decades. The mouse is much more sensitive to touch than a joystick. Furthermore, it is less prone to breakage, doesn't trap dirt and has a smaller "footprint".

In the automotive industry, 3D coordinate measuring devices are used to input three-dimensional information from clay models, to be later smoothed and rationalized by a CAD system.

Right 4.10   This Logitech MX 610 laser cordless mouse also has a tilt wheel that scrolls horizontally or vertically.

Far right 4.11   Rolling balls such as this Logitech Trakman FX are used in gaming and air-traffic control. Only the ball moves, and it offers greater precision than a mouse.

Top 4.12 The SenseAble Phantom is a haptic input device with three degrees of freedom positional sensing and six degrees of freedom force feedback (three perpendicular axes plus the rotations of yaw, pitch and roll) to make you feel as though you are actually "sculpting" a real 3D object.

Right 4.13 The Epson Perfection 4990 Photo A4 scanner has an optical resolution of 4800 x 9600 pixels, a transparency unit and film holders for film formats from 35 mm to 5 x 4 inch, and it will scan a 216 x 297 mm (8^1/$_2$ x 11^5/$_8$ in) document. Digital ICE (Image Correction and Enhancement) automatically removes defects such as dust and scratches from prints or film.

For drawing directly in 3D space, designers can make use of haptic (meaning pertaining to the technology of touch) devices (Fig. 4.12), more commonly found in robotics and medical applications. Products such as the SenseAble Phantom can speed up the transition by digitizing sketches or clay models. A stylus is mounted in a device with six degrees of freedom positional sensing, which feeds back stiffness and forces so that the designer has the perception that he or she is actually sculpting the virtual clay into a real physical object.

Desktop scanners (Fig. 4.13) allow the designer to input already existing images—manual drawings and sketches for further manipulation, commissioned photographs or images plagiarized from books or magazines—or the silhouettes of small 3D objects into the system. In this way, a paint system can be used to generate electronic collages (Fig. 4.14), useful to the product designer for presentation drawing backgrounds or for mapping textures such as wood grain onto a surface. Be aware of copyright implications, however.

Above 4.14 PiliPili, Waterproof Televic nurse calling system, 2004. This Belgian design group collaged together UGS NG computer models and a heartbeat graph to produce this presentation graphic.

Hardcopy output

In the theoretical "paperless" design office of the future, there would be no need for hardcopy. A designer would be able to visualize a concept on-screen, work up the detailed production data and generate the information required by the machine tools to make the product, without leaving his or her seat. In reality, however, computers have created an unprecedented demand for paper. Designers still want something to hold in their hands and to scribble on and modify; clients prefer to spread out the different hardcopy options so they can be compared and contrasted with one another; production engineers, despite the availability of "ruggedized" terminals designed for factory floor use, still crave the reassurance of fully dimensioned orthographic drawings on paper.

A hardcopy device, such as a pen plotter, was once one of the highest priced components of a CAD system. Plotters with real pens that moved point to point have been supplanted (and, in many cases, made obsolete) by large-format raster devices, such as inkjet printers, still known as plotters and using the Hewlett-Packard plotter output language HP-GL/2. Plotters were used primarily in drafting and CAD applications, where they had the advantage of working on very large paper sizes while maintaining high resolution. They are still found in

Right 4.15 The Epson 9400 wide-format inkjet printer prints B0+ wide (44 in, 1200 mm) on matte or glossy media up to 1.5mm thick.

Above 4.16   The HP Laserjet 1020 printer is a "personal" monochrome laser printer that delivers 1200 dpi-like quality A4, in a space-saving design.

Below 4.17   The Canon Selphy CP710 dye-sublimation thermal transfer printer produces postcard-size 5 ⅞ x 4 in (148 x 100mm) output at 300 dpi. The results are photographic because the technology blends the ink while it is in a vapour state.

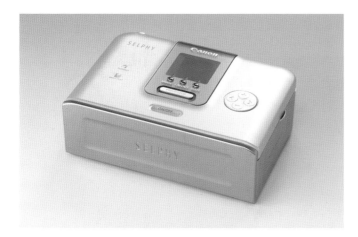

use in the garment trade, silk-screen printing and at vinyl sign makers where the pens have been replaced by cutters.

If you need large plots (A1 size or larger), you will have to choose between an electrostatic plotter and an inkjet (Fig. 4.15). For smaller formats (A4 and A3), these are joined by laser, dye-sublimation and thermal-transfer printers.

Electrostatic plotters were first introduced by Versatec (now absorbed into Xerox Engineering Systems) as an alternative to pen plotters. Unlike pen plotters, which draw vectors from point to point, these plot in horizontal lines, raster fashion, like large-scale laser printers. They too have largely been superseded by inkjet printers.

Laser printers (Fig. 4.16) work on a similar principle to laser photocopiers. In a photocopier, the light reflected from the white areas of an image causes a rotating drum charged with static electricity to lose its charge, so the toner doesn't stick. In a laser printer, however, there is no "original", so a laser draws a negative image onto the drum, removing charge from the white areas.

Inkjet printers spray jets of microscopic electrically charged droplets of ink onto moving paper. These jets of ink are deflected by electromagnets—just like the electron beam in a CRT tube—to build up the image. Bubblejet printers have an array of thin nozzles in the print head, each of which is full of ink, held there by surface tension. A small heating element causes a bubble to form that forces the ink out of the nozzle and onto the paper. Another variation is the thermojet printer, which sprays melted plastic onto the paper.

Perhaps the best contender yet for near photographic colour hardcopy is the dye-sublimation printer (Fig. 4.17), which mixes the ink on the treated paper, without dots or dithering. Sublimation is the phenomenon whereby certain substances go directly from a solid to a gaseous form, without the usual intermediate liquid stage. The thermal head on a dye-sublimation printer varies the temperature so that the amount of dye emitted is continuously controlled. They have currently found a niche in small-scale photographic printers, but may well be the technology of the future.

3D output devices

A numerically controlled (NC) machine tool can also be considered as an output device. Low-cost milling machines (Fig. 4.18) are available that can be wired up to a designer's

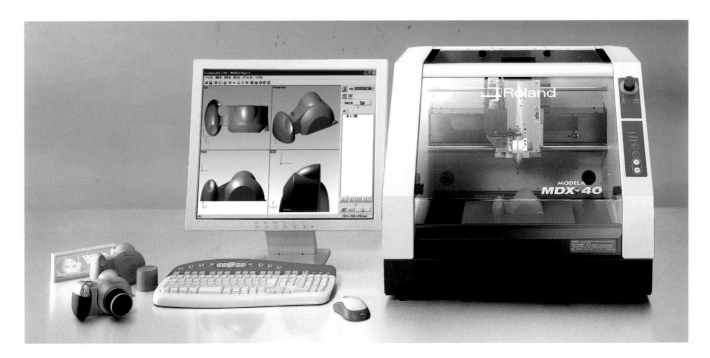

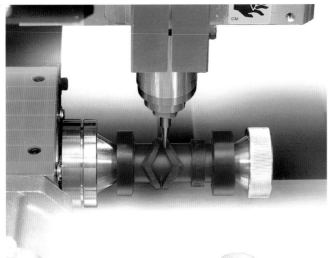

CAD system to produce 3D wax or polystyrene models direct from a computer database (Fig. 4.19).

A stereolithography machine (Fig. 4.20) creates real 3D objects layer-by-layer by solidifying cross-sectional "slices" of ultraviolet-curable polymer. The photopolymer is sensitive to ultraviolet light, so when the laser touches the photopolymer, the polymer hardens. You first create a 3D model of your object in a CAD program, then software chops your CAD model up into thin layers—typically five to 10 layers per millimetre. The 3D printer's laser "paints" one of the layers, exposing the liquid plastic in

Top 4.18   The Roland MDX-40 3D milling machine can produce smooth prototypes, parts and models in ABS, acrylic, chemical woods, plaster, styrene foam and wax of a maximum size 12 x 12 x 4 $^1/_8$ in (305 [x] x 305 [y] x 105 [z] mm).

Above 4.19   A 3D wax model is being cut on a Roland JWX-10 milling machine, a four-axis model aimed at jewellery designers.

Right 4.20   There are several different technologies used in rapid prototying, including stereolithography, selective laser sintering, and direct composite manufacture. The 3D Systems Thermojet is described as a solid object printer that uses multijet modeling (MJM) technology with adapted inkjet printheads used to deposit layers of thermoplastic powder as the prototype drops downwards.

Right 4.21   An automobile wheel prototype is being created on a 3D Systems SLA7000 stereolithography machine from UV-sensitive resin.

the tank and hardening it. The platform drops down into the tank a fraction of a millimetre and the laser paints the next layer, and so on, until your model is complete (Fig. 4.21). Once the run is complete, the objects are rinsed with a solvent and then "baked" in an ultraviolet oven to thoroughly cure the plastic.

This process is known as rapid prototyping (RP) and other fabrication technologies include selective laser sintering, laminated object manufacturing and fused-deposition modeling.

The RepRap project at Bath University is looking into the future when every home will possess a refrigerator-sized RP machine, at around the cost of today's inkjet printer, which could download designs via the internet and manufacture plastic parts and complete objects, including the RP machine itself, for the cost of the polymer or low-temperature metal alloy.

Networking

Computer hardware is only so much silicon, plastic and steel without the applications software packages required to bring it to life, and these will be discussed as they are encountered in subsequent chapters. Computers,

however, are being used earlier and earlier in the design-to-production cycle. They were already being used in designers' offices for word processing, general administration and project management. It was only a small step to buy image processing software and use computer graphics for concepts and proposals.

As soon as you have more than one system, they can be networked together (Fig. 4.22). There are three main reasons for networking: to exchange files and messages with nearby members of your team; to share resources such as laser printers and disk drives; and to co-operate jointly with others on large-scale projects—in a workgroup.

The best-known LAN (local-area network) is Ethernet. It was developed by Xerox, DEC and Intel, and introduced in 1980. With Ethernet it is possible to mix PCs and Macs on the same network, by cables or wirelessly (by WiFi).

Workstations were designed from the outset to be networked, so there should be no problem there. When more than two systems are linked, one system is designated the server—the place where files are stored—and the others are called clients. Any computer in the network can act as a server. This provides shared storage for programs (though it is faster to keep your own local copy) and files that everyone on the network can access. It is the responsibility of the applications software manager to

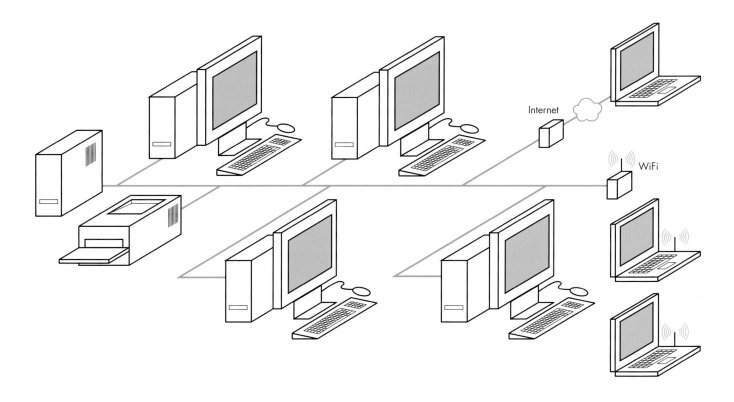

Above 4.22 Computer systems and workgroups can be linked together by networking. The most common local-area network is Ethernet. PCs and Macs can be connected by cables or wirelessly, or can communicate remotely over the internet.

Below 4.23 To prevent unnecessary stress and injuries, the designer's workspace ergonomics should be taken seriously. While sitting on a chair, your upper and lower legs should be at right angles; with your feet comfortably on the floor or a footrest. The angle between your upper and lower arm, when typing or drawing, should also be about 90 degrees.

say who has read-only access, and who has the authority to make changes to the master files. With broadband and the internet, members of the workgroup can be located around the globe and be working on the same project.

Health and safety

As computers become commonplace, so must health and safety issues be taken seriously (Fig. 4.23). It is rare indeed, for example, to find ergonomically adjustable desks and chairs in large organizations, so what chance does the smaller design studio have? But they cost little compared with the total investment in hardware and software, and can prevent lower-back damage to the most valuable component of the system—the designer. If that is not an incentive, then it should be noted that many of the recommendations are or will become legal requirements.

Desks should be as thin as possible and adjustable for height; chairs should be grounded sturdily and give good lumbar (lower-back) support. When you sit on your chair, upper and lower legs should be at right angles and feet comfortably on the floor. A footrest may have to be provided, subject to sufficient leg clearance, if desk height is not adjustable. The angle between your upper and lower arm, when typing, should be around 90 degrees.

There is a body of knowledge existing on such hazards as WRULD (work-related upper-limb disorders) and RSI (repetitive strain injury)—a disorder of the hands and wrists causing numbness, swelling, tingling and ultimately complete seizure. Keyboard operators have already suffered severe damage, and employers have been sued for large sums, so do not wait until it is too late. Take frequent "thinking" breaks away from the system, perhaps relocating to a drawing board and sketchpad. To rest the eyes, a break of 15 minutes in every 75 minutes of continuous computer use is recommended.

Lighting should be diffuse and indirect. Fluorescent lights should have diffuser shades and should run parallel to the user's line of vision. Avoid glare and reflections, and excessively bright or dark colour schemes. No user should have to face a window directly, and vertical blinds should be fitted, to be closed on sunny days. Regular eye tests are recommended. Because of the possibility of radiation, pregnant women should have the right to keep away from computers and laser printers, without loss of pay or career prospects.

The health risk from static build-up and electromagnetic radiation from computers is an issue still hotly debated. Emissions from the front of a computer, for example through a CRT screen, are in fact lower than from the sides or back. The computer screen should be at arm's length from your body—anyone sitting closer than 28 inches (711 mm) from the front is at some risk. Nobody should sit closer than 36 inches (914 mm) from the sides or back of a computer screen.

Photocopiers and laser printers should be placed where the air is changed at least once an hour, 3¼ yards (3 m) away from the nearest person, and preferably in a separate, well-ventilated room to disperse the fumes produced by the toner.

Finally, stress and anxiety can be reduced through appropriate and thorough training. This can be as simple as sitting down with the software manual for an hour or two each week to practice shortcuts, or spending time looking over the shoulder of the "resident guru" at work. Or it can involve taking time off from your paying projects regularly to attend more formal training courses.

Conclusion

Training can make or break a CAD installation, and it is the way designers are paid that usually militates against successful implementation. Top designers are often thought too busy to be taken off fee-earning projects to learn how to operate a computer program, a system that, if properly used, could be giving them even more earning power. CAD is an investment in both money and time. The temptation is to train only junior designers, or technician-like operators. The result is that the juniors get headhunted by other more enlightened consultancies; the company using dedicated operators loses many of the potential benefits of CAD.

Used and managed properly, a CAD system can do more than pay for its keep. It can allow a design consultancy to take on more work and handle larger projects, as well as reducing leadtimes and, hopefully, increasing the quality of the work produced. Computers are a neutral technology: they are not an end in themselves nor something with which to impress the clients, but just another tool—albeit a potentially powerful means of assisting the designer through each and every stage of the design process.

Hot tip:
Being resourceful

Illustrator John Nez says he couldn't stand drawing on the hard plastic surface of his Wacom Inuos 2 tablet. He felt as though he was drawing with a ballpoint pen on a marble bank countertop. Also, he found the plastic surface got pitted very quickly.

His solution was to cut out a piece of hard plastic from the cover of a school notebook and tape it across the top of the tablet like a hinge. This greatly improves the feel of the pen, which now moves smoothly and naturally. He couldn't source a plastic that worked for the mouse as well as the original surface, so he flips the plastic up to use the mouse and flips it back down to draw.

Case Study 2: David Goodwin's mesh ball ring 2004

David Goodwin designs jewellery that combines traditional craft techniques with modern manufacturing processes, such as rapid prototyping, and he's proud they look computer-generated. His 18-carat gold wire structures—spheres, cushions, mushroom clouds and ovals—are often set with precious gemstones that play with light to create optical effects, but the inspiration for his mesh rings came from experimenting with computer 3D modelers and liking the way the wireframe representation (usually just a short-cut means to an end) looked (with its moiré patterns) so much that he wanted to replicate it as the finished effect—serendipity in action.

David received his BA (Hons) Design: Silversmithing and Jewellery at Glasgow School of Art in 2001, then moved to London's Royal College of Art where he graduated in 2004 with an MA in Goldsmithing, Silversmithing, Metalwork & Jewellery.

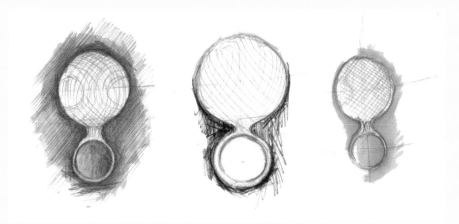

He says that working within a 3D environment allowed him to visualize his ideas more clearly than if he were designing on paper. However, he still sketches out initial ideas on paper (and in his diaries) (Fig. CS 2.1) but he makes his final design choices within the 3D virtual world. The ability to see designs in their entirety makes selective decision-making easier. Designing using Rhinoceros 3D CAD software and ray tracing in Flamingo (both developed by Robert McNeel & Associates in Seattle) produces a photo-real image of a possible physical object almost as good as the real thing (Figs. CS 2.2–CS 2.4).

Models of dyed polymer resin are then "3D printed" using the 3D Systems Viper SLA (stereolithography apparatus) in the RCA's in-house rapid-prototyping facility RapidformRCA (Fig. CS 2.5). The same 3D data with attached sprues (solid pathways that will become the channels in a mould through which molten plastic or metal can be poured) is used to make the gold ring by first "printing" the design in a special resin that burns out cleanly and then using this disposable model in high-pressure vacuum casting equipment. SLA laser-cured epoxy resin components can be built within an envelope size of a 250mm cube. This material creates semi-flexible parts with strength enough for snap-fit parts. Prototypes are built to +/-0.1mm as standard. A range of finishes can be applied, as for any epoxy resin component, including painting and texturing.

Right CS 2.1 Pencil and marker concept sketches.

Opposite top left CS 2.2 A Rhinoceros screenshot, showing the finished piped ring.

Opposite top centre CS 2.3 The 3D model rendered in Rhinoceros.

Opposite top right CS 2.4 The ring ray-traced using Flamingo.

Opposite below left CS 2.5 The laser-cured epoxy resin model straight out of the stereolithography machine.

Opposite below right CS 2.6 The finished gold ring, with sprues removed.

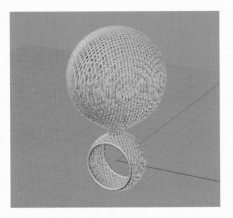

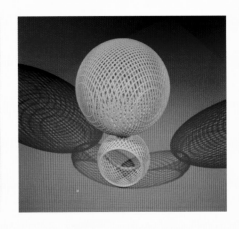

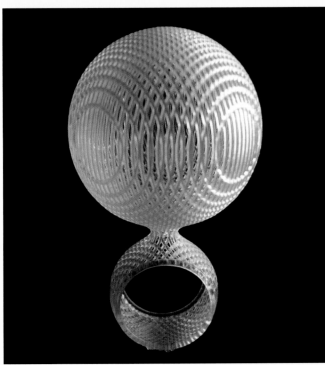

There were certain restrictions on the 3D system that had to be considered when designing the ring. All objects must be considered solid, and as Rhinoceros is predominately a NURBS-based surface modeler he had to ensure that all surfaces were joined, thus creating a closed polysurface.

To model the mesh ring, David first generated two spheres, sliced off a portion of each with cutting planes, then used the "blend surface" command to join the two. Next he contoured the object using a spacing of 1.5mm between each contour line. The polysurface was then hidden to show the entirety of the curves, and the curves then piped to make the wireframe solid. In this instance he used a 0.3mm radius for each pipe. The pipes were mirrored then the original base polysurface was "un-hidden". A cylinder was generated through the lower sphere to create the finger hole by Boolean difference. The resulting ragged edge was covered by ring pipes of double thickness.

These delicate rings, difficult if not impossible to fabricate by hand (Fig. CS 2.6), won him both the World Gold Council Grima Award and New Designer of the Year award at the Business Design Centre in 2004.

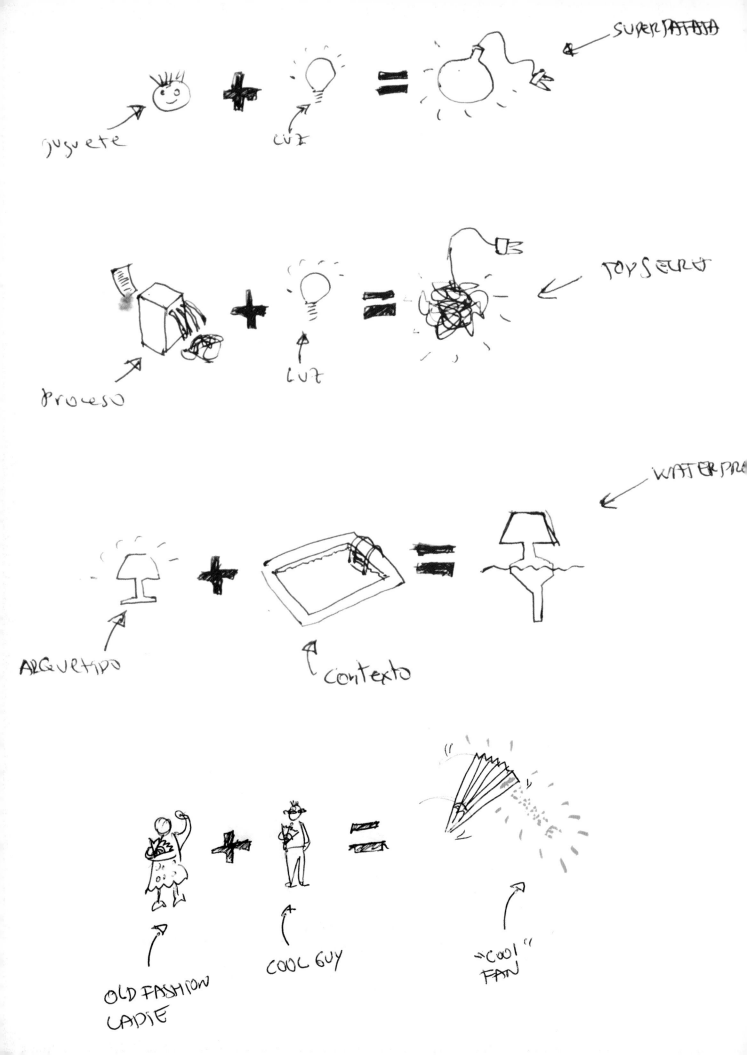

juguete + Luz = SUPER PATATA

proceso + Luz = TOYS EURT

ARQUETIPO + contexto = WATER PRO

OLD FASHION LADIE + COOL GUY = "COOL" FAN

> *"Drawing has always been an essential medium for the designer …
> for drawing is not just a medium of expression. We do not use
> drawings just to communicate our ideas to others. Designers need
> to draw in order to externalize their thoughts and make them
> concrete. It could even be argued that, if an artifact has not
> undergone this process of externalization, it cannot claim to have
> been designed at all."*
>
> John Lansdown *Computer-Aided Architectural Design Futures* 1986

5

Concept design

Opposite Héctor Serrano, Waterproof pool
lamp, 2003. The designer's mind can be seen
at work in these concept sketches.

Right 5.1   King and Miranda
Design, Tam Tam lamp, 1996.
The concept drawings of King
and Miranda, such as this sketch
for Sirrah, show the hand and mind
of the designer working together
freely, crystallizing an idea into
reality.

The concept stage in the design cycle is where the designer can have most fun, sketching out the wildest ideas before having to think of practicalities. The tool of choice will be the pencil or ballpoint pen, on anything that comes to hand: the back of an envelope, or even—for the more methodical—a dedicated sketchbook. However, the designer rarely has the completely free hand of the fine artist as there are also the needs of the client to consider, and downstream in the design process the engineers wait patiently for a set of 2D drawings or a 3D computer model on which they can begin to work. The computer has yet to make a useful contribution to concept design but researchers are busily working on computer-aided concept systems, for the earlier the design and engineering teams are able to work together, the shorter the product leadtime and the lower the overall cost of the design-to-production cycle.

At the concept stage, the product/industrial designer has two roles: to visualize the as yet non-existent product and to present to the client a choice of alternative design solutions.

Ideally, this stage should be as short as possible, leading quickly to a satisfactory design that can then be specified for manufacture. Representing this proposal visually is a fundamental part of the design process and conventionally these representations are 2D drawings and/or 3D physical models. The presentation requirements are driven by the intervention points of the client or, in the case of a large organization such as an automobile manufacturer, the company management.

Concept drawings show us the designer's mind at work: crystallizing a thought, evaluating it and moving on iteratively to a more refined design. As Corrado Bosi says in the introduction of the catalogue to a Milan exhibition of King and Miranda's concept sketches: "We should think of drawing as the quickest route from an idea to its depiction. We ask a lot of a drawing: in fact we think we can find out more from a sketch than from a working drawing, we want more intensity from a draft than a frescoed wall. Drawing uses up ideas and then creates others. The new drawing supersedes the preceding one, which is then forgotten. But for us—the viewers—all the drawings are part of the construction of a bridge that leads from the idea to the work" (Fig. 5.1).

Satisfying the client

Designers, unlike fine artists, rarely work in a vacuum and have to be aware of the demands of their clients. A designer would ideally like to be left alone to represent the concept quickly, with flexibility and with the option to modify it easily once created. If a computer is to be of use at this stage (see below), any input of geometric information would have to be quick and easy to do, not be overly precise, be easy to modify, user friendly and with a visual quality adequate for rapid evaluation. The client, on the other hand, would like the concept (and presentation) stages to integrate well with the downstream engineering design process, and allow other professionals to participate in the design decisions at all stages of the design process.

A concept sketch can be defined theoretically as "a collection of visual cues sufficient to suggest a design to an informed observer". A typical design comprises a "skin" of styling that contains a package of pre-sourced components, such as motors or power supplies. Sketches can be categorized as either free "theme" sketches, with little regard yet for the components to be contained within, or "package-constrained" schematic sketches, with less emphasis on the final outward appearance of the product. A theme sketch (Fig. 5.2) is the initial expression of how a proposed design is intended to look, drawn with as free a rein as possible without the designer getting bogged down with considerations of any internal constraints. An informed observer should be able to understand what is implied about the design proposal, the visual impact of the design as a whole and its specific visual characteristics.

The package-constrained representation (Fig. 5.3) of a proposed design is a sketch that communicates the fixed dimensional parameters of a design that has to incorporate off-the-shelf components, as most designs will. It allows an observer to understand the dimensional

Below 5.2   George Sowden, Isilys toaster, 2004. A "theme sketch" is the first expression of how a proposed design could look, drawn without the designer being restricted by internal constraints, as in this initial sketch for Moulinex.

Above 5.3   The "package-constrained" representation is a sketch that must incorporate off-the-shelf components, as in this schematic by Sony Ericsson of the K800 mobile phone, 2005.

constraints and proportions of the proposal, as well as the fit or interference of the theme proposal with the package.

For sketches like these to be useful in the design process, and not just redrawn or thrown away, it is necessary for them to be used directly as a source and input to computer models that can then be evaluated and easily modified. These models would allow for a 3D concept to be evaluated much earlier in the process than is traditionally possible. The availability of this virtual 3D model would also allow other professionals to participate and engineers to work concurrently with the designers much earlier in the design-to-production cycle than is possible using conventional drawing methods.

The design process starts here

As outlined in the Introduction, the design process is initiated when a designer or design practice receives a design brief from the client, identifying the need for a new product. A design team is established, and timescales, fees and a product design specification (PDS) are discussed with the client. The designers retire to work and reconvene with the client on an agreed date to submit a series of proposals (*see* Chapter 6), usually accompanied by presentation drawings and models.

Below 5.4   Karim Rashid, *Liquid* chair, 2005. In a simple concept sketch the designer attempts to give form to a future product. Here the designer tries out several ideas for his *Liquid* chair.

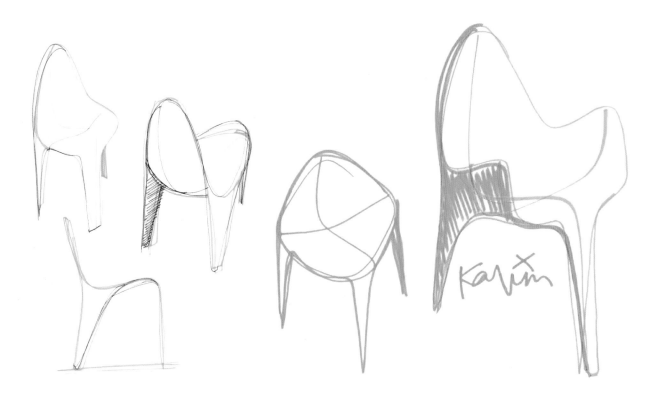

In some cases, the designers and the client will part company at this stage, with the latter taking concept documentation to manufacture. In other cases, the designers may be brought back into the project after the package-constrained object has been sketched, to carry out a "packaging" or styling job.

A design brief can be presented as top-down or bottom-up (*see* Introduction, p. 23). In either case, the first stage of the design-to-production cycle is called concept design.

The concept sketch close up

The concept sketch is the designer thinking aloud with a pencil; what Aldo Rossi calls "private visions". The designer may be putting on paper—usually on a translucent layout pad—an *aide-mémoire* of a totally thought-out 3D idea to be worked up later into production drawings; alternatively, and what is more likely, the very act of drawing can be a means of crystallizing a vague inkling that may or may not be worth pursuing. Frequently, the making of a simple sketch to express a concept can, in itself, suggest further conceptual ideas. Sketches, according to Bryan Lawson in *How Designers Think*, act as a kind of additional external memory to freeze and store spatial ideas that can then be evaluated and manipulated to produce further ideas. The designer is wrestling with future possibilities, attempting to give form to uncertainty (Fig. 5.4).

In the London design consultancy of Seymourpowell, partner Richard Seymour is a concept designer of the first category—he claims to reveal the picture he has in his mind like the picture in a child's magic watercolour book becoming visible as a wet brush is washed over it, or like the image appearing in a developing bromide print. His partner, Dick Powell, on the other hand, admits to being less mechanical. Drawing to him is a more interactive process, a process of exploration and understanding.

Concept sketches may look inexpensive to produce, but the designer must be conscious that it is here that the cost implications of the project are at their most sensitive; it is at this stage that the overall look—as defined by the 3D spatial and proportional relationships—of the product is decided. Concept sketches also focus on various perceived problem areas or challenges associated with the as yet non-existent product. Unless the designer has specific instructions to fit all the various components into a specific shape or size—the space envelope—prescribed by the client, there is no measurable content yet.

Sketch or schematic

Initial sketches may be of the overall form of the product, of certain difficult details, or may be a system schematic—a collection of interconnected boxes labeled "motor", "keyboard", "display", and so on (Fig. 5.5). The designer may include a few rough calculations to estimate the final

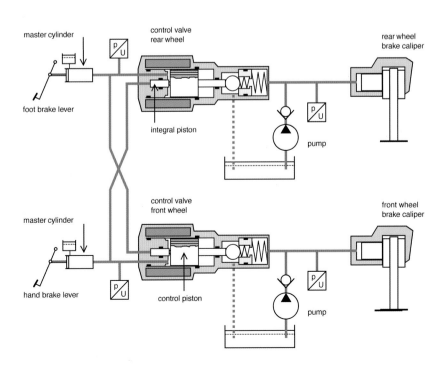

Right 5.5 A system schematic, such as this of a BMW ABS brake system, is an abstract layout drawing bearing little relation to physical reality.

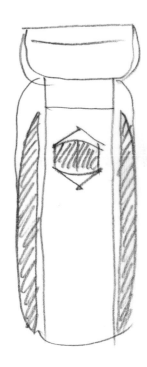

Above 5.6 In a shaver, such as this early pencil concept for the Braun 360° Complete, there is a well-defined space envelope, dictated by the shape of the human hand and the components that must fit inside.

size and proportions of the product. Concept sketches do not have to be to scale, need be neither neat nor clean; they are a hardcopy record of the ideas taking shape in the designer's mind (Fig. 5.6). Ideally they should all be retained, bound together in a sketchbook, as even those judged no-hopers at the time might be useful in future projects, or when the designer is sent "back to the drawing board" by a difficult client or by a change in the brief.

The medium used is that preferred by the individual designer—pencil, fibretip pen, fountain pen—for initial concept drawings are rarely shown to the client, or to other designers in the team. The Spanish designer Oscar Tusquets Blanca, for example, typically uses soft Derwent pencils (B or 3B) in A4 squared notebooks (Fig. 5.7). Other designers say the medium does not matter. As Tucker Viemeister of New York's Springtime-USA puts it: "I do not have a favourite pen or pencil. I do not have special lucky socks that I wear on opening nights either. Ballpoints on napkins work just as well as mechanical pencils on Mylar."

Concept sketches are usually incomplete descriptions of the object being designed. The rest of the information remains locked inside the designer's head or has yet to be thought out. Direct-communication sketches for the benefit of another designer or the client, done on the spur of the moment following a statement such as "Here, let me show you what I mean …" need an additional commentary from the designer to be fully understood. More committed

Right 5.7 Oscar Tusquets Blanca, *Carlitos* bench, 2003. Pen and coloured pencils, 11⁷/₈ x 8¹/₄ in (30 x 21 cm). The Spanish designer examines various design details for his design for Figueras Internacional Seating.

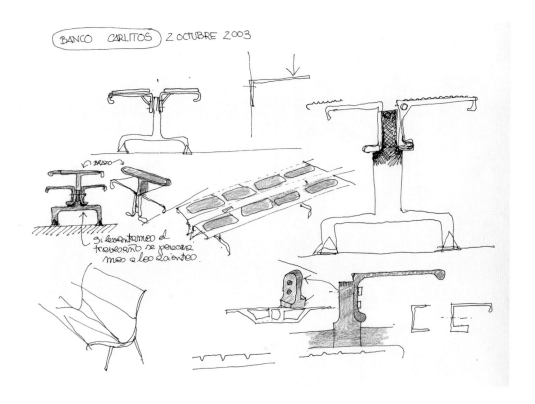

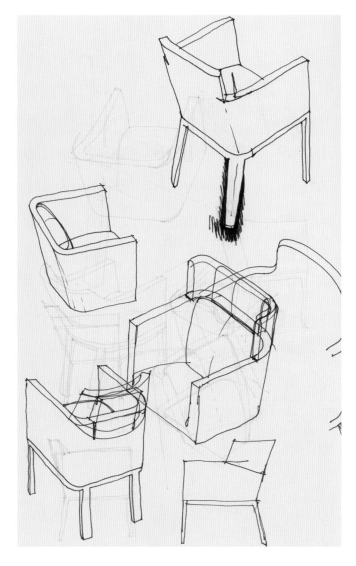

sketches often begin with an overall light outline, with the designer darkening selected lines, filling in details and adding notes and perhaps key dimensions. If a sketch is to be copied, paper with feint blue lines or squares should be used, unless of course the grid is to be made a feature of the drawing.

Evaluating the design

As the project progresses, the concept drawings will be modified and reshaped in line with any new information, and the results of analyses into performance, durability, cost, reliability and ease of manufacture (Figs. 5.8–5.13).

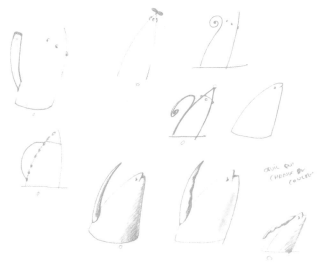

Above 5.8   Paul Sayers (Drum Design Studios), Chairs, 2004. Drawing on translucent paper in a series of stacked overlays, as here, allows the designer to build on and refine previous sketches into more finished concepts.

Top right 5.9   Philippe Starck, Hot Bertaa kettle, 1990–97. The designer's sketches for this Alessi kettle show different handles.

Bottom right 5.10   Philippe Starck, Hot Bertaa kettle, 1990–97. This product shot of the final design for Alessi shows the spout and handle as one.

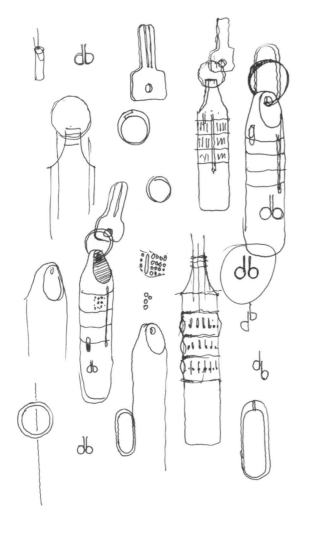

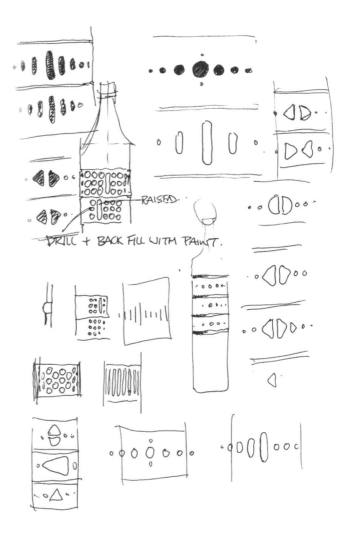

Top 5.11   Priestman Goode, Decibel keyring
earplugs, 2005. These concept sketches for
a keyring containing earplugs concentrate on
the surface finish of the keyring enclosure.

Above 5.12   Priestman Goode, Decibel keyring
earplugs, 2005. The Decibel tones down disruptive
ambient noise from public transport, so commuters
don't have to turn their MP3 players up to hear
their favourite tracks.

And as the concepts develop, so more accurate drawings
will be needed to confirm to the designer that the original
loose concepts will, in fact, work. Using the initial concept
sketches, plus information from calculations, codes of
practice, standards, additional requests from the client and
catalogues of proprietary items, the designer will then
attempt a scale layout drawing to see if and how everything
will fit together. This will establish the key dimensions
and will probably be drawn freehand in orthographic
projection, as a rough first try at a general arrangement
drawing (*see* Chapter 7).

Overlays on translucent layout paper, tracing paper or
Mylar film can be used to experiment with the placement
of components, to check they do not clash with one
another and to evaluate the parameters of any movement
envelopes (Fig. 5.8). If the layout is drawn in orthographic
projection, all three views must be drawn together in
scale—the components may fit nicely in one view, but
clash badly in another. Sections, auxiliary views (the
axes easiest to draw may not be the easiest to use in

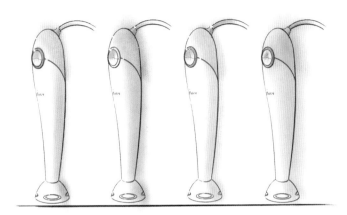

Above 5.13   Youmeus Design, Kitchen tools, 2004. Biro pen and pastel. These concept sketches for Kenwood were rendered in biro and pastel dust applied by absorbent cotton.

manufacture) and scrap views (close-ups) may be included with the orthographic to help clarify the proposed solution, and to try to eliminate any ambiguity.

The concept tested, the contented designer is now ready to move on to the presentation drawings of Chapter 6 (to convince the client and financiers that the solution proposed is the right way to proceed) and then to the general arrangement drawings of Chapter 7, which will become the key to the enormous number of working drawings required for manufacture and assembly.

Can the computer help?

Until recently, computers have played only a very minor role at the concept stage of product design, the stage when the designer is alone, thinking aloud with pencil and paper, in a solitary quest to produce something new and never seen before, but something that also fulfills the design brief. It is an iterative process of sketching, evaluation and re-sketching. There would be obvious benefits if these sketches, instead of being isolated from the rest of the design-to-manufacture process, could form part of the input into an integrated computer model that could be used again downstream.

The problem is that, despite the needs of the client and engineers, the designer does not want to commit

to a fixed geometry and dimensions at this stage, but wishes to remain flexible and undecided for as long as possible. Current computer systems, however, demand too much precision too soon.

The use of computers to aid in concept design is a highly charged and controversial area. To many, it is synonymous with artificial intelligence and computer-automated design, if there is such a thing, promoting the idea that computers can *think* for themselves. But if there is such a possibility as systematic design, and if all that designers are doing when they design is problem solving— that is, matching a set of manufacturing parameters to a perceived set of performance criteria set out in a specification laid down by marketing people, and constrained by cost considerations and the technological state of the art—then surely all jug kettles would look the same, there would be an ideal and optimum shape at any given time, with form following function. That electrical white goods—refrigerators, washing machines, microwaves—(even cars) do look more or less the same, does not blunt the argument.

In the capitalist world, designers are in the fast-change fashion business—design as differentiation. Computers— even so-called expert systems—don't yet have the kind of brain that can absorb, recycle and appropriate all the diverse ideas and influences a designer is bombarded with from the worlds of fine art, popular culture and elsewhere. If a computer can't yet do the designing, what it *can* do is act as an able and tireless assistant, doing the computer equivalent of running errands and sharpening the pencils, keeping accessible archives and performing tedious calculations—but never intruding where it is not wanted (Fig. 5.14).

Concept design has always been the Cinderella of CAD. Back in the heady days of the 1960s, excited theorists— especially in systems architecture and electronics—mapped out schemes for automated or "systematic" design, comfortable perhaps that the means of implementing their visionary systems existed only in a distant future of cheap and plentiful hardware and was far beyond the capability of their contemporary mainframe computers (which were probably equivalent to the power of the microprocessor in today's disposable digital watch or calculator).

More pragmatic and modest applications for computers, such as the 2D drafting systems that emulate the manual methods of the traditional drawing office, have dominated ever since—the ubiquitous low-cost PC-based drafting systems, rather than liberating designers, merely perpetuate outdated Victorian conventions.

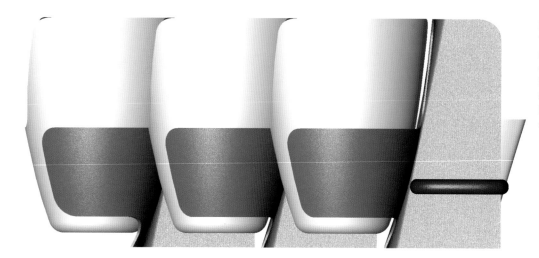

Left 5.14 Pearson Lloyd Design, Virgin Atlantic Upper Class Suite seating, 2001. These CAD concepts were modeled in Cobalt to visualize early conceptual thinking and material ideas, and to see how the forms relate to one another in multiples.

3D solid modeling concepts

Now the processor and memory chip developers are calling the shots, and the hardware with the horsepower to handle computer-intensive tasks and manage large amounts of memory has become much more affordable. CAD developers are using this excess processing power to make the interfaces to their systems more user-friendly and the software more "intelligent"—employing OOP (object-oriented programming) techniques so that designers can have more confidence that their designs will be right first time, can try out "what if?" scenarios and can take more responsibility for the ultimate success of the designed product.

What is object-oriented programming (OOP), you may ask? Historically, programs have been viewed as procedures (that we may think of as "verbs") that operate on data. OOP is a modular approach taking the view that programs should start by thinking about the data (or "nouns") first. The result is software that is simpler and more robust to develop and to maintain, with tried and tested modules and components called "objects" being reused and inheriting the attributes of other objects—more below.

The problem with many mainstream CAD systems has been that designers usually have to know exactly what they want before sitting down in front of the screen. And this is exactly what the conceptual designer does *not* want—the initial sketch phase of design is the back-of-the-envelope stuff, in which designers are struggling to formulate and externalize their ideas. The last thing they want is a computer pestering them for precise dimensions, angles and tolerances good enough to build a working prototype. Not yet, at least.

The paradox is that most present-day systems need to know everything about the finished design before they can start modeling. But free from that "prior condition of completeness" that rigid present-day CAD systems insist on, designers can really begin to design creatively, telling the system as much as they want it to know now, and more later; telling it what they want it to do rather than having to spend time explaining to the machine how to go about doing it and where to find the information.

Object-oriented systems

In object-oriented systems, an "object"—which can be as primitive as a line or arc, or as complex as an assembly—is defined in terms of a set of data items plus all the procedures for manipulating and controlling it. The object not only knows what it is, but also what it is realistically capable of doing and how it goes about doing it, and is aware of its relationship to other objects with which it may have to interact.

Similar objects are grouped into "classes" and these can be broken down into sub-classes that can "inherit" the data structures and functionality of the "parent". The class "line" can have a sub-class "pipe" that will inherit the methods for moving, displaying and deleting, but whose data structure will also include such attributes as material and diameter. Thus new graphic elements can be defined with the minimum of duplication and least amount of disturbance, making the maintenance of the software considerably easier.

Common codes can be shared by many classes in the system and where differences do exist, it is only necessary to indicate the changes. OOP allows software engineers, and designers, to develop new applications by taking advantage of previously developed objects, and all the "intelligence" inherent in them. Objects take CAD beyond the confines of physical geometry; the designer can try out variations of a design using different materials, sending a stack of designs off, say, for stress analysis, each of which can then be explored more readily.

The whole history of the design process can be automatically recorded so it can be rerun, altered or evaluated at any time—a feature indispensable to concept designers who like to play around with ideas before committing themselves to a physical prototype. A "history" function also enables designers to gain an insight into the manufacturing implications of their styling decisions on a component's physical properties (weight, volume, moment of inertia) and the likely production cost penalties. "Programs should allow designers to change their minds," says design research guru John Frazer, "allowing precise definitions of components for the purposes of evaluation, but at the same time permitting the easy change of fundamental shapes or proportions. With CSG (constructive solid geometry) solid modelers [*see* Chapter 2], this is not always possible. Unless you can get at the tree of Boolean operators used to arrive at the geometry, the design process is irreversible."

Design programs also need to be sympathetic to a designer's needs, using familiar words—taken from a manufacturing vocabulary, rather than computer-oriented jargon such as Boolean and Euler—creating computer models of components from virtual reality blocks, billets, sheets, turned parts or extrusions, using industry-understandable operations such as drill, punch and chamfer, just as real metal components are made in the workshop.

What this boils down to is that software vendors are aiming to produce 3D solid modelers that are more easy-going and flexible, in terms of requiring less precision, and easier to use than the ones currently on the market, so that they can be used earlier on in the design process.

A hybrid approach

Until more flexible and responsive modelers are available commercially, designers have adopted a hybrid approach, combining manual methods with computer aids and different kinds of software. Although there are software packages designed specifically for quick and easy 2D sketching, using a digitizing tablet and stylus for input, such as Alias SketchBook Pro (Fig. 5.15), most designers will most probably still begin the process using a pencil and paper, then scan in the resulting drawing to be cleaned up and coloured in using a "paint" program such as Adobe Photoshop. Using layers and tracings (both physical translucent sheets of paper and their computer equivalents) makes the process slightly more flexible and understandable. The challenge is to convert these 2D sketches into a reasonably faithful 3D computer model

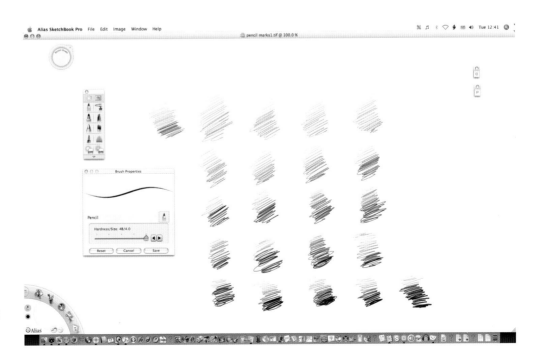

Right 5.15   Screenshot of Alias SketchBook Pro showing simulated pencil grades from 4H to 4B in different mark sizes.

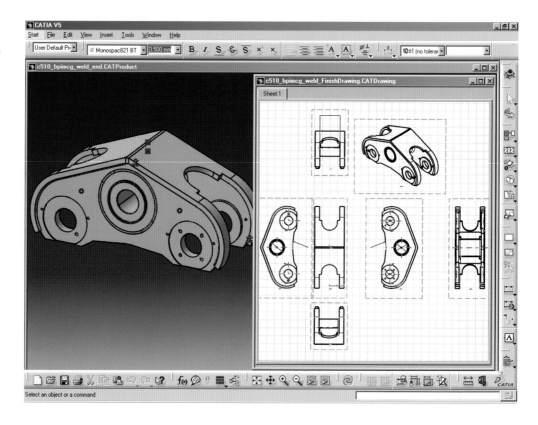

with the minimum of effort, which can then be used later
to make rendered presentation drawings, instructions for
NC milling machines, and other data for manufacturing.

Orthographic (plan and elevation) sketches appear at
present to be best suited for taking off measurements and
for establishing anchor points and curves as a basis for
a 3D model, especially if there is some symmetry involved
in the product, around the centreline of an automobile or
mobile phone, for example (Fig. 5.16). Perspective sketches
may look convincing, but are in effect distortions and not
really accurate enough to extract data from in order to help
create a useful 3D model.

Commercial computer solutions

There are several software products on the market aimed
at bringing together the tools needed to carry a concept
through to the next stage of design. Some designers may
work with real or virtual clay to input into a 3D solid
modeler such as SolidWorks (*see* Step-by-step 2) to capture
the rough geometry of the concept. Pro/Concept is a
program specifically aimed at concept design, and is the
front-end to PTC's parametric solid modeler Pro/Engineer.

Using Pro/Concept, the designer selects a virtual
pencil, marker or other drawing tool from the toolbar and
starts to create the concept sketch. There are image-editing
tools to apply, such as warp, stretch and colour
replacement, to generate alternative sketches. The sketch
can then be expanded into a wireframe model by drawing
key lines and sections through the model. This may already
be enough information to capture the concept and hand
off the design to the CAD engineers, for them to create
the solid model. Or the designer may wish to develop the
3D forms further by combining lofting techniques and
primitive objects to build basic 3D forms, using various
local and global editing tools to refine them and add detail.

When the model is complete, tools similar to those
used on the original sketch—warp, bend, paint and so
on—can be used directly on the model. The software is
claimed to be flexible enough to let designers start at any
point in the conceptual workflow—at sketch, layout or
virtual clay—and then move to any other point from there.
To start at the layout phase, for example, a designer might
begin by inputting "legacy" curves from an existing design,
or scanning an existing model. To start at the virtual clay
phase, facet data from existing 3D models can be input.
Then, or at any point, the designer can simply grab the
sketching tool, or the eraser, or the paintbrush, and go
from there.

To fine-tune a design, a designer can "paint" onto
the 3D model to explore ideas before committing geometry

to the model. To try out several different keypad ideas on a new mobile phone, for example, a designer can map a 2D picture of the keypad onto the model, review it, remove it, and try another. Once the preferred style is found, the actual geometry of the painted keypad can be added to the model. With realistic rendering and lighting, the design team can present and evaluate designs with greater realism much earlier on in the product development cycle.

Drawing in space

The biggest handicap to working in 3D on a flattish 2D screen is being able to picture exactly where you are in space. The 2D computer screen is merely a window into the virtual world of the 3D solid modeler. And unlike the solid models used for movie animations and games, which are merely visual representations of 3D objects, the CAD solid model has far more properties, such as weight and volume.

For drawing and sculpting directly in 3D space with tactile feedback, designers can make use of haptic devices (Fig. 5.17), more commonly found in robotics and medical applications. Products such as the Omega can speed up the transition from sketches to model by importing 2D files from drawing and illustration packages, build 3D models from 2D curves and hand over a single 3D model rather than multiple 2D drawings that may be misinterpreted. It can also create affordable 3D interpretations of designs earlier in the design cycle by reshaping and decorating clay models, rendering and animating models to test out different design directions before committing to physical prototypes and more detailed designs.

To reiterate the point made in the previous chapter, a stylus is mounted in a device with six degrees of freedom positional sensing, which feeds back stiffness and forces so that the designer has the perception that he or she is actually sculpting the virtual clay into a real physical object. The system output includes photo-realistic renderings, files for rapid prototyping and selected 3D formats for downstream processes.

As mentioned in Chapter 2, Pro/Engineer (Fig. 5.18) is an example of a parametric solid modeler that allows models to be constructed and modified dynamically—the designer adding to or deleting from the base model without suffering the penalties incurred with conventional "static" solid modelers. The need for exact dimensional information has almost been eliminated—the general shape is captured parametrically, and dimensions can be modified by inputting a value, by establishing a relationship to other parametric dimensions or by defining a relationship to a table of parts. A designer can establish datum points, axes and space envelopes, can sketch a part,

Right 5.17 A commercial three-degrees-of-freedom Omega haptic force feedback device. Courtesy Force Dimension, Switzerland.

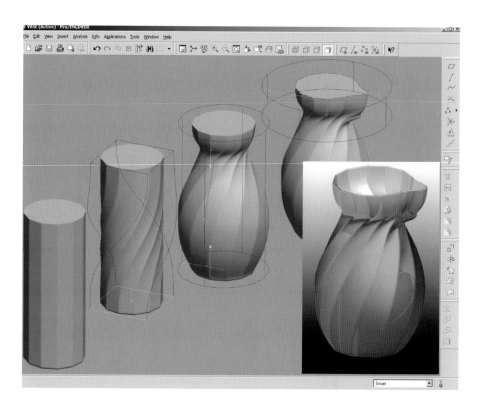

Right 5.18   A Pro/E screenshot of a rendered vase created from a twisted and manipulated prism/cylinder.

Below 5.19   Pearson Lloyd, Soul advanced cantilever chair, 2006. Pearson Lloyd used Pro/E to draw the elevational line drawing for Fritz Hansen (subsequently produced by the British company Senator International). It would have been almost impossible to draw this chair in 2D by hand, because the form was a fluid injection moulding.

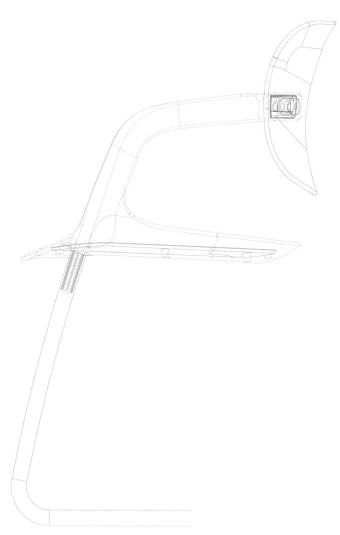

then generate a component model that can be further refined by adding features, such as holes, bosses and flanges.

It is capable of modeling objects with any number of planar, cylindrical, conical, spherical, toroidal or sculptured surfaces. Models of assemblies or parts can be viewed and shaded from pre-set angles, interrogated for mass-property data, used to produce associative and automatically dimensioned 2D drawings and exploded diagrams (Fig. 5.19). The term "associative" means that amendments to the drawing are automatically updated in the model and vice versa.

Creating organic forms

While block-like shapes are easy to construct using a CSG solid modeler, the ability to create freeform unconstrained forms easily and controllably has been the Holy Grail for CAD researchers (Figs. 5.20, 5.21). Sculptor William Latham (Fig. 5.22) is a pioneer of teasing "organic" forms from solid modelers more used to handling chunky engineering components. He developed his inspirational rule-based "evolutionary tree" shape at the Royal College of Art in London. He then became a Research Fellow at IBM's UK Scientific Centre in Winchester working towards a PhD thesis entitled "An Interactive Computer Graphics System

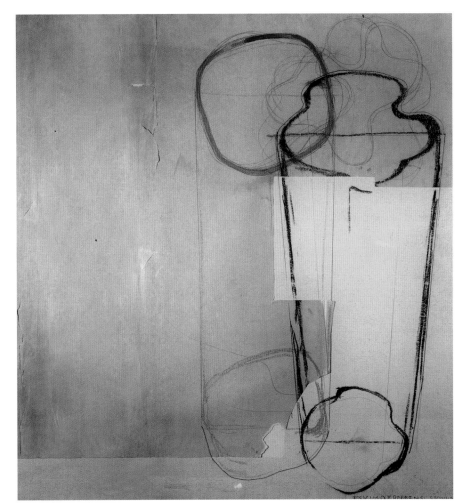

Right 5.20   Alvar Aalto, Glass vases, 1936. Crayon and cardboard collage. The designer made these concept drawings for Iittala Glassworks, Finland, for the 1937 Paris World's Fair. These vases were the precursors of Aalto's Savoy vases and were inspired by Eskimoerinden Skinnbuxa (the leather trousers of an Eskimo woman). Courtesy Iittala Group, Helsinki, Finland. (*See also* fig. 14)

Below 5.21   Alvar Aalto, Savoy vase, 2006. For the seventieth anniversary of the Savoy vase, so named because the Savoy restaurant in Helsinki was the first to use them, Iittala brought out this version in petrol blue. Courtesy Iittala Group, Helsinki, Finland.

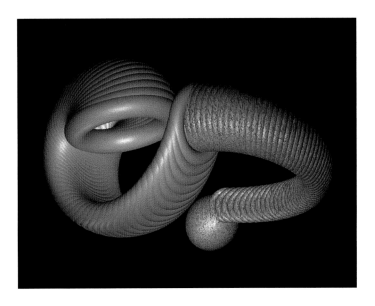

Above 5.22   William Latham, Mutation X Ribbed, 1993. William Latham became a pioneer in teasing organic shapes from solid modelers while he worked as artist-in-residence at the IBM UK Scientific Centre, Winchester, Hampshire.

Below 5.23 El Ultimo Grito, Land Ho! seat and planter, 2003. This deceptively simple sketch for Nola shows an urban oasis based on the concept of a desert island.

for Designing Complex Forms". Latham's Form Synth was intended to help designers with the sort of 3D products that have to fulfill certain functional requirements, but are still allowed scope in the overall shape of the form: products such as sofas, light fittings and bottles.

Wireframes, which can be created and oriented interactively, are sent off to be textured, lit, blended (softened by rounding off edges and filleting joins) and finally ray traced for an authentic appearance according to the laws of optics. Texture is generated in 3D using fractal techniques so the object looks as if it has been carved from a solid textured block. Latham found that the smallest amount of texture added to a polished metal or glossy plastic object makes it appear even more realistic (more on computer rendering in Chapter 6).

Conclusion

At the concept stage of the design process, the designer is mostly concerned with evolving new and novel product forms whilst resolving the constraints of the design brief to his or her satisfaction (Fig. 5.23). Rough sketches and freehand layouts, plus associated notes and calculations, have been sufficient for this task in the past.

Conventional CAD at this early stage can stifle creativity by its insistence on the designer providing the system with exact dimensional and geometric information. But there are systems in development that can provide the designer with valuable analyses—weights, volumes, moments of inertia and information on clearance and clash detection—while not committing him or her to a final shape or form. But until they are intuitive, inexpensive and user-friendly, designers will still rely on the clutch pencil and the nearest used envelope to record their spontaneous conceptual thoughts.

Hot tip: Practising freehand drawing

Practice your freehand drawing by choosing a common item and drawing it in perspective from unusual viewpoints and at different extreme scales. Be like American pop artist Claes Oldenburg and scale up a small object such as a pen or watch into a monumental object, using exaggeration for dramatic effect, high against the horizon and with the vanishing points closer together than they ordinarily should be.

Case Study 3:
Linda Andersson's punk concept car

Linda Andersson was brought up in Sweden and was intrigued that the country so famous for its progressive liberal attitudes to social welfare issues could also embrace American-style custom cars and hotrods, in a rockabilly subculture known as raggare *(a word roughly corresponding to the English term "pick-up artist"). She set to work researching how in a mass-production culture defined by brands someone—in this case her hypothetical John, age 49—could express himself through the car he drives. The result was her final-year project at London's Royal College of Art, the Punk Car.*

Linda comes from near Gothenburg and studied mechanical engineering design for two years at Luleå. She also loved art so she took an evening drawing course at Umeå. She worked for three summers as an intern at Volvo, where she developed an interest in studying transportation design. She then joined the third year of the MDes (Master of Design) course at Coventry University in England. Sponsored by Saab, she developed a hovercraft with two front wheels for extra manoeuverability. She was spotted by Julian Thomson of Jaguar, also

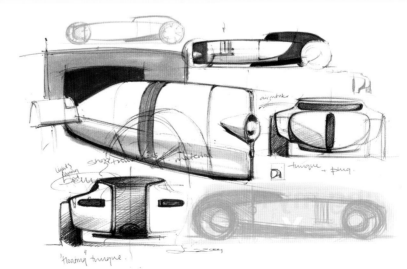

Right top CS 3.1 Concept car for Jaguar Advanced Design, 2003: pencil drawing airbrushed in Photoshop and collaged with interior detail.

Right bottom CS 3.2 Concept sketches for the Punk Car, 2004: pencil, ballpoint pen and marker, finished and collaged in Photoshop.

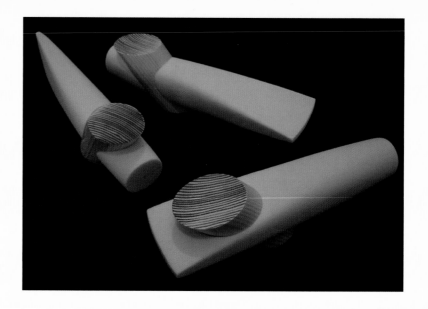

based in Coventry, who sponsored her through the Royal College of Art's MA in Vehicle Design course. Since graduating from the RCA she has been working at Jaguar Advanced Design, one of four designers developing concept cars (Fig. CS 3.1).

The title of her project at RCA was "Self-Expression and Individualization". She targeted the forty-five to sixty year-old age group with disposable income who grew up in the 1950s and 1960s. "There is a need for a provocative and rebellious concept," she explained, "a rebel against the blank car, to show a new direction on and off the road. A car with a personal 'face' which strives to fulfil the user's yearning for individuality." Her idea was for a car that could be customized by the user so as to have different detachable faces in different materials, contrasting the front of the car against back (Fig. CS 3.2).

Linda wondered how to encapsulate the essence of *raggare* through form and decided on the cube. To emphasize this, she evolved a car form that changed subtly from a soft round back to a sharp aggressive front end, the toothpaste tube (Fig. CS 3.3). She developed this form further by using contrasting materials: wood at the fluid emotional end; metal at the mechanical end, much like a handgun with its ergonomic wooden handle and cold functional barrel (Fig. CS 3.4). Other details included split tyres with neon light shining through and dark visor-like sunglasses.

Linda considered carefully the use of personal space in her car design. She researched which room in their houses people's cars represented—

bathroom, bedroom, living room? The exterior of her car concept was for show, to express oneself to others, but the interior was living space for one's self, or for entertaining. For Linda, what the space within a car felt like was more important than what it looked like.

Linda used ballpoint pen and marker in her drawings, then collaged and finished them on her computer using Photoshop (Fig. CS 3.5). She also made a quarter-scale wooden and clay model, which was photographed and added to the drawings (Fig. CS 3.6). All she needs now is a wealthy patron to make this concept a reality, although with its exposed wheels the present version wouldn't be street legal.

Opposite top CS 3.3   Wooden concept models examining the "toothpaste tube" shape.

Opposite bottom CS 3.4   Collage of rendered elevation, airbrushed in Photoshop, with concept sketches (including context drawing of handgun).

Top CS 3.5   Dramatic rear-view perspective of Punk Car drawn using pencil, with spattered ink and airbrushed in Photoshop.

Right CS 3.6   Photograph of a quarter-scale model of finished Punk Car collaged in Photoshop with scene of salt flats and type added.

"The designer has never resembled Rodin's Thinker *who sits in solitary meditation, but has in contrast always externalized his thoughts, not only as an end product in the form of a design, but as an integral part of the process itself in the form of drawings and sketches."*
Bryan Lawson *How Designers Think* 1980

6

Presentation drawings and visuals

Opposite   Mario and Claudio Bellini, My Lady steel cooking pot, 2003. This is a photo-real part rendering in Rhinoceros for Barazzoni SpA.

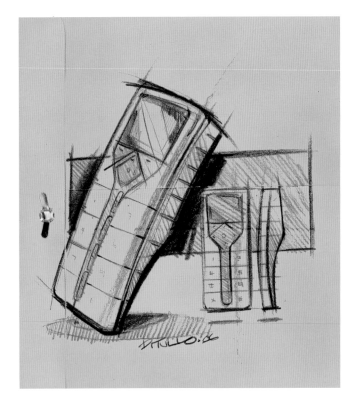

After the often solitary concept stage of design, it is now time for the designer to become a team player and, correspondingly, there will be a need to communicate those vague sketches to other professionals using more finished drawings in marker or coloured on the computer (Fig. 6.1). Various details contributing to the finished design, such as ergonomic, technological and aesthetic factors, have yet to be satisfied. The presentation phase has to cover each and every aspect of the product, so that marketing and engineering departments are able to sign off the design intent for the production stage.

This is called the design-development phase. There is now a choice of workable designs, and the outcome will be a single design proposal, even though some aspects of the design may not yet be fully thought out. The fine details will be worked out in the next phase (Chapter 7).

Highly rendered 3D pictorial presentation drawings (Fig. 6.2) have become increasingly important, as engineers' 2D orthographic drawings—the set of plan and elevations developed over the years in the quest for a complete and unambiguous representation of a designed object—have become increasingly difficult to understand, or to "read", especially for those being asked to foot the bills (the client, manager or accountant). This is regretted by designers such as Dick Powell, of London consultancy

Above 6.1   Michael DiTullo, Mobile phone, 2005. Indigo blue prisma pencil on the back of an envelope.

Right 6.2   Factory Design, Concorde seats, 1998. Markers and pastel with pen. This design was part of a collaborative team including the British Airways in-house design team and Conran & Partners to create a new interior for the aircraft's return to service.

Right 6.3   Pilipili Product Design, Household
cleaning products, 2004. A rendered 3D model of
household cleaning items for PDC Brush, using
UGS NG software.

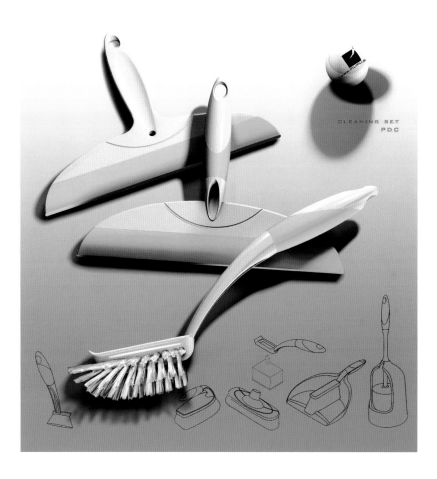

Seymourpowell, who lament the passing of a generation brought up on engineering drawing practice and who, through experience, can visualize a 3D form in their heads from just looking at a set of orthographic drawings— and be able to use rendered plans and elevations as presentation drawings and to make physical models.

For example, to make a quick model, a side elevation can be attached to a block of polystyrene foam and the shape cut with a band saw. The foam is re-assembled and the top view attached to the foam to be cut out with the saw. Finally, the foam pieces are put back together and the end elevation is cut to shape. Result: a rapid and easy method of producing a rough model. Of course, not all designers bring in CAD so early in the process and we will leave further discussion on 2D drafting for Chapter 7.

A set of 2D drawings on paper, whether drawn by hand or with the aid of a CAD system, is still necessary, a convention going back to Victorian times. A 3D computer model encapsulating a complete description of the product is a much more desirable aspiration. A computer surface or solid model is able to fulfill both roles: as an accurate geometric representation of the virtual product and as a photo-realistic visualization, complete with shading, shadows and lighting effects (Fig. 6.3).

The computer can't do it all by itself, however, and some designers still like to show the "hand of the artist" in their presentations, in the form of hand-rendered drawings in pen, pencil or marker, albeit often finished and "air-brushed" using a computer "paint" program such as Adobe Photoshop (Figs. 6.4 and 6.5) or Corel Painter. Some designers also produce presentation drawings using vector programs such as Adobe Illustrator, with CAD geometry (either 2D or 3D) as input. Vector images have an advantage over "paint" (bitmap) packages in that they can be scaled to any size without loss of resolution and occupy less disk space. The quality of rendering textures, however, is not as realistic.

Presenting highly rendered computer models too early in the design process does, however, have its dangers: clients may perceive the slick rendering to represent a finished product design already "set in stone"; and the hassle of changing the model may, even at a subconscious level, lead designers to allow through various aspects of the design they might otherwise have second thoughts about and would have preferred to change.

Right 6.4   Georg Baldele, Glitterbox chandelier, 2002–05. Ballpoint pen and Photoshop. The designer drew this chandelier for the Swarovski Crystal Palace Project by taking a ballpoint pen sketch, reversing it out in Photoshop, and then colouring it blue.

Below 6.5   Factory Design, Remington Big Shot hairdryer, 2005. This presentation drawing started as a hand-drawn sketch, and then was scanned and coloured in using Photoshop.

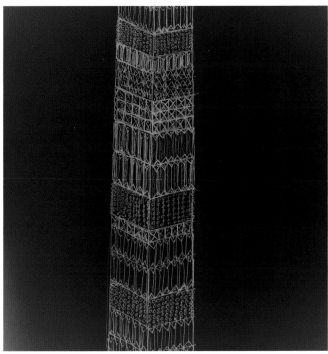

From watercolour washes to markers

In Victorian times, presentation drawings were merely grander versions of 2D working drawings, executed in pen and ink with an added watercolour wash, often—as their name suggests—presented to the client on the completion of the job (Fig. 6.6). As there became a requirement for the reprographic duplication of the drawings—there were no colour photocopiers in those days!—in the form of cruder blueprints, it became common, for the sake of legibility, for the colour washes to be replaced by black line cross-hatching and other shading patterns.

With the growth of independent design consultancies from the 1940s, there became a need to "sell" concepts to the client, and a cold engineering drawing was inadequate and inappropriate. Designers had to present a realistic rendering, showing the client exactly what he was going to get for his money. Rendering skills became important again. Some designers employed watercolour artists to produce their presentation graphics. Raymond Loewy, a fashion illustrator by training, was able to do his own (Fig. 6.7). Italian designers, such as the Memphis group, who were mostly architecturally trained, had the edge: the act of drawing has always been a joy to architects. Gouache (body colour) and airbrush, a device originally developed for retouching photographs, ruled during the mid-twentieth

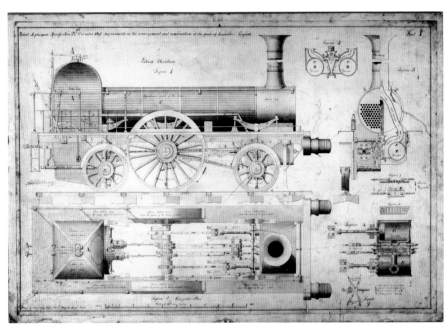

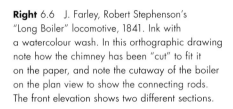

Right 6.6   J. Farley, Robert Stephenson's "Long Boiler" locomotive, 1841. Ink with a watercolour wash. In this orthographic drawing note how the chimney has been "cut" to fit it on the paper, and note the cutaway of the boiler on the plan view to show the connecting rods. The front elevation shows two different sections.

Below 6.7   Raymond Loewy, The S-1 locomotive for the Pennsylvania Railroad, 1936. Perspective drawing on yellow tracing paper. The pencil marks on the back facilitate tracing the image to another sheet but also enhance the feeling of streamlined speed. Courtesy Cooper-Hewitt National Design Museum, Smithsonian Institution, Washington, DC.

century, and a designer such as Syd Mead in his work for Ford and US Steel was king, but today of all the manual methods, only pen, pencil or marker drawings remain.

Painting by numbers

The skills needed to produce presentation drawings or visuals are very different from those required in concept design. Designer Richard Seymour, the other partner in the London practice Seymourpowell, contends that a presentation drawing is "painting by numbers" and anyone following the exercises in his partner Dick Powell's excellent book *Presentation Techniques* will be able to produce acceptable results. Drawing for presentation is all about colouring and rendering, and is an aside from the process of designing a product. Nevertheless, without a successful presentation—and the subsequent approval of the client—the design process is unlikely to proceed.

Interestingly, after he wrote the book, Powell simplified his presentation style: using more physical models, with concept drawings conforming to a standard colour scheme—rendered in white on graduated colour board with the shading in blue—so that a client was not distracted or influenced in the choice of a design alternative so early in the process by the colours used in the presentation drawing (*see* Case study 1). Now he draws using a fibretip pen and renders the drawing in Photoshop, to be printed in an A4 report, or projected from his computer at a meeting using PowerPoint.

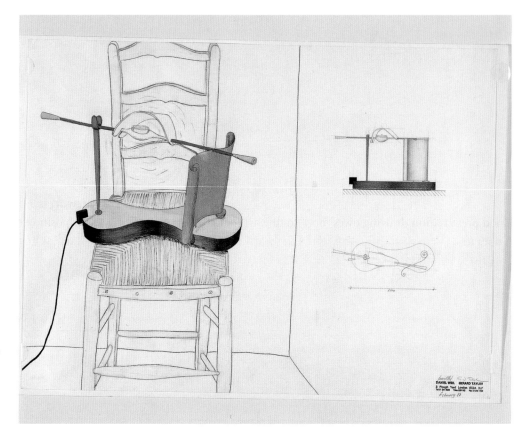

Right 6.8 Daniel Weil (now of Pentagram) and Gerard Taylor, *H-Arp* lamp, 1987. These designs were made for Anthologie Quartett in Germany. In Weil's view bland boxes are a hopelessly inadequate reflection of the marvels they contain. Weil and Taylor usually drew chaotically onto huge rolls of wallpaper liner, but here they constrain the object to a van Gogh chair.

Below 6.9 Dieter Rams and Hans Gugelot, SK4 radio/record player (nicknamed Snow White's coffin), 1956. These drawings were made by Rams for Braun.

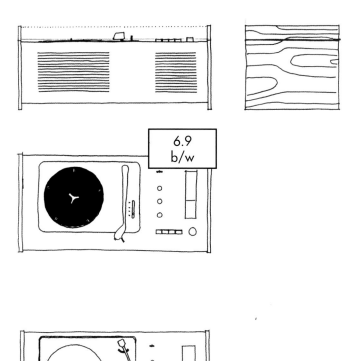

It is also true to say that the more famous the designer, the fewer presentation drawings he or she may need to submit. Star designers are known quantities and are engaged by a client to put their personality stamp on a product (Fig. 6.8). They are often given *carte blanche* and will come up with one solution that in his or her consideration is the one that is right for this particular client. An "average" design consultancy, however, will be expected to present three or four concepts, of which one may be the designer's own favourite, and it is down to the designer's persuasive powers and diplomacy to direct the client into choosing that particular approach.

Drawing for presentation is all about producing a stylish drawing—likely to appeal to the client—as quickly as possible. Shortcuts and conventions will be used here as elsewhere later in the process. Designers will also strive to make drawings recognizably theirs, whether they deny it or not. They are also not immune to changes in fashion. Thus Syd Mead's colourful fantasy cars for Ford or Dieter Rams' Hi-Fi designs can be placed squarely into the 1950s and 60s (Fig. 6.9); drawings with looser striated marker lines identify that particular technique as belonging to the 1980s and 90s.

As the profession of *design* evolved from "applied art", and commercial artists became designers, so they seemed almost ashamed of their artistic roots, preferring the businesslike tag of industrial problem-solver. Rendering skills inevitably suffered. But as design became styling and threatened to become just another branch of marketing, a backlash in the form of Post-Modernism restored detail and decoration to product design (and why not?). Drawing skills have never been so greatly sought after.

The art of design

Good presentation drawing owes more to fine art than it does to reality, whether it is interpreting what we see directly or what we see photographically, as through the lens of a camera. Prospective designers will do well to study the masters—London designer David Crisp sets Degas (whose compositions were influenced by photography with its cropping of forms and motion blur) as an example for students learning to draw; Tucker Viemeister of New York practice Springtime-USA lists Leonardo de Vinci as a hero.

Photographic realism—for the photograph with its single viewpoint and fixed depth of field is the present-day paradigm for "reality"—is a limited aspiration. The lessons that painters have developed over the centuries for presenting visual cues and clues that exploit the mind's ability to relate to previous experience and emotions should not be ignored.

Art—and presentation drawing—is more concerned with conveying a desired impression, and not necessarily to present geometric and physical accuracy. That comes later, in the general arrangement and detail production drawings (Chapter 7). Put bluntly, a presentation drawing should be more like a cartoon, where features are exaggerated, albeit subtly and by choice of view, to convey a message with an economy of effort. It should be remembered that artists such as Matisse and Picasso worked hard to make their drawings appear simple—Matisse would draw all day "to get his hand in", discarding pictures as he went along, to produce in the evening perhaps just one perfect and fluid drawing that looked as if it had been dashed off in seconds.

Visuals of a designer's concept should be convincing enough for a client to make that important decision to commit the finance to take the design further along the design cycle. The designer should be bold, and approach the rendering in the knowledge that it will probably take two or three attempts to build up the confidence to attack the final version. If using markers, an outline "underlay"

inserted beneath the translucent paper can be used as a guide, and it is well worth spending time to get it right in the first place—no amount of rendering skill can disguise a badly produced perspective.

Designers should develop a strong sense of graphic balance. That means composition, and there are rules and conventions (the golden section, the law of thirds and so on) that can be used—and abused. The very act of drawing helps us understand the structure of objects. Drawing from life—observational drawing—is practice never wasted. Drawing is all about looking—carefully scrutinizing the disposition of tone, reflections, highlights and shadow in a scene. The process is iterative, with the designer's skills improving and the visual vocabulary increasing all the time. The designer at work, however, is more than likely faced with a blank piece of paper, or some concept sketches, and is expected to produce a drawing from nothing but imagination—no mean feat.

Visual tricks

Economy of style can lead to visual clichés, and these can be put to good use only if the designer is aware of them. "California chrome" for example, a trick of the airbrush artist, assumes that the shiny object being drawn stands surrounded by bright yellow sand under a deep blue sky, which graduates to white at the horizon where it meets the dark desert. This is patently ludicrous in many situations, but it was once used with great effect almost universally, regardless of the product's actual location and background. Shiny automobile bodies often reflect a city roofline of skyscrapers. The details, not always apparent on first viewing, give the viewer visual clues as to the lifestyle of the aspiring end user. These effects can be applied manually or are built into rendering software.

There are other conventions that add to the vocabulary of the presentation drawing. When a curved object is depicted, it is common to leave a thin band of "reflected" light, instead of taking the shadow right to the edge bounding the surface. Square windows, preferably with old-fashioned quartered panes, make effective highlights (also called "farkles" or "chings") on a glossy product, even if such windows are not to be found in the depicted environment. Comic books are a good source to be studied for tips on rendering, for example how to use high-contrast reflections and theatrical lighting. Marker drawings in particular exaggerate the qualities of a surface to be informative and convey excitement (Fig. 6.10).

Right 6.10 This 2002 concept sketch of a Sony Ericsson T610 mobile phone was executed in pencil and markers, with the construction lines retained for a more immediate feel.

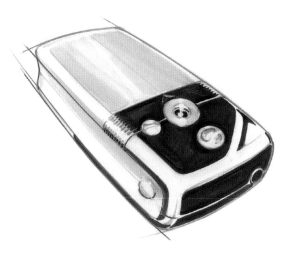

Making marker drawings

Markers are used for presentation drawings for their immediacy and quick results (Fig. 6.11), their colour range and their compatibility with other media. Unlike watercolour, they require little preparation and no cleaning up afterwards, but do need to be used on bleed-proof translucent layout paper, usually bound together as marker pads. Marker drawings are at least as good as and often more appropriate than drawings done in gouache or watercolour. They offer only a limited opportunity to blend

Below 6.11 Jonas Hultqvist, Concrete-project waterproof urban training shoes, 2002. The designer uses marker freely to render these sketches for the Swedish footwear manufacturer Tretorn. As well as using markers, Hultqvist also employed dry pastel for fading effects and gouache for highlighting. For postproduction he used Adobe Photoshop to place the logo and adjust colour and contrast.

 Tretorn   c o n c r e t e

and manipulate tonal value but, nevertheless, they help the design process move at the throwaway pace expected of today's designer, and allow a greater number of concepts to be communicated to the client and the other members of the design team.

Presentation drawings are created on marker pads and collaged or mounted onto boards, drawn directly onto proprietary boards or, if they have been subsequently touched up and cleaned on the computer, printed out and mounted on foam boards. The designer first has to develop an accurate line drawing in pencil or ballpoint pen (the latter preferable because it will not smear when marker is applied) with enough delineation to define the appropriate amount of detail. This can be traced from the concept layout drawing (it is quite common to present a rendered 2D elevation of the product—for example, a mobile phone or bicycle—if it can be read easily that way), otherwise a 3D pictorial representation—a paraline (isometric) or perspective—must be generated.

Next, it is usual to establish the shadows in a contrasting marker colour to prevent confusion. When rendering on translucent marker paper, the line drawing can be positioned under a clean sheet of paper onto which the first marker lines go. Areas of marker strokes can be edge-masked, as in traditional airbrushing, to restrict rendering to a specific tightly controlled area. As marker rendering proceeds, edge lines can be made more crisp (using coloured pencil or black fibretip pen) and highlights introduced (using white gouache, typing correction fluid or coloured pencil) during the final stages, making sure that all the initial ballpoint lines are concealed.

Value adjustments can sometimes be made by applying a marker to the back of the translucent paper, with a toned-down colour showing through. Coloured pencil, pastel or airbrush can be used for more subtle shading and blending, added to a marker base. Or the marker can be blended to a limited amount using lighter fuel on baby cotton swabs. Overlays or stick-on pieces can be used to build up a product story: for example, starting with a car chassis, adding the engine and component parts, then finishing with the body panels.

2D computer programs: "paint" and vector

Most designers nowadays will start a drawing using a pencil or fibretip pen on paper and will then scan the image into the computer to be coloured and rendered using a computer program. As mentioned in Chapter 5, there are some programs, such as Alias SketchBook Pro, specifically developed for freehand sketching—they are quicker to learn and use, and have a simpler interface than mainstream "paint" programs such as Photoshop and Painter. As its name implies, Photoshop, like the airbrush it has made obsolete, was designed originally as a photographic retouching tool, but has quickly become the de facto industry standard for "painting" on the computer.

In computer software, there are two distinctly different ways of producing images, referred to as "draw" (or vector) and "paint" (or bitmap). A "paint" document is stored in the computer's memory as a bitmap, a one-to-one array corresponding to the pixels (dots) appearing on the screen—although the virtual image can be much larger than the size of the screen. In a paint program, a circle intersected by a line, say, is just a pattern of dots and can only be moved en bloc. It is not possible to edit "globally" —modify every circle in a picture, for example—using just one command.

A "draw" or vector document is stored in the computer's memory as a "display list" of the points and lines that make up the illustration, plus the formulas for any circles, ellipses and curves, using a language called PostScript (the same format used to describe the letter forms in a font). This is similar to a 2D CAD system and is also known as object-oriented graphics, because every object—a circle, line, or curve—can be accounted for separately. In draw programs, it is possible to move the line without affecting the circle because they exist as two separate entities, but they can be grouped together to form another object. Because they are not stored in terms of bitmaps, the output resolution to, say, a laser printer is independent of the image's resolution.

The original paint system was the Quantel Paintbox, best known for producing special effects for broadcast television. With ever more powerful computers and cheaper memory, much of the functionality of the Paintbox can now be reproduced by programs such as Adobe Photoshop. There are also paint systems available that do their best to emulate "natural" media such as oil paint and watercolour. Corel's Painter, for example, can produce convincing chalk and pastel effects through the use of a pressure-sensitive stylus and tablet (Fig. 6.12).

Some designers also use paint systems as a collage tool. A convincing presentation can be montaged from a concept sketch and contextual images "grabbed" by a scanner or digital camera from books or other sources (but be aware of copyright infringement).

Step by step 3:
Automotive marker
rendering by Etienne Salomé

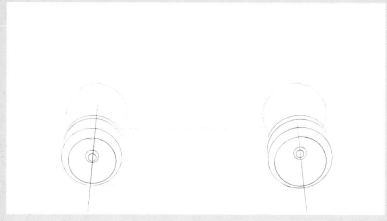

SS 3.1   Etienne begins construction with a virtual chassis of four wheels using a Bic Cristal ballpoint pen. He draws the car using one-point perspective, the vanishing point being behind the car. Note that he can treat the wheels as circles because the plane they are in is normal to his sight line.

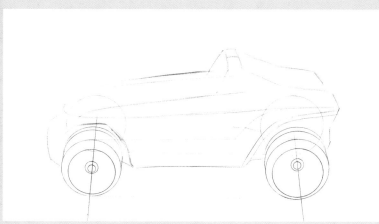

SS 3.2   He sketches in the outline of the car.

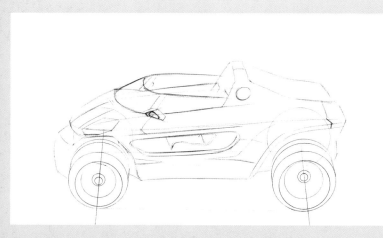

SS 3.3   Etienne adds the windows, headlamps and other major elements.

SS 3.4 He establishes details such as mirrors, lamps, alloys and rocker.

SS 3.5 Etienne next adds tyres, the fuel cap and the shadow on the ground in more detail, and then he can map in interior details such as the seats.

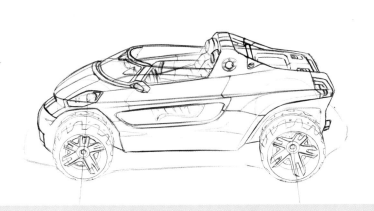

SS 3.6 He starts rendering with an AD marker basic gray 4, to block in the bumpers and rocker.

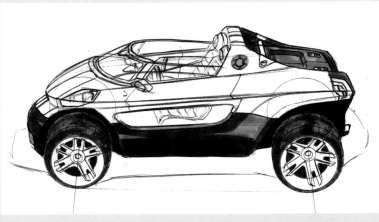

SS 3.7 He adds shadows and definition to the bumpers and rocker using AD marker basic greys 5 and 6, with AD marker cool greys 3 to 5 for the wheels.

SS 3.8 Etienne renders the side of the body using Naples yellow P-135 and grass green P-122 AD markers.

SS 3.9 He colours in the wheels using AD marker Naples yellow P-135 and grass green P-122, the seats using Naples yellow. He blocks in the rest of the interior using AD marker warm grey 3.

SS 3.10 Etienne draws the reflection on the windows using AD markers warm greys (1 to 4), and the front and rear lamps using AD markers deep salmon P-206 and cool grey 5.

SS 3.11 Finally, he colours in the ground shadow using AD markers warm greys (1 to 6), and he picks out highlights using white pencil and white Posca paint marker.

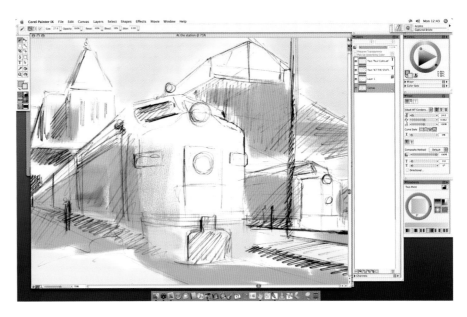

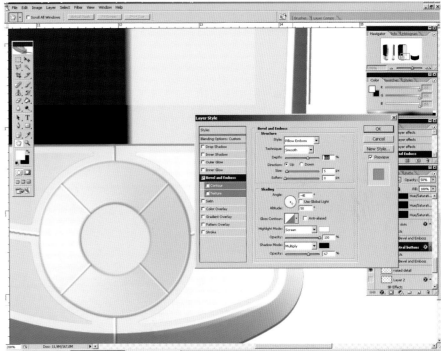

Above right 6.12 Paul Collicut, *At the Station*, 2006. Corel Painter aims to reproduce natural media such as oil paint and watercolour and is a favourite of Ron Arad. In this screenshot, illustrator Paul Collicut simulates acrylic paint applied using a bristle brush.

Right 6.13 Mark Jones, Cell phone, 2006. Adobe Photoshop was originally developed as an image-processing program for photographers but has become the de facto standard for all image manipulation, including drawing. Here Mark Jones uses the "bevel and emboss" tool on his cell phone demo. (*See also* Step-by-step 4)

The computer allows you to play around with ideas—trying out different type for captions, alternative positioning of elements, another background colour and so on—for as long as your schedule will allow. As the American designer April Greiman says: "The paint never dries." And so long as you save the different versions, there is no chance of ever spoiling the original.

Brothers Thomas and John Knoll began developing Photoshop in 1987 and Version 1 was released by Adobe in 1990. From the start, the program was designed as a tool for manipulating images that had been digitized by a scanner, which was then a very expensive device. At the time of

Right 6.14 Alexander Åhnebrink, Mountaineer watch, 2000. Many designers begin a drawing in a precise vector program such as Illustrator, as here, and then transfer the image to Photoshop for airbrushing and finishing off. (*See also* figs. 3.20 and 7.18)

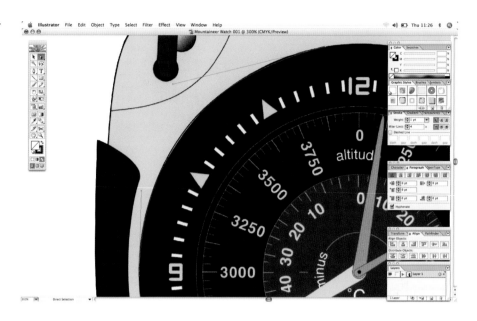

writing, the most recent version is marketed as Photoshop CS2. CS refers to its integration with Adobe's Creative Suite (which also includes Illustrator) and 2 because it is the second version released under the CS brand (Fig. 6.13).

Since 1994, the program has the ability to work on many different layers (the equivalent of physical overlays), so that the original scan can remain unaltered in its own background layer while work can be carried out on a duplicate layer, adding further layers for colours and variations. Layers can then be toggled active or inactive, visible or invisible, and the layer "stack" re-ordered to produce various different images for printing out.

Typically, the designer would draw and interact with the computer using a pen-like stylus on a digitizing tablet, such as made by Wacom. To "airbrush" a drawing, one would first construct masks, equivalent to the Frisk low-tack film masks used in physical airbrushing—virtual "paint" is prevented from appearing on the "paper" wherever the mask covers it. The big difference is that a physical mask has a sharp edge (unless you hold a piece of card above the surface of the paper to blur the resulting edge); a Photoshop mask can have a soft graduated edge. And the virtual mask will never stick to the paper or allow leakage beneath its edge. In Photoshop, the eraser tool can also act as an airbrush, to remove colour. And if a mistake is made, there is always the "Undo" command.

Paint programs such as Photoshop do have some limited vector capabilities, to draw editable "paths" for example, useful for creating masks or cutout illustrations. Draw programs such as Adobe Illustrator can be used not only for drawing, but also to manipulate type and lay out pages for presentation documentation.

Adobe Illustrator was first developed for the Apple Macintosh in 1985 as an application of Adobe's in-house font development software and PostScript file format, filling a niche between paint and CAD programs (Fig. 6.14).

Both Illustrator and the similar program Macromedia FreeHand (a program recently acquired by Adobe whose future is uncertain at the time of writing) use controllable freeform curves (called Bézier curves, after the French engineer who invented them), which can be manipulated and filled to produce complex precise drawings. Scanned images or bitmapped drawings from a paint program can be imported and traced to convert them to paths. Despite its name, FreeHand is not an easy program with which to draw freehand, and is more akin to a 2D CAD program in the way drawings are constructed from lines and shapes. Colour fills can be either flat or graduated, but despite more sophisticated tools for producing subtle blends by using a mesh to control the transitions between colours, "draw" programs still cannot airbrush quite as freely as paint programs. Designers will most likely use a combination of draw and paint programs (and CAD programs), passing files back and forth between programs, to produce a finished presentation drawing—using whatever it takes to produce the desired result.

Other tools in vector programs are used to create boxes, lines, ellipses and corners. Layers (overlays) are also available, so that the drawing can be split up into separate elements that can be displayed and edited individually. Line attributes, pattern fills and colours can be saved in a computer style sheet and applied to other elements later to maintain a consistency throughout a series of drawings.

Step by step 4:
"Airbrush" computer rendering by Mark Jones

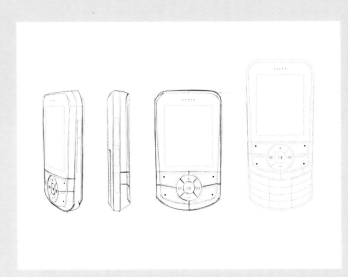

SS 4.1   Mark traces his concept sketches in Adobe Illustrator using the Pen Tool with a 0.5pt line thickness, ensuring there are no gaps between adjoining lines.

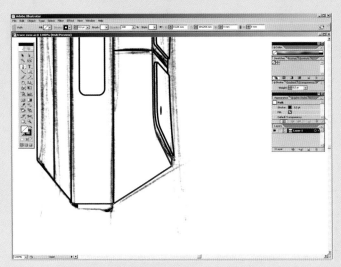

SS 4.2   He pastes the artwork as pixels into a 300dpi RGB Photoshop document, and renames the layer "line art". He would paste graphical elements such as logos, button text or small speaker holes onto separate layers to make Magic Wand selections easier later. He then re-pastes the Illustrator artwork as paths, ensuring that the two line up correctly. Finally, he creates layer groups for each of the views and names them appropriately, for example, "Front view" or "Side view".

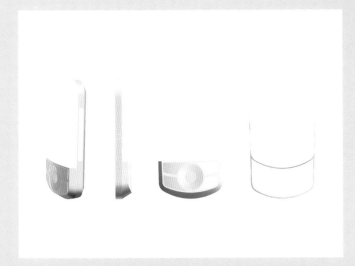

SS 4.3   Mark uses the Magic Wand tool to select an area of the product for shading. He can correct the selection manually using the Polygonal Lasso to add (hold Shift key) or subtract (hold Alt key) areas. From the Select menu bar, he chooses Modify>Expand and expands by one pixel. The selection now lies in the centre of the 0.5pt artwork line. It is important that there are no gaps between the shaded areas.

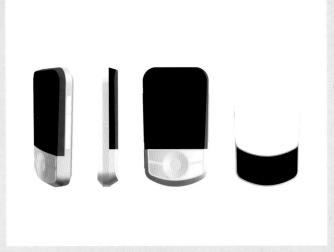

SS 4.4   To shade with the paintbrush, Mark makes his selection and creates a new layer in the appropriate layer group. He adjusts the layer opacity to 50%. This will allow for adjustments later, should some areas appear too light or dark. Mark prefers to work in black and white, adding colour later using a Hue/Saturation layer. This allows him to concentrate on achieving the correct tonal values. Using a large, soft brush, and with the brush opacity set to around 25% (to prevent immediate saturation), Mark begins shading the area.

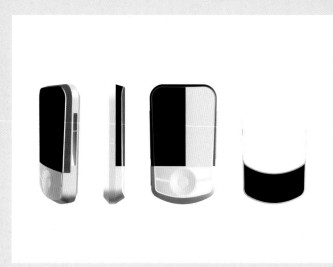

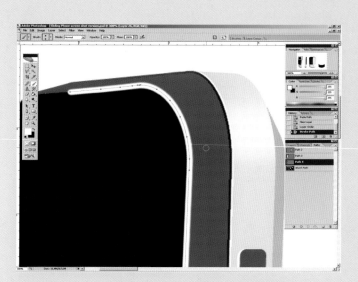

SS 4.5   To create edge highlights, such as the ones running around the black screen casing, Mark first creates a new layer for the highlight, remembering to name the layer appropriately. In the Paths window he selects the path layer created at the beginning. Using the Path Selection tool, he clicks on the individual path that defines where he wants the highlight to be.

SS 4.6   Mark clicks on the Brush tool and selects a size 8 brush of 70% hardness. He makes the brush opacity 100% and ensures that his foreground colour is set at either white for a highlight or black for a shadow. He clicks the stroke path symbol at the bottom of the path window. The line will be stroked accurately with the brush that Mark has chosen. Now with a soft eraser he can dim down or remove the areas where the highlight is not required. Tip: This technique can also be used for creating quick (but inaccurate) split lines. Simply perform the process twice, once in white, then on a separate layer in black, then nudge the layers diagonally apart from each other.

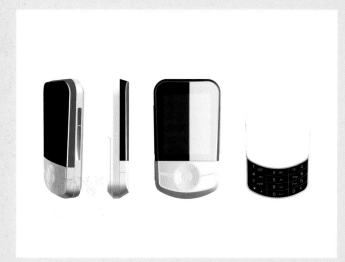

SS 4.7   To create accurate split lines and edge fillets, Mark goes back to the "line art" layer and selects an area to one side of the desired split line. From the Select menu he chooses Modify>Border and sets the border at 2 pixels. The outer edge of the selection now lies at the centre point of the line. Using the Lasso tools, he may have to correct the selection manually at sharp intersections and remove unwanted areas. Mark now creates a new layer and shades it with the Airbrush according to the direction of the light source, adjusting the opacity of the layers to get the correct balance.

SS 4.8   Mark double-clicks on the layer containing the shading. The Layer Style window appears. He selects the Bevel and Emboss option. There are numerous parameters with which he can experiment to achieve the desired effect. Once chosen, layer effects can be re-adjusted later should they need it.

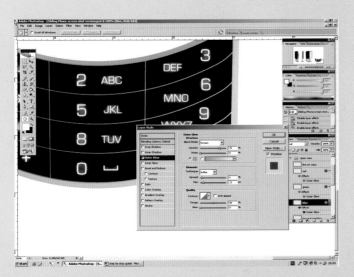

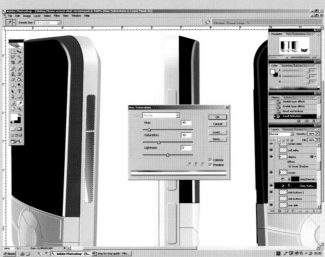

SS 4.9   There are many other useful layer effects. For example, Mark used an inner shadow on the screen display area to add depth, a drop shadow behind the speaker holes to give a back-painted effect and gave the keypad numbers an outer glow.

SS 4.10   Mark selects areas where he wants to add colour. He presses Ctrl and clicks on the layer thumbnail to select the areas. He creates a new adjustment layer by clicking on the circular icon at the bottom of the layer palette. He chooses Hue>Saturation, then the Colorise option and adjusts the parameters to achieve the desired colour. He can alter the adjustment layers again at any time by double clicking on the thumbnail that appears on the layer bar.

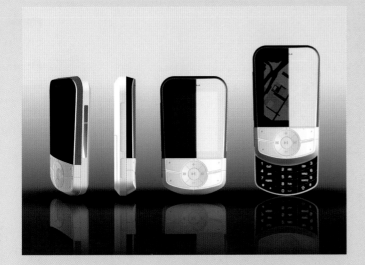

SS 4.11   To create a background scene, Mark first saves the finished rendering as a JPEG and places it into a new document. He uses Magic Wand to select the white background and delete it. He duplicates this layer and flips it along the horizontal plane so that he has a mirrored image. Using a very large, soft eraser, he strokes along the bottom so that the image fades to nothing. He lowers the layer opacity to achieve a convincing reflection. To get the correct reflection image for the perspective view, he skews the image and redraws some areas with the Pen tool, then shades them. On a new layer, beneath the rendering, Mark uses the gradient tool to create a gradual background fade. Again on a separate layer, this time above the rendering, he airbrushes a soft line across the horizon. This creates the ground plane and completes the rendering.

There are commands for rotating, scaling, mirroring, skewing and stretching elements. Drawings thus created can be exported directly, as EPS (Encapsulated PostScript) files to page-layout packages such as QuarkXPress or Adobe InDesign. There they can be combined with text originated on a word processing system to produce presentation documents.

More and more, designers will be creating presentations on computer—images that can be shipped directly to page make-up programs with no intermediate artwork needed. There will always be a place, however, for images produced using traditional materials, and today's designer will need to know how to make the best use of both, for years yet to come.

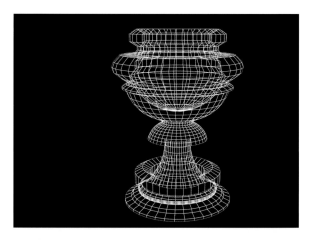

3D computer-aided styling

The main and most fundamental difference between a marker drawing rendered manually, or an image created using a "paint" or "draw" program, and a CGI (computer-generated imagery) visualization is that the former is a 2D illusion; the computer drawing, if it has been modeled in 3D, exists in three virtual dimensions.

A CGI visualization can be rotated and looked at from any angle or viewpoint (though not necessarily in real time—a new view may take some time to compute, depending on complexity) and the aim of a so-called "computer-aided styling" system is to shade, texture and light a wireframe model, sending the same stimuli to the brain as a viewer might experience seeing a real physical object in a naturalistic setting.

The search for photo-realism (and a simulated photograph with its restricted depth of field, motion blur and out-of-focus background seems somehow more "real" than pin-sharp reality) has added some weird and wonderful words to the computer graphics vocabulary: Phong and Gouraud shading, fractals, ray tracing and radiosity.

Creating virtual reality

There are five steps to the creation of a synthetic scene. First a 3D model must be built within the computer that defines the entire geometry of the object and its environment.

The simplest way of constructing the model is to use the software tool called a solid modeler (discussed in Chapter 2), which will produce a complete and

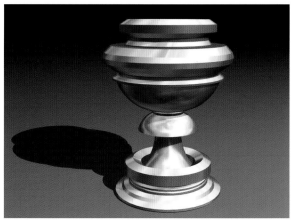

Opposite top 6.15   Raysan Al-Kubaisi, Uccello's chalice, 2003. The designer used 3D Studio Max to recreate Uccello's chalice (*see* fig. 1.1). This is the wireframe view, which resembles the original perspective construction. The model is made from polygonal facets: the more facets there are, the more detailed the rendering but the bigger the file.

Opposite middle 6.16   Raysan Al-Kubaisi, Uccello's chalice, 2003 The first step is to shade the facets of the model and light them. With flat shading, the discontinuities at the edges of the facets are obvious and give rise to the Mach effect, which accentuates the contrast.

Opposite below 6.17   Raysan Al-Kubaisi, Uccello's chalice, 2003. Gouraud shading calculates the surface normals at the vertices of the polygons, which are then averaged for all the polygons that meet at each point. These color values are then interpolated along the edges of the polygons. Phong shading is used to add specular reflections (highlights).

Opposite bottom 6.18   Raysan Al-Kubaisi, Uccello's chalice, 2003. Finally, a background is added, with shadows used to increase the realism of the virtual object.

unambiguous description of the model in 3D space by performing either Boolean operations (union, difference, intersection) on "primitive" shapes such as cones, cubes, cylinders and spheres, by extruding a 2D profile, by sweeping a profile around an axis or by some combination of all of these methods. The resulting shapes are welded together or bits are subtracted until the designer arrives at the desired form. Built-in checks make sure the topology is always correct and that Escher-like impossible objects are not being created.

Alternatively, a designer can use a "skin-deep" object generated on a surface modeler as input. This class of modeler is more adept at handling the doubly-curved "fair" shapes loved by the designers of automobile bodies and telephone handsets, which are more freeform and organic than forms created from simple chunky geometric shapes. When rendered, they may look as substantial as a "solid" modeler, but they won't be able to yield any information about mass properties such as material density, centre of gravity and moments of inertia.

Next, each vertex of the model is mathematically transformed to generate a perspective picture of the object in wireframe on the image plane, and the correct depth information is stored in the computer's database (Fig. 6.15).

On most systems the model can be moved around at this stage, to find the most aesthetically pleasing position, then the "hollow" wireframe is rendered and lit, with the computer working out which surfaces should be visible and which are hidden to the viewer (Fig. 6.16). A light reflection routine is used to predict the colours and spatial distribution of the light rays reflected from, refracted through or absorbed by each surface in the scene (Fig. 6.17). Finally, the image is rendered on the screen of the display by the computer selecting the appropriate red, green and blue intensities for each pixel (Fig. 6.18).

Because of constraints imposed by available processing power and the overhead of computer memory, many shortcuts have been taken to produce acceptable results. Models are often displayed as a collection of planar facets—so that a cylinder will look like the kind of pencil designed not to roll off your desk, or like a Greek column. Doubly curved shapes will be made up from a mesh of polygonal facets. The more facets there are, the smoother the object, but adding more facets means increasing the time needed for computation.

Subdivision surface modeling uses a process of repeated refinement—a sequence of meshes is generated that converges from a crude construction to a smoother mesh with more polygonal elements. Areas of smaller

facets are concentrated around important features of
the object. Carpenters use a similar technique to round
off a corner of wood. First they make a cut at 45 degrees,
then another two cuts through the sharp edges, and
so on until the cuts are too small to notice and there
is a smooth rounded edge.

Shading a computer model

Early attempts at computer rendering used constant-
value shading—the computer calculated a single intensity
for the whole polygonal facet, coloured lighter or darker
depending on whether it was pointing towards or away
from the light source.

Now a cylinder really does look like a fluted column
from a Greek temple, as something called the Mach
band effect accentuates the boundaries of the faceted
surfaces. Gouraud shading was invented in 1971 by Henri
Gouraud to interpolate linearly the shading across each
polygon to provide a smooth transition from one edge
to the next.

Specular reflection introduces highlights, and
a shading scheme developed by Bui Tuong Phong in
1973 is based on an empirical observation that shiny
surfaces reflect light unequally in different directions.
Only with a perfect mirror are the angles of incidence
and reflection equal—the rule we learn in school optics.

An illuminated object does not look real unless
shadows are present; a shadowing algorithm determines
which surfaces can be "seen" by the virtual light source.
These techniques can take account of multiple light
sources, both ambient and local, and the lights can be
of any colour. The designer is thus able to light the object
dramatically and theatrically, with no restrictions
on where the lights are placed.

Diffuse shadows are tedious to calculate, but a trick
that is sometimes effective is to place a "negative" light
source, which has the effect of sucking away the light,
behind the object.

None of the techniques discussed so far take account
of the light-transmitting properties of surfaces. A study
of paintings will show that it is the subtle colours found
in shadows and reflections that help bring a picture
to life.

Ray tracing and radiosity

In 1980, Turner Whitted went back to basics and applied
the laws of physics to a light ray's journey around a scene.
He established that every time a ray encounters a surface,
it divides into three parts: diffusely reflected light,
specularly reflected light and transmitted or refracted
light. Each ray leaving a surface is the sum of varying
contributions from these three sources.

Right 6.19 Miroslav Mitrovic, Valve
system parts, 2004. Ray tracing has been
used here to calculate the pathways of
light rays bouncing around this scene
of Ducati Desmo valve system parts,
producing convincing reflections and
shadows. It was modelled by Miroslav
Mitrovic of Bluming, Inc., using Solid
Edge, and rendered in Virtual Studio+
for promotional use by Ducati USA at
motorcycle shows throughout North
America. Courtesy UGS and Solid Edge.

Right 6.20 Solid models are lit using light
sources of various kinds located in 3D virtual
space and renderings made by placing a virtual
camera, with all the attributes of a real camera,
in 3D space, as shown by this SolidWorks
screenshot. Courtesy SolidWorks Corporation.

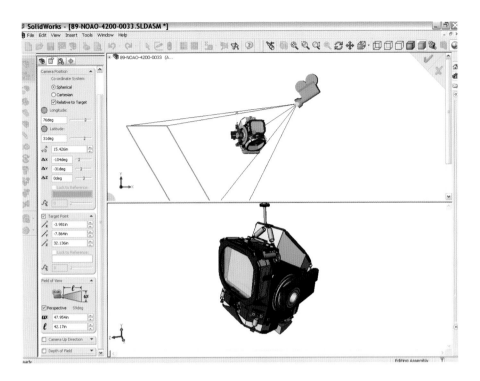

If you think of each ray growing a "tree" of reflected rays each time it hits a facet, it doesn't take a great deal of mathematical ability to deduce that the amount of computation required to arrive at the correct optics for a scene will be enormous, if not infinite, especially when there may be multiple light sources illuminating a scene.

Luckily, most of these rays shoot off to oblivion and so, to pare down the number of sums needed, the calculation is done in reverse—rays are traced back from the viewer's eyes (shot, in effect, through the pixels of the display's screen), and bounced around the scene, arriving back eventually at the light source. Hence the term ray tracing (Fig. 6.19).

Even with these economies, we are still talking about a colossal task for the processor. A display with a resolution of 1280 × 1024 pixels has over a million rays to deal with, and with even a modest scene containing, say, 10,000 polygons, you can see how the technique can strain the most powerful computer. Early ray-traced images were created on Cray supercomputers taking hours of number-crunching. Special graphics engines dedicated to the task are coming to the rescue, however, and ray tracing is now possible on workstations and PCs turbocharged with a go-faster graphics card.

Despite the global approach, ray tracing does fall down in certain circumstances—it won't show the glow from obscured local lights, colour bleeding or "blushes" from one object to another, for example. And each image

is dependent on the current position of the observer—shift the viewpoint or the position of the virtual camera and the whole scene has to be recalculated (Fig. 6.20).

Radiosity is an approach that determines the light energy equilibrium of all the surfaces in a static environment, which is independent of the observer's position. This requires the computer to solve large numbers of simultaneous equations, but once the scene has been computed in terms of its form factors and intensities, it is only then necessary to render any further views.

After the first picture has been computed, lights can be altered or turned off without having to recalculate the geometry, and the next view can be produced relatively quickly. Change the position of the viewer and only the rendering process has to be repeated.

Maxwell Render from Next Limit is a stand-alone program or plug-in for modelers such as 3D Studio Max, Lightwave and Maya. It considers light as an electro-magnetic wave defined by a frequency spectrum, which ranges from the infrared to the ultraviolet (Fig. 6.21).

Once Maxwell has completed the rendering procedure, each pixel in the output image contains different amounts of spectral energy—sourced from the lights in the scene—and arrives at the conceptual film/ccd of the virtual camera, or at the retina of the viewer. It is described as an unbiased renderer—with sufficient render time the rendered solution will always converge to the correct result without the introduction of artefacts.

Right 6.21 Peter Schuster, Hairdryer, 2005. Maxwell Render is a standalone or plug-in render engine that uses neither ray tracing nor radiosity but is based on the physics of real light using global illumination. All light emitters, material shaders and cameras are based on physically accurate models.

Adding texture

Most real surfaces are not smooth, they have texture, and various techniques have been developed to give a surface microscopic detail. The earliest method was to "map" or wrap around the curved surface of the object a scanned-in photograph or artificial 2D texture produced on a "paint" system.

James Blinn of the Jet Propulsion Labs in Pasadena was the pioneer of this effect, using it successfully on his simulations of planets. When the real image-processed pictures arrived from space vehicles, they turned out to be remarkably similar to the simulations. Other methods "perturb" the surface to render the effect of roughness. It is now possible to reproduce synthetically almost any surface texture, and it is not difficult these days to produce 3D textures such as wood or marbling (Figs. 6.22 and 6.23) that go right through the object and appear as they should if the object is sliced.

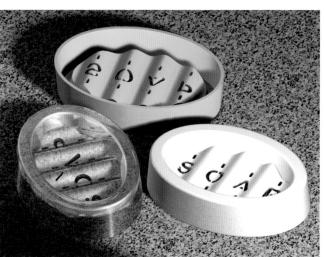

Top left 6.22 Various material textures can be mapped onto a surface or solid to make them look more realistic. This soap holder, modeled by Rio21 using Ashlar-Vellum's Cobalt, is shown in different colours and degrees of transparency sitting on a woodgrain surface. (*See also* figs. 2.38, 2.39)

Bottom left 6.23 Here the same scene and 3D geometry as in fig. 6.22 has been rendered this time with the soap holders sitting on a marble surface.

Above 6.24   David O'Connor, Screenshot.
2006. Bryce is a program that uses fractals
to render seemingly random naturalistic
textures such as mountains, clouds and water,
as in this screenshot.

Fractals

Using facets to create natural-looking objects, such as
mountain ranges and clouds, would be a herculean task,
and, being fabricated by humans, would probably not look
random enough. So computer graphics enthusiasts turned
to the work done in the 1930s by a man called Benoit
Mandlebrot to make sense of the seemingly haphazard
aspects of nature. He had originally set out to measure
the length of a coastline, but found the job frustratingly
difficult. The details are just as complicated as you home
in from a bay, to a cove, to individual groups of pebbles.
What he did discover, however, was that there is a degree
of self-similarity between the macro shape and the micro
shape and, looking around, found this principle repeated
throughout nature—a twig, for instance, looks like a tree,
a fact not unnoticed by model railway enthusiasts. The
result of his research was a book entitled *The Fractal
Geometry of Nature*.

Fractals in computer graphics start with a generator—
a series of coordinate points or, for a mountain range,
a mesh of polygons. This shape is scaled and rotated to
fit between an initial pair of points, called the initiator,
and each new pair of points on the resulting shape further
subdivided recursively. All this can be implemented with
just a few lines of code and produces a surface of infinite
complexity. A fractal is defined as "a curve of infinite
length with an infinite level of detail". No matter how
closely you look, fresh detail will be forever revealed. The
most spectacular examples of fractals are mountainscapes
(Fig. 6.24), but they have also been put to practical use
to generate textures. Particles are similar to fractals,

but are free floating and are used to create naturalistic "assemblies" like fire, smoke, clouds and leaves in CGI.

Commercial modelers

The 3D surface modeling and rendering package of choice for many designers is Maya, from Alias, a company formed in 1995 when workstation vendor Silicon Graphics bought Alias Research (founded in 1983) and Wavefront Technologies (founded in 1984), then merged the two. Alias was then taken over by CAD vendor Autodesk.

The surface modeler Maya, named after the Sanskrit word for "illusion," was first delivered in 1998 and is now in its seventh version. It has tools for NURBS (non-uniform rational B-splines, a technique for generating and representing curves and surfaces, a generalization of the Bézier splines found in draw programs), polygon facets and subdivision surface modeling, particles, texture mapping and ray tracing using proprietary software called Mental Ray. Other modelers with rendering include 3D Studio Max (sometimes called 3ds Max), Cinema 4D, and Ashlar-Vellum's Cobalt (Fig. 6.25).

But beware: as mentioned earlier, commercial surface and solid modelers do at present have that prior condition of completeness—the design has to be 100 percent complete in order for it to produce a presentation model.

And, as Dick Powell points out, before computer rendering was commonplace, clients used to be able to judge a designer's designing ability by the quality of his or her presentation drawings, but now only the most dedicated CGI nerd can tell how good the designer really is from a computer visualization.

While the 3D solid modelers on the market have been used mainly to produce visualizations or check out potential clashes in complex assemblies only *after* the design has been fixed and signed-off as a set of 2D orthographic projections, the impetus for using the computer as a tool for designing at the concept stage is more likely to come from work in television computer graphics or computer-aided fine art.

In many applications, for consumer-oriented products such as cars, there is a demand for a much closer relationship than already exists between stylists and engineers. Expensive automobiles are bought for their looks, and the specular reflection on a car's surface is a design element now as important as its profile or proportions.

Cost-effective and credible realism early in the design process, when financiers are making up their minds to underwrite a project, and integration with manufacture to maintain the designer's intentions throughout the design process, are key parameters in any future 3D CAD system.

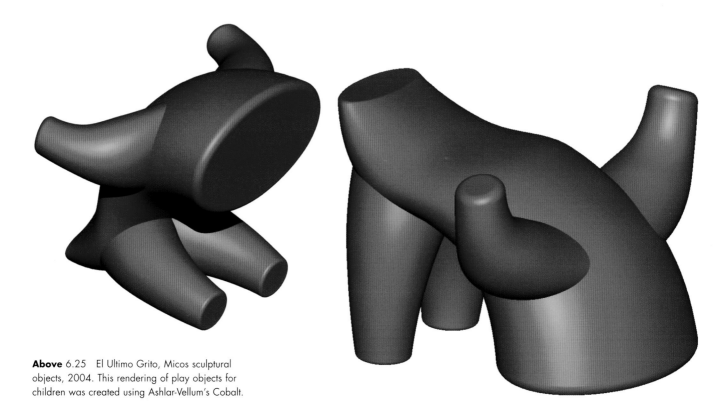

Above 6.25   El Ultimo Grito, Micos sculptural objects, 2004. This rendering of play objects for children was created using Ashlar-Vellum's Cobalt.

Conclusion

It must not be forgotten that the principal role of
a presentation drawing is to make the client feel happy
that the project is proceeding satisfactorily and that they
were right in their choice of designer. Anything goes,
and the presentation style is often carefully tailored to the
client. With a longstanding relationship, a designer may
be able to get away with the most cursory and sketchy
presentation visuals—and these may be appropriate for
a more design- and fashion-conscious client.

A more conventional captain of industry, using
a particular consultancy for the first time, may require
more subtle wooing and a theatrical ad-agency
performance (which could include video and computer-
generated concepts). The idea is to get the ideas across
successfully and to inspire confidence in a client—who
may be committing substantial development costs
to an as yet intangible project—as expediently, but as
effectively, as is humanly possible. The designer must
also bear in mind that if the project goes ahead the
product will have to be manufactured and assembled,
and the presentation drawings or computer models will
become the basis for the detail drawings and models
required in the next phase of design, as discussed in the
next chapter.

211.3

87.6

106.7

53.4

7

From general arrangement drawing to production

Opposite Torsten Neeland, Stackable
porcelain bowl, 2005. This is a 2D CAD
drawing made using VectorWorks for Guzzini.

Above 7.1 Charles Voysey, Oak table, 1903. Ink on tracing linen. This traditional general arrangement drawing by the Arts and Crafts designer is a design for an oak table, with leg details shown at full size. Courtesy RIBA (Royal Institute of British Architects), Library Drawings and Archives Collections, London.

One day, this whole chapter may become redundant, but not yet, not for a long time. Design theorists might wish for, and work towards, a complete computer model of the designed object good enough to drive all the machines needed to make it and its component parts, with no paper interpretations required between the stages of the design process. Until that day, however, designers and engineers will continue to use 2D drafts—whether manually produced (rare, these days) or computer-generated— at some point, to communicate their designs to those responsible for production and manufacturing. There will inevitably be a whole set of drawings, with the key to them all being the general arrangement (GA) drawing (also know as the assembly drawing), which takes the form of an orthographic plan and elevations. The GA shows the complete product and will lead to other separate drawings of close-up details, component parts and sub-assemblies (Fig. 7.1).

Engineering drawings may seem boring to the aspiring high-flying designer, but as German artist George Grosz once pointed out: "The neutrality and clarity of an engineering drawing is a better model for teaching about art than all the uncontrollable drivel about the cabbala and metaphysics and the ecstasy of sainthood." So let's get serious, and take a trip back to Victorian times in the quest to turn the designer's concept and presentation drawings into a precise and unambiguous detailed description that can be used to manufacture the product and all its parts.

In the future, a single all-embracing 3D computer solid model will encapsulate the product's geometry and all its associated specifications, but we're not quite there yet and the best we have at present is the plan and elevation orthographic drawing—the blueprint—albeit created with the help of a CAD system.

Unambiguous is the key word. A memorable segment of the rockumentary film parody *This is Spinal Tap* occurs when a miniature replica of Stonehenge is lowered onto the stage behind the band—they look surprised because they were expecting a full-size 18-foot replica of the ancient monument, but were instead presented with a pathetic 18-inch model, made exactly as indicated on the original drawing that Christopher Guest's character, Nigel Tufnel, had sketched in too much of a hurry (with two emphatic tick marks after the 18") and handed to the band's manager to be mocked up. Mistakes can easily be made, especially when you think the computer is infallible. Just consider how spell checkers will let through the wrong word, so long as it is spelled correctly!

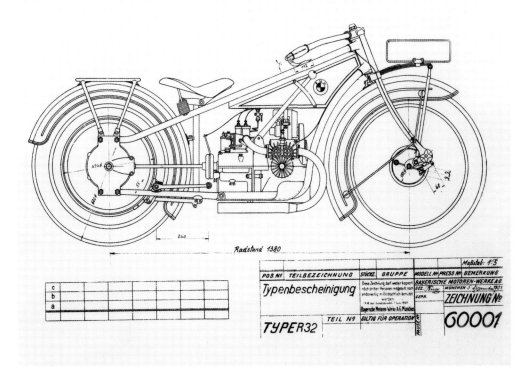

Right 7.2   Max Friz, BMW RS2 motorcycle, 1923. A side elevation of the first BMW motorcycle, with a flat-twin engine and shaft drive, seems to have a minimal amount of dimensioning. Courtesy BMW AG.

Below 7.3   With a 2D drafting system it is easy to create objects that look all right but would be impossible to manufacture. A 3D solid modeling system would ensure that the geometry and topology were correct.

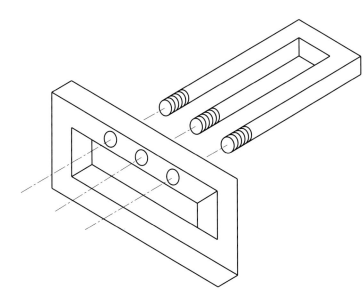

A product designer's background can always be detected from the detail drawings—a product "engineer" will do them by the book; more artistic types might take liberties, and are in real danger of infuriating the sticklers down on the shopfloor in production or even in the designer's own model workshop.

Engineering drawings are basically much neater versions of the concept sketches, with lines straightened out, to scale and with real dimensions added, taken perhaps from the already existing components that must be incorporated within the product being designed (Fig. 7.2). The familiar engineering drawing, or blueprint, once drawn in ink or polymer pencil on Mylar film and copied to blue dyeline paper, but now more likely to be a computer printout, has one purpose: to communicate a designer's concepts to those responsible for manufacturing the components of the product and assembling them, along with pre-sourced proprietary items, to create the finished object. As such, the drawings must be complete, reliable and, as I keep saying, unambiguous (Fig. 7.3).

To prevent any misinterpretation, production drawings are highly codified, and to the untrained eye can appear confusing and difficult to read; it is often hard to see the form of the object, lost amongst all the dimensioning and tolerancing information. As the manufacturing and assembly of the product is often carried out in different countries, or even continents, the drawings need to be language-independent. The rules that dictate these conventions are set down by standards organizations and although each country will have its own, the most important is the ISO (International Standards Organization).

Technical Product Documentation

The modern term for a set of engineering drawings is TPD (Technical Product Documentation) or TPS (Technical Product Specification), which encompasses not only the traditional paper-based drawings but also other forms of information, such as the methodology for design implementation, the means for verification (metrology and precision measurements), quality assurance, technical documentation, and information on any other related

tools and equipment. Whenever a new standard is published or an old one updated, the year is appended to the identifying ISO number, for example ISO5456-2:1996 is entitled "Technical drawings—Projection methods—Part 2: Orthographic representations".

Engineering drawings are always executed in orthographic projection: in the USA and the UK using third-angle projection, elsewhere in first-angle projection (*see* Chapter 4). A designer may, however, use a form appropriate to the type of object being designed. For a long and thin object, such as a railway locomotive, it will be expedient to use third-angle projection so that the front elevation, for example, will be to the right and adjacent to the side elevation. The type of projection must always be indicated on the drawing, usually by means of a conventional symbol (Fig. 7.4). The orthographic projection is often accompanied by auxiliary views (that is, ones not orthogonal to the x, y or z axes), so-called "scrap views" of details requiring close scrutiny and perhaps a 3D pictorial view in isometric or perspective.

The general arrangement drawing

The GA drawing is the master drawing and key to all the other drawings (Fig. 7.5). It is here that the final layout is

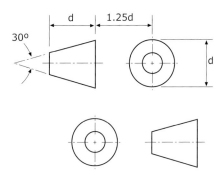

Above 7.4   To indicate whether a drawing has been created using first-angle projection (Europe) or third-angle projection (US), it is common to include one of these truncated cone symbols: first angle is at the top, third angle below.

Right 7.5   A general arrangement drawing for the rear frame assembly of a Brompton folding bicycle. Note the symbol for third-angle projection. The numbers in circles are called callouts and refer to other drawings or annotations (listed top right).

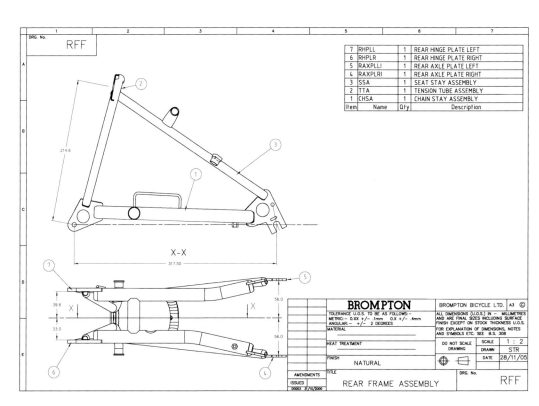

Item	Name	Qty	Description
7	RHPLL	1	REAR HINGE PLATE LEFT
6	RHPLR	1	REAR HINGE PLATE RIGHT
5	RAXPLLI	1	REAR AXLE PLATE LEFT
4	RAXPLRI	1	REAR AXLE PLATE RIGHT
3	SSA	1	SEAT STAY ASSEMBLY
2	TTA	1	TENSION TUBE ASSEMBLY
1	CHSA	1	CHAIN STAY ASSEMBLY

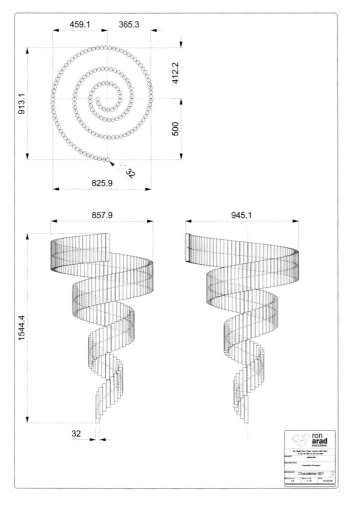

Above 7.6   Ron Arad, *Lolita* chandelier, 2004. This MicroStation general arrangement drawing for Swarovski indicates that if the drawing were printed out at A1 the scale would be 1:5 but at A3 it would be 1:10.

Right 7.7   David Lewis, CD player/radio detail, 2003. This is a hand-drawn general arrangement drawing for the Bang & Olufsen BeoSound4 CD player/DAB radio with built-in SD memory card.

decided upon, dimensions are fixed, ergonomic considerations resolved and the methods of production finalized. The client is satisfied and the designer is, in theory, ready to embark on the task of producing the fully dimensioned drawings required by production: the detail drawings, the drawings of the press tools, progressive dies or moulds, plus all the assorted jigs and fixtures that will be needed to manufacture the product. There may also be a need for assembly drawings showing how the component parts are to be put together (Fig. 7.6). All these drawings, which could run to hundreds, might be at different scales and are coordinated with reference to the GA (Fig. 7.7).

In the early days of the Industrial Revolution, one drawing—a rendered GA—often sufficed. A drawing of a pump or steam engine by Boulton and Watt (*see* Fig. 1.2), for example, would incorporate the basic dimensions for erection, but none concerned with manufacture. As they were almost invariably one-offs, the production of the parts was left to skilled craftsmen. As machinery became more standardized, more and more drawings were needed and their production was delegated to draftsmen and (mainly female) tracers.

The GA gives the overall disposition of the product, the arrangement of its component parts and the way in which they are to be put together (Fig. 7.8). It gives the overall dimensions and usually includes a parts list that refers the reader to the whole hierarchy of the other more

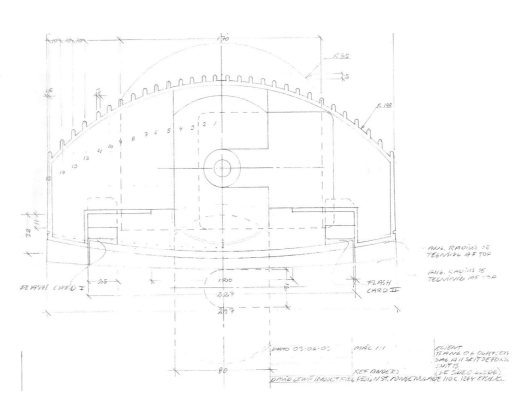

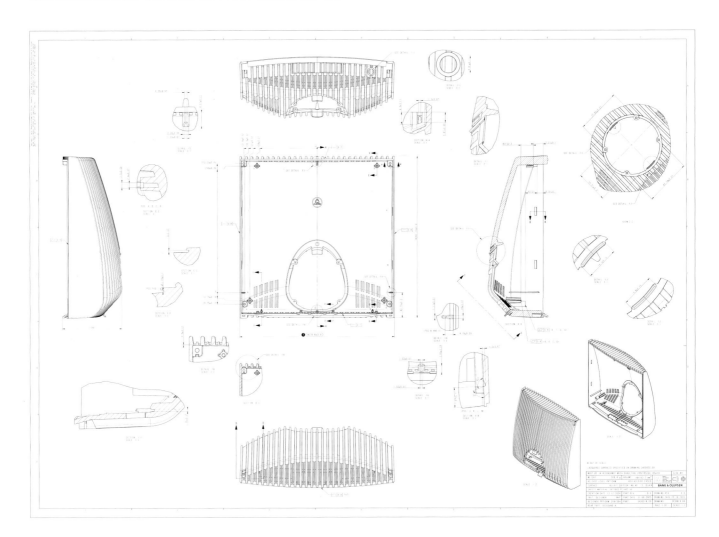

Above 7.8   BeoSound4 CD player/radio,
2005. A Pro/E drawing (with half-size
isometrics) for the rear panel of the Bang &
Olufsen BeoSound4 CD player/DAB radio.
Note the symbol for first-angle projection and
all the sections and scrap details.

detailed drawings: subassembly and discrete assemblies,
and the individual detail and sub-detail drawings. These
show more manageable sections of the product, with every
essential dimension and allowable tolerance documented
(Fig. 7.9). These drawings also include information
detailing the material the part is to be made from, its
surface finish and treatment (ground, anodized, painted
and so on) (Fig. 7.10). The tolerance and finish of a part
have a significant effect on the type and precision of tools
that can be used and hence the cost of manufacturing, so
must be chosen and documented with great care. If a part
is to be cast and subsequently machined, the designer may
be expected to provide as-cast drawings. Any way in which
the designer can help optimize the design-to-production
cycle will always be appreciated (Figs. 7.11 and 7.12).

The drawings following the GA were once produced
using technical pens and ink, or polymer pencil, onto
sheets of Mylar film, preprinted with a border and a title
block into which was placed information about the
drawing: its unique number and its relationship with any
other drawings, the name of the designer, the date,

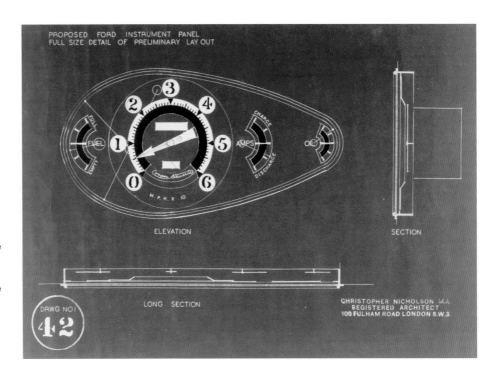

ELEVATION   SECTION

LONG SECTION

Top 7.9   Christopher Nicholson, Ford automobile instrument panel, 1936. This is a blueprint copy of a detail drawing for the Cooper-Steward Engineering Company Limited. Blueprints, produced by the cyanotype contact-printing process, were the only way to reproduce ink drawings before photocopiers and inkjet printers became commonplace. Courtesy RIBA (Royal Institute of British Architects), Library Drawings and Archives Collections, London.

Right 7.10   A screenshot of an Arctic Cat gear pinion part, 2004. Drawn using UGS NX software, this shows a non-orthogonal section (A-A) and a rendered preview. CAD allows designers to show gears and screw threads accurately. Previously they were indicated using conventional symbols.

Below left 7.11   Rio21 Design, Soap holder, 2004. This simple general arrangement drawing using Ashlar-Vellum's Cobalt betrays quite a complex geometry. It shows a plan, two sections taken orthogonally and a blown-up detail.

Below right 7.12   Ron Arad, Oh Void table, 2005. The designer leaves nothing to chance in this MicroStation installation drawing for the "Paved with Good Intentions" exhibition in Miami (2005). As well as indicating the different scales at different printout sizes, he includes a 10mm square and an instruction not to scale from this drawing!

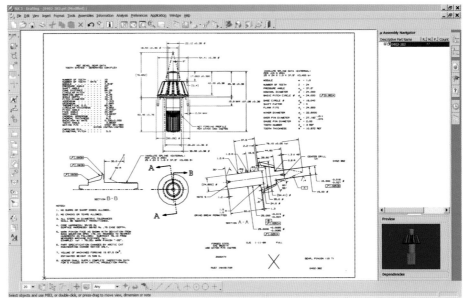

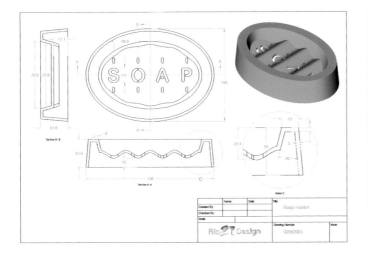

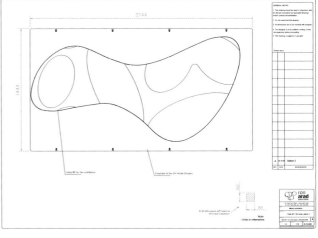

a symbol indicating the projection being used (first- or third-angle), the original scale and the title of the drawing. These will now be output from the computer as inkjet or laser prints or, less so these days, drawn by a pen plotter.

Drafting standards

BS308, the first standard in the world for orthographic engineering drawings, has been the designer/draughtsman's bible since 1927 and in 1972 grew to three large volumes (two of which were devoted solely to tolerancing) in which were detailed the way dimensions, tolerances, cross-hatching and so on, ought to be presented for consistency and clarity. It was probably unique in that it was universally accepted in the UK by both industry and the armed forces. A metric version was introduced in 1985, but as the pace of technological advance quickened during the late 1980s, BS308 couldn't keep up and in 1992 the BSI (British Standards Institution) decided to accept all new ISO standards and rebrand them as British Standards. By this time, BS308 comprised 260 pages of standards; the ISO handbook, containing 155 standards, worked out at 1496 pages! In 2000, BS308 was withdrawn and replaced by BS8888:2000, which is basically a road map to the 106 appropriate ISO standards, but also carries forward valuable clauses contained in BS308, but not present in ISO documentation.

The full title of BS8888:2000 was *Technical Product Documentation (TPD). Specification for Defining, Specifying and Graphically Representing Products*. At the time of writing, the latest update is BS8888:2004 *Technical Product Specification* and references 151 ISO standards, including the new BS ISO 1101 that takes into account 20 years of GPS (Geometrical Product Specification) development, BS ISO 1209-1 for the dimensioning of technical drawings, and BS ISO 16792 for technical product documentation. It must be stressed that these standards do not refer to any particular drawing method: a manual drawing and the output of the latest CAD system must both conform to the same standards and be incapable of misinterpretation.

The US standard ASME Y14.5M-1994, published by the American Society of Mechanical Engineers, is only one of a number of standards issued by bodies such as NASA, the utilities and the armed services. The USA is one of the few countries in the world still using imperial units (feet and inches) and, despite its global influence, tends to go its own way where standards are concerned.

Why standards?

The purpose of a drawing standard is twofold: first and foremost it is a universally agreed codification of practice to aid in the communication of ideas between different professionals and disciplines; second, as stated in the 1943 foreword to BS308, it is "a useful guide which will enable young engineers and draughtsmen to proceed with much of their work without too frequent reference to their seniors". Drawing standards such as BS308 advise the designer on such matters as recommended scales (1:1, 1:2, 1:5, 1:10, 1:20 and so on), the type of linework to be used (continuous thick lines for visible outlines and edges; chained thin lines for centrelines, trajectories and pitch lines; continuous thin lines with zigzags for indicating the limits of partial or interrupted views and so on, and how to draw the arrowheads used on dimension and leader lines. There are recommendations on lettering, how to simplify the representation of symmetrical parts, how to draw "interrupted" views of long simple objects and repetitive features such as holes on a circular pitch. The drawing of sections and sectional views is treated in great detail, as are the methods and conventions of hatching.

All is not so straightforward: by convention, when a sectional view passes longitudinally through fasteners such as bolts, nuts, shafts, ribs, webs and the spokes of wheels, it is the practice to show them in external view. Intersection lines too are often approximated by arcs and straight lines where the projection of true lines of intersection is unnecessary. Flat surfaces on a shaft for example can be indicated by crossed diagonals and knurling is hinted at by showing only part of the surface so treated. There are also conventional representations for bearings and screw threads. Surface finish is indicated by a tick symbol with the maximum permissible roughness shown numerically. Commonly used items, such as bolts, springs and gears are not drawn realistically, but are represented by symbols.

According to the standard, each dimension necessary for the complete definition of a finished product should be given on the drawing and should appear once only. There are all kinds of regulations governing the placement of dimension lines and the method of dimensioning (parallel, superimposed running or chained dimensioning). American and European methods of dimensioning differ in that all dimensions on drawings produced in the USA can be read from the horizontal; drawings produced in Europe keep the dimensions parallel to the dimensioning lines—vertical dimensions are thus turned onto their sides and so must be read from the right.

It can be gathered from the above that engineering drawings, in their quest for simplicity and a desire to be universally understood, have, in fact, moved further and further from a realistic depiction of the object and have thus become inscrutable to anyone untrained in technical drawing.

Tolerances

All dimensions are subject to tolerances, and tolerances are a whole subject in themselves. More than two thirds of BS308 is devoted to tolerancing and most of the major revisions to the standard since it was introduced in 1927 have a direct relationship to the way tolerance information is represented.

A tolerance specifies the limits of size of a particular dimension and is crucially important if an assembly of parts is to fit together and function properly. There is a trade-off to be made: a tolerance should not be too stringent or the cost of machining the part will begin to escalate dramatically. It has to be just right, and selecting the correct tolerance is part of the skill of the designer. What the standard does is ensure that the designer's instructions are conveyed to production with the minimum possibility of misinterpretation.

Most designers will claim that, of course, they can produce drawings to BS308 or other equivalent national standards if they are really pushed. The good news is that these rules and conventions can be programmed into 2D CAD systems to ensure that designers always keep on the straight and narrow. Some systems will even convert a drawing done to BS308 to its American ANSI (American National Standards Institute) or European DIN (Deutsches Institut für Normung) or ISO equivalent at the push of a button, or allow dimensions to be input in a mixture of imperial and metric units. This is not considered best practice, however.

Computer-aided drafting

The rudiments of engineering drawing have always been taught by example, and have been well documented elsewhere. This chapter will show what a 2D CAD (which can stand for computer-aided design or the more modest computer-aided drafting) system can do to help designers produce the necessary evil of fully dimensioned and toleranced orthographic drawings.

With CAD, it is possible for the designer to work at full-size (1:1) on a "master" drawing of the product, regardless of its size and complexity, using pan and zoom on the computer to window into the portion of the overall product currently being worked on. Most commercial CAD systems arrange the drawing in layers or levels, equivalent to overlays, so that, for example, a relatively uncomplicated GA can be put on one layer with detail kept separate on further layers. However, because the computer has so many layers available, as well as the means for managing them, it is usual—to aid later modification—to install even the simplest drawing on several layers: the construction lines on one, the outline on another, the text on a third and so on.

These layers can be viewed and worked on in isolation or combination, and coordinated variations output in various forms and scales. All the different

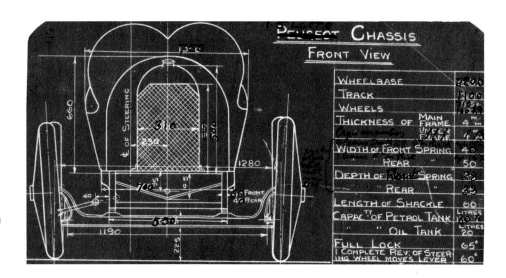

Right 7.13   G. H. Roesch, Peugeot design, 1923. This is a blueprint from a front elevation drawing, annotated with design changes to go back to the drawing board, 3 1/8 x 5 1/2 in (8 cm x 14 cm). Courtesy Institution of Mechanical Engineers, London.

craftspeople involved in the production process can then have their own individual customized drawing, up-to-date and signed off with any recent amendments, rather than, as was common, a barely legible scribbled-on dyeline blueprint (Fig. 7.13). With systems connected together in a network, it is also possible for different members of a multi-disciplinary team to work on the same master—with some having only read-only access, others having the authority to make changes.

Geometric constructions

CAD systems are at their most productive at the detail design stage. These productivity increases are usually attributed to the use of "library" symbols or components—that can be drawn once, and used over and over again—or by using parametric programming (more of which later) for generating families of parts. But even on one-off products, it is possible to score over manual methods by making use of all the geometric constructions that a CAD system has to offer.

The simplest PC-based systems have commands that can draw circles tangent to lines, arcs or other circles. A circle can be drawn through any three points, inscribed inside a triangle or polygon, or, say, tangent to two converging lines and another given circle lying between those lines. Fillets, blends and chamfers can be generated automatically. Commands like these, plus on-screen rulers and calculators, can sometimes make the tedious preliminaries of setting up construction lines unnecessary. Lines will always be straight, circles always true, and right angles always square. Goodbye to "draughtsman's licence".

Manual dimensioning is a matter of annotating a drawing with the number you know it ought to be.

A designer would never "scale" a drawing to ascertain the true length, because you know that manually produced drawings are too inaccurate for fabrication. With CAD, it is the other way round: entering points accurately in the first place ensures that the drawing (or more correctly, the computer model from which the drawing is generated) is precise. You can also "take-off" other dimensions from the drawing with confidence, and most systems will have some form of automatic and associative dimensioning in metric or imperial units conforming to a national or international standard such as BS308.

The snapping of points to a pre-defined grid ensures that a profile, for example, is closed with no gaps, so fudging is not allowed. Manual drawing is limited by visual accuracy, not so with CAD. Editing—with commands such as delete, alter, move, rotate, translate, mirror, trim, copy—is simpler with CAD and so it is more likely to be carried out.

Controlling curves

Before computers, designers didn't seem to care very much about the accuracy of their curves. If it couldn't be done with compasses or an ellipse template, they would reach for the nearest French curve or a bendy ruler and leave the rest to the patternmaker on the shopfloor to sort out. Freeway designers and the skilled loftsmen of the automotive and aerospace industries had their own tricks of the trade—using piano wire and weights, or plywood "splines" held in positions of tension with lead "ducks"—to generate the long "fair" lines required by their particular applications (Fig. 7.14).

When NC (numerically controlled) point-to-point contouring machine tools became available in the 1960s,

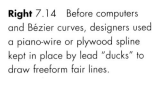

Right 7.14   Before computers and Bézier curves, designers used a piano-wire or plywood spline kept in place by lead "ducks" to draw freeform fair lines.

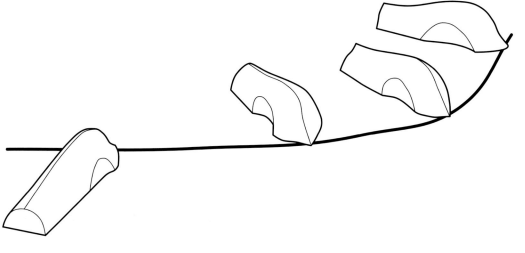

they demanded software that dealt with parametric spaces and complex doubly-curved surfaces that were totally and accurately defined. Strangely enough, the problems associated with 3D surfaces were tackled before simple 2D curves in the work of Steven Coons in the USA and Pierre Bézier at Renault in France.

Complex surfaces are important to the designer for two different reasons. First, there are the shapes that have been optimized by rigorous experimentation—turbine blades, boat hulls and so on—and second, there are the aesthetic curves created by stylists—like car body panels—that must assemble with, or keep clear of, neighbouring parts. In both cases, an accurate, predictable and controllable means of defining the curves and surfaces is paramount. The representation should also be economical in terms of computer memory and speed of response.

Early systems joined up the dots defined by the x, y, z Cartesian coordinates measured at various points on the surface to create a net of curves, with each mesh of the net (the "patch") defined by an algorithm which ensured smooth slope or curvature continuity between adjacent patches. Sometimes the operator can adjust the mathematical derivatives to improve the general shape, but care has to be taken not to alter the general continuity.

The parametric cubic segment is the most commonly used curve in CAD. This requires the Cartesian coordinates x, y, z to be expressed in terms of a parameter t, and the x, y, z coordinates vary as polynomials of t, in this case

containing a term of t to the power of 3. The Bézier form is defined in terms of four points: a start point, an end point and two points lying on the respective end tangents. The positioning of the tangent points is critical—the further they are moved along the tangent line, the more highly curved the segment.

The designer starts with an initial first guess—say placing the tangent point a distance along the tangent line, a third the chord length—and successively improves the positioning interactively until the overall curve shape is right (Fig. 7.15).

Most CAD systems have a spline routine that automates the definition of curves built up of several parametric cubic segments. The designer specifies the end points of the segments and the system supplies the end tangent vectors. The result is called a spline curve and models the physical lath or piano wire of the loftsman, which always rests in the position of least tension. Spline routines are simply programs for assigning tangent vectors in a reasonably sensible way to achieve overall smoothness.

Modifying the curve thus created is another problem altogether. A spline is an entity in its own right and can only be altered into another spline. Direct and total control is a chimera, especially if you only want to change bits of the curve. Local data changes can cause global shape changes. The B-spline is an optimal definition that confines the extent of shape changes and gives designers direct—but not total—control over their creations. A B-spline with two segments is defined by five points; one

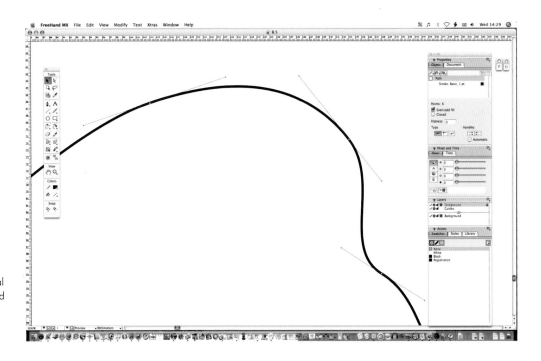

Right 7.15 The mathematics of Bézier curves were invented by Pierre Bézier of Renault during the late 1940s in his work on numerically controlled milling machines, and are now an integral part (along with more sophisticated math) of all CAD and 2D drawing programs, as in this Freehand screenshot.

with three segments by six points and so on. The designer inputs the segment end points V_1, V_2 … V_{n+1} and the system creates a polygon framework of points P_1, P_2 … P_{n+3} around the curve. From then on the designer works with the "polygon" points and the disturbing effects of localized changes are restricted to around four segments at most.

Higher order Bézier curves are often offered as an alternative form in some CAD systems. The designer specifies the points and the program generates a curve passing through them. Subsequently, the designer works directly with the vertices of the Bézier polygon with direct and total control of the definition, but without the ability to make localized shape changes.

The rational cubic is a versatile form and can define a wide range of shapes including spline curves and cubic sections (such as circles, ellipses, parabolas and hyperbolas). It has been the basis of in-house systems in the aerospace and automotive industries for some time and has now become available commercially. The non-uniform rational B-spline (known lovingly as NURBS— *see* Chapter 6) has been adopted by most vendors as a mathematical means of unifying their wireframe, surfacing and solid modellers.

NURBS can be trimmed to arbitrary boundaries, and have more modest database requirements. Large curves, such as an entire automobile body panel, can be modelled with single, low-degree entities. Operations such as smoothing, intersecting and offsetting are faster and more stable, and NURBS are very good for fitting fair curves through large numbers of points, even when the points are unevenly spaced. Furthermore, NURBS geometry can exactly represent points, arcs, conics, Bézier curves and uniform B-spline curves without approximation, for better geometry transfer between different makes of system.

Parametric design

Early CAD systems merely modelled the drafting task, simulating pencil on paper. Most present-day CAD systems contain some degree of "intelligence". A system may remember how items connect with one another, when items are tangent to others, and it may associate fillets and chamfers with their master lines. These features save time when making alterations to the drawing, and reassure the designer that the drawing has not lost its integrity.

Parametrics are useful for creating a set of parts having a family resemblance from an initial "generalized" drawing.

Below 7.16   By defining dimensions as parameters instead of fixed numbers, a change to the parameter will automatically change the design, but not the topology, of the shape. Thus a bolt, for example, can be made short and fat or long and thin, but with the same head.

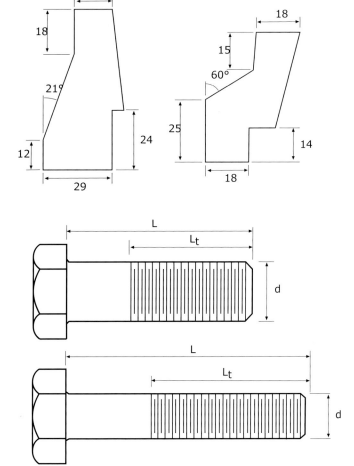

Below 7.17   Héctor Serrano, Waterproof swimming-pool lamp, 2003. This is a detail drawing showing cross-hatching of sections. (*See also* figs. 2.30 and 3.30)

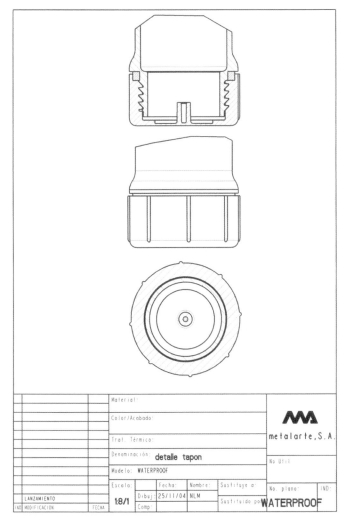

A bolt, for example, can be short and fat, or long and thin (Fig. 7.16). The topology is the same; the dimensions (angles and lengths) may be different. By replacing the exact dimensions with parameters: *l* for length, *d* for diameter, and so on, the real dimensions can be keyed in at a later stage to generate automatically the production drawings for the specific part. Parametrization is also a useful tool at the concept stage of design when final dimensions—to fit around a sourced component, for example—may not be known.

Conventionally, parametrization is achieved by entering into a computer file all the commands necessary to draw a part, perhaps by recording the keystrokes made during the construction of a drawing. The designer defines the parameters as the shape is drawn. Once drawn, the shape can be altered interactively by a command to change the parameter to a new value. Any items dependent on that parameter will be automatically redefined. Any parametrized geometry can be converted into a "symbol" by pointing to the appropriate area. The symbol can then be stored in a library and recalled onto another drawing. On recall, the system will prompt the designer for each parameter value in turn. This kind of relational geometry can also be used to draw linked views and mechanisms.

Over the years CAD has become less like copying and much more akin to designing (Figs. 7.17–7.21). Designers

Below 7.18   Alexander Åhnebrink, Mountaineer watch. This is a CAD general arrangement drawing using Illustrator, then exported to Ashlar-Vellum's Graphite for dimensioning and annotating, then back to Illustrator again for final touches. (*See also* figs. 3.20 and 6.14)

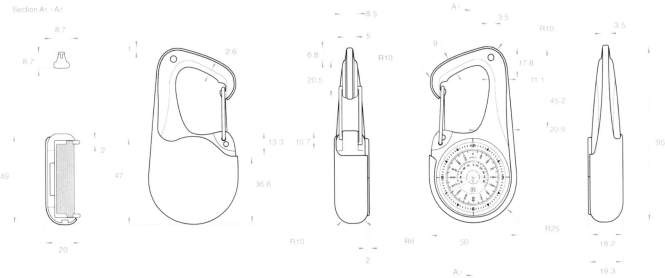

may have the time to try out "what if?" scenarios with the confidence that they can always return to the original design if the variant being tested does not look likely to succeed. Whether the 2D orthographic drawings are derived from a 3D solid or surface model, or worked up from scratch from the original concept sketch, the designer can rest assured that the CAD drawing will be accurate, legible, coordinated and easily amended should the client have a change of mind or should a pre-sourced component turn out to have different dimensions from its original specification.

Many design consultancies, especially those practising in Europe and those from a more architectural background, do not usually concern themselves with the nuts and bolts of engineering drawing. Their involvement with a design project ends with the layout drawing or the GA. In the USA and UK, on the other hand, there is a longstanding tradition in engineering, and designers

Above 7.19 Torsten Neeland, Tank wall lamp, 2002. This is a 3D-rendered version for Anta, modeled and lit using 3D Studio Max.

Right 7.20 Ito Morabito (Ora Ito), Cinderella shoes, 1998. Orthographic projections designed using Autodesk Alias Studio (formerly Alias StudioTools), albeit coloured and rendered, remain a popular way of showing designed objects, as in these ones for Roger Vivier.

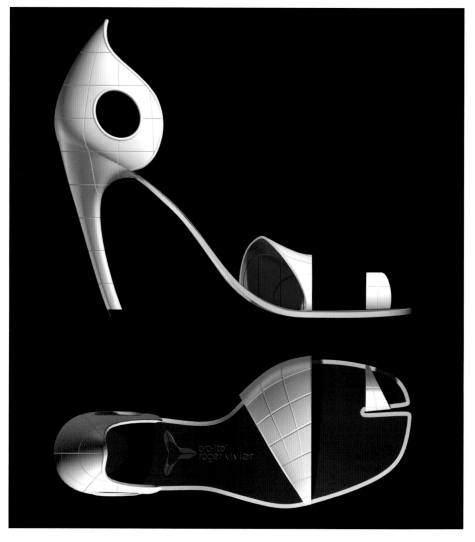

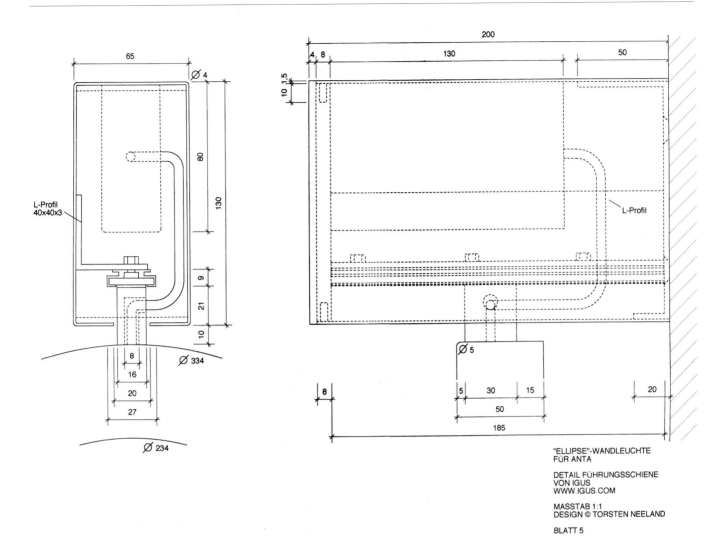

"ELLIPSE"-WANDLEUCHTE
FÜR ANTA

DETAIL FÜHRUNGSSCHIENE
VON IGUS
WWW.IGUS.COM

MASSTAB 1:1
DESIGN © TORSTEN NEELAND

BLATT 5

Above 7.21   Torsten Neeland, Tank lamp, 2002.
This is a full-scale detail drawing for Anta, drawn
using Ashlar-Vellum's Graphite. Note the dotted lines
for hidden components.

will wish to see the design right through to production.
Some designers insist that this is the only way that their
original concepts can be realized with integrity and
without compromise. The production of all the many
hundreds of detail drawings needed to manufacture a
product is a very labour-intensive and time-consuming
activity, and the designer often has to rely on the
cooperation of the client and the client's drawing office,
or possibly use contract draughtsmen to carry out the
work. A CAD system in-house, while not a panacea, can
give the design consultancy control over the entire design-
to-production cycle and the means of compressing time
scales, thus giving them a competitive edge in fast-
moving markets.

CAD data-exchange standards

Early CAD systems were hugely expensive and affordable only by large corporations. They were based on mainframes and minicomputers, requiring their own air-conditioned rooms, and huge vector displays that had to be physically close to the computer, often the other side of a wall. Vendors included Computervision, Intergraph and Applicon. Software was usually proprietary—developed in-house and incompatible with every other vendor's software—and the systems were sold as turnkey packages—complete packages of software and hardware—locking in the customer to a particular non-standard system.

To overcome incompatibilities between systems, the development of IGES (Initial Graphics Exchange Specification) was started in 1979 by a group of CAD users and vendors, including Boeing and General Electric, with the support of the US National Bureau of Standards. The idea was to define a neutral data format so that drawings could be exchanged between one CAD system and another. The emerging shift to 3D CAD software using solid models, and the need for such software to manage product data such as material properties, surface finish, engineering tolerances and so on, was, however, creating a need for a new data exchange standard.

In 1984 the PDES (Product Data Exchange Specification) initiative was started in Europe to address these needs. These have both been superseded by STEP (Standard for the Exchange of Product model data), officially designated as ISO 10303 *Industrial Automation Systems and Integration—Product Data Representation and Exchange*. It is an international standard for the computer-interpretable representation and exchange of industrial product data. The objective is to provide a mechanism that is capable of describing product data throughout the lifecycle of a product, independent of any particular system. The nature of this description makes it suitable not only for neutral file exchange, but also as a basis for implementing and sharing product databases and archiving.

All change in the CAD market

The CAD market was transformed almost overnight in 1982, with the introduction of the affordable IBM PC and a simple 2D program from Autodesk called AutoCAD. It quickly became the top-selling CAD program and

by 1994, Autodesk announced that it had sold its millionth license. The twentieth release, AutoCAD 2006, has amongst its features dynamic "blocks" (the company's term for standard library components), representing objects that engineers use frequently, such as bolts. Special "grips" allow stretching, scaling, rotating, adding or removing threads as needed and dynamic input settings that enable users to enter dimensions at the cursor.

AutoCAD's DWG (pronounced *drawing*) and DXF (Drawing Interchange Format, or Drawing Exchange Format) have become de facto CAD data-exchange file formats. But despite the ubiquity of AutoCAD, many design companies prefer other, Mac-based systems, such as Ashlar-Vellum's Graphite. A version of AutoCAD for the Mac was released in the late 1980s, but met with limited market acceptance and was soon dropped.

Parametric Technology Corporation launched the first Unix workstation-based 3D CAD software, Pro/Engineer, in 1987. The leading CAD software vendors of the day—Computervision, Intergraph, McDonnell-Douglas Unigraphics, GE/CALMA, IBM/Dassault and SDRC—initially dismissed it as irrelevant, immature and unstable, yet within 18 months of its release, the CAD establishment was in turmoil as Parametric Technology sold new licences of 3D CAD software at a record pace. Today most of the founding CAD vendors have gone out of business.

As well as being able to draw geometric constructions and "fair" curves, a useful CAD system should be capable of:
– automatically generating standard components
– reusing design components
– design modification and versioning
– validating and verifying designs against specifications and design rules
– simulating designs without having to build physical prototypes
– direct output to a rapid prototyping or rapid manufacture machine for producing industrial prototypes
– automated design of assemblies, collections of parts and/or other assemblies
– outputting of engineering documentation, such as manufacturing drawings and Bills of Materials
– output of designs directly to manufacturing facilities.

The big problem smaller design consultancies have is that whatever system they prefer to use in the studio, they will usually have to transfer the design files to the client's own 3D CAD system, whether it be Catia from Dassault Systèmes or NX Unigraphics, both popular in the automotive and aerospace sectors, or the more widespread Pro/Engineer. A combination of IGES and DWG/DXF is the pragmatic solution as we await further standards such as STEPS to come into use.

Conclusion

With the production of the engineering drawings and all the associated paperwork—whether manually produced or output from a CAD system—we are now at the end of the design-to-manufacturing process for this particular job and the product (once merely a sketch on the back of an envelope) is away being fabricated. PLM (Product Lifecyle Management) is a buzzword used for the process of managing the entire business lifecycle of a product, from its conception, through design and manufacture, to its servicing and eventual disposal.

Drawings are necessary in every stage of a product's life. Soon it will be in the shops or with the end user, but there is just one drawing job left in the product's lifecycle, that of producing the technical illustrations associated with the product, its assembly and operation, packaging and marketing.

Case Study 4:
Nelson Au's USB pocket hard drive for Seagate

Nelson Au is a practising industrial designer based in California's Silicon Valley. He has over twenty years' experience and was a founding designer of IDEO. While at IDEO, he developed products for many clients, including Apple, Silicon Graphics, Palm, Xerox, Sega of America and Alaris Medical Systems. He was also a program manager for a joint venture between Samsung and IDEO when Samsung came to IDEO to learn the IDEO methodology for innovation. The Seagate Pocket Drive was designed after he left IDEO as an independent designer working with Lunar Design. He is currently with designafairs USA.

While he managed projects and junior designers at IDEO, he also designed products and worked with engineers within the firm and outside. Some of the younger designers were using Alias StudioTools and Maya (now known as Autodesk AliasStudio) and the engineers used Pro/E. The industrial designers within his group mainly used Ashlar-Vellum 2D (now called Graphite) to define the design. He felt he needed a 3D CAD application to define his designs more precisely for the engineers and model makers—not so much to do cool renderings but rather to have complete control over the design of the surface appearance. He chose to learn Cobalt from Ashlar-Vellum, even though he assumed at the time that the ability to do photo-realistic renderings was the domain of Alias; although his colleagues considered the choice unusual, it has proven to be a good choice.

Having used Ashlar-Vellum 2D software since 1989, Au took to Cobalt because it was easy to learn and compatible with his Mac. Says Au: "My co-workers used Rhino, Alias, SolidWorks, or Pro/E, and then whined a lot about their software. I use Cobalt without all of the aggravation, and can still exchange information with all these applications using the built-in translators."

He first used Cobalt to create the Digi-Pix digital camera concept for the Design-Engine 2002 Photoreal Electronics Competition. To his amazement, he won the Grand Prize! (Ironically, the grand prize was a copy of Alias StudioTools.)

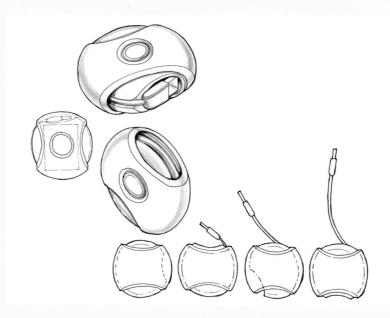

Right CS 4.1 Initial concept sketches of the Seagate Technology pocket drive in felt-tip pens and coloured pencil. Courtesy Seagate Technology.

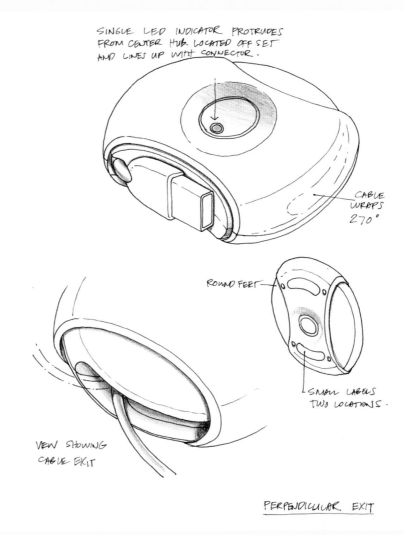

SINGLE LED INDICATOR PROTRUDES FROM CENTER HUB. LOCATED OFFSET AND LINES UP WITH CONNECTOR.

CABLE WRAPS 270°

ROUND FEET

SMALL LABELS TWO LOCATIONS.

VIEW SHOWING CABLE EXIT

PERPENDICULAR. EXIT

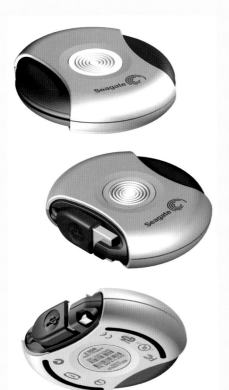

Cobalt is history-driven with associations and 2D equation-driven parametrics and constraints. Like Alias and Rhino, it has surfacing tools and is also a solid modeling program. Once a design is roughed out in surfaces, it can be stitched together and converted to a solid with operations such as blends and chamfers on corners and edges. Holes can be drilled though or into solids. Boolean operations can be used to add, remove or intersect the solid shapes. Au built the Digi-Pix digital camera concept by extruding closed arcs and splines along curves and rails to form a solid object.

Anytime Au needed to modify a part, the history tree allowed for it. For example, if a client didn't like the radii, a Get Info box allowed him to type in the new radius. If a hole was added earlier and was no longer needed, he could either remove it or alter its dimensions. When a model is built with changes in mind, most things are easy to modify. Where a product has an LCD—a PDA for example—and the engineer tells you that the LCD vendor has changed and the screen opening is wider and no longer symmetrical, this can be changed using the associative capability.

Users of Graphite 2D will know how easy it is to select the end points of a line or closed object and drag it to a new location. If the LCD opening, say, has to move, the same can be done either numerically or using the mouse. The opening will move and update the surfaces around it.

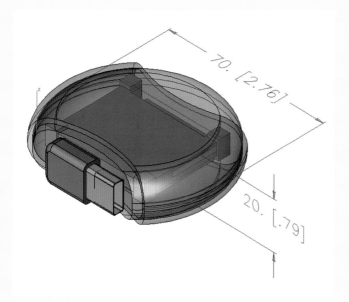

It took about a week for Au to take a design through
to a completed 3D model for a photo-realistic rendering,
including lighting and graphics (Figs. CS 4.1 and 4.2). This
included the time to refine the design in doodle and sketch
form, 2D layout to refine proportions and sizes, then actual
3D modeling. For things such as logos and graphics on
the products, Au created decal art in Illustrator and
Photoshop, and then applied them to the model.

Lighting took some time to fine tune. As in
photography, you need time to set up the environment to
create the kinds of reflections you'd like to affect the model
and best show off the contours, form and details. The
result is a photo-realistic image of something that you've
created, an image that serves to communicate the design
intent in a realistic way, including colour, materials and
graphics (Fig. CS 4.3).

The Mac version's IGES export has flavours for Pro/E,
Alias, SolidWorks and AutoCAD. Another export option is STL for rapid
prototyping. It can also use QuickTime to create flyby movies—useful
presentation tools, particularly if you will not be there to explain the design.

Cobalt can also be used in the early design process, as a 3D sketch tool
(Fig. CS 4.4). Rather than using traditional hand sketches or Photoshop
renderings, concepts can be built up as 3D CAD models. Real component sizes
can be input to assure they fit inside the design. The beauty is that a concept can
be developed in roughly a day (depending on the design) and output as a full
rendering. The output JPEG images can be blended together in Photoshop for a
presentation page per concept with titles, notes, or other information, to be
printed or emailed. Without a background surface in the rendering or complex
lighting set-up, each rendering will take less than two minutes on a 450MHz
Mac G4.

Cobalt is Au's choice, but he also works in Alias: "You can never know
enough CAD," says Au. "A good friend once said to me, it's the work that
counts, not the tools."

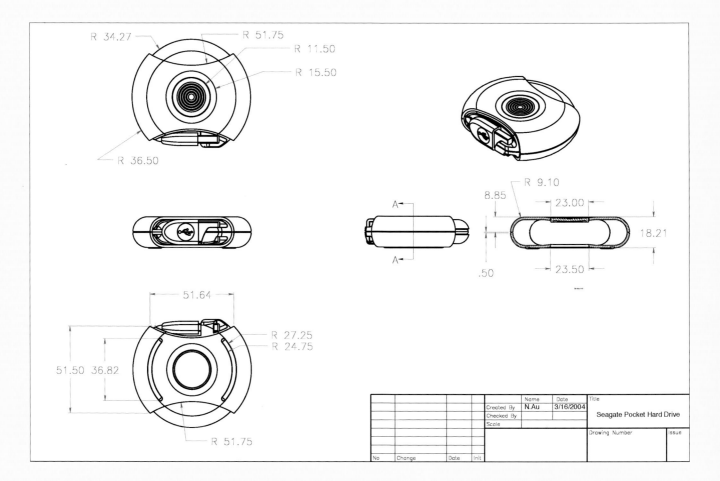

R 34.27 — R 51.75
R 11.50
R 15.50
R 36.50

A→
A→

8.85
R 9.10
23.00
18.21
.50
23.50

51.64
R 27.25
R 24.75
51.50 36.82
R 51.75

					Name	Date	Title	
				Created By	N.Au	3/16/2004		
				Checked By			Seagate Pocket Hard Drive	
				Scale				
							Drawing Number	Issue
No	Change	Date	Init					

Above CS 4.6 Orthographic drawings were not necessary for this project, but Nelson Au produced these especially to show how they can be generated from the 3D model.

Seagate Technology of Scotts Valley, California, wanted an iconic design for their new portable drive, to compete successfully in an already crowded market. William Watkins, chief executive of Seagate Technology, says: "Disk drives have been a $20 billion market for five years. All of a sudden you're going to see phenomenal growth. People want to be able to take their pictures, videos and music and move them around." Given a physical model of a previous design, a printed circuit board and several other components, Au used Cobalt to produce several concepts, taking advantage of the software's ability to create shapes quickly.

Au created an outer enclosure to house the retractable USB 2.0 cable, and an inner portion to house the 5Gbyte memory and other electronic components. Using Cobalt's transparency features, he was able to communicate to the client that the design and inner workings of the drive would fit and work together. The client approved the design, and the 3D model went directly to a rapid prototyping house to create an STL (stereolithography) model, validating the touch and feel of his tactile design (Fig. CS 4.5). No 2D CAD drawings were necessary for this project, but to demonstrate how easy they are to produce Au generated a set especially for this Case Study (Fig. CS 4.6).

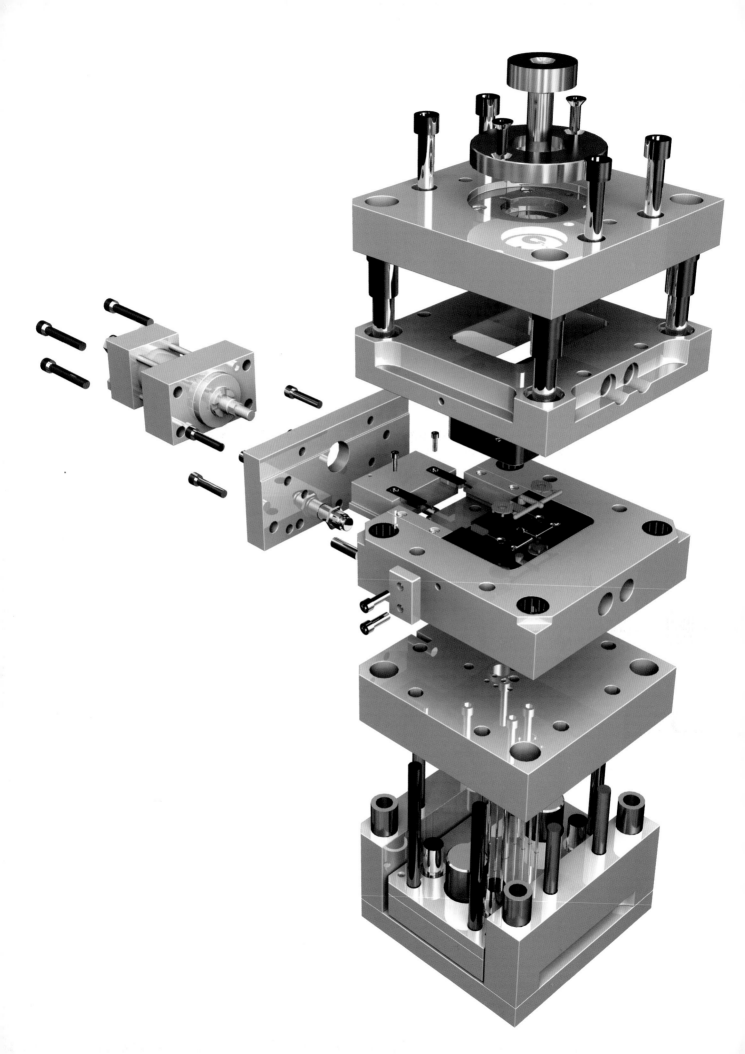

8 Technical illustration

Opposite JK Mold Design, Two-cavity mold for making valve caps, 2004. Exploded diagram modelled and rendered in SolidWorks. Courtesy SolidWorks Corporation.

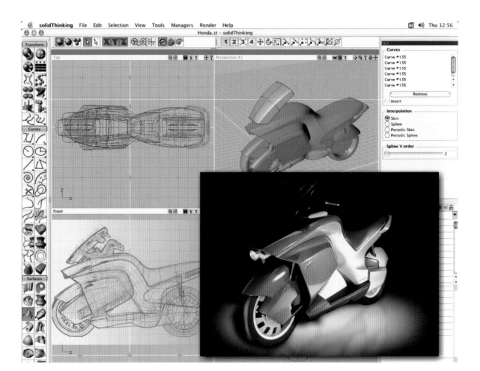

Right 8.1   Screenshot showing an orthographic projection of a Honda motorcycle and a 3D model, both in its raw form and fully rendered. Courtesy solidThinking Ltd.

Below 8.2   Andrew Ritchie, Brompton folding bicycle, 1977. Patent drawing.

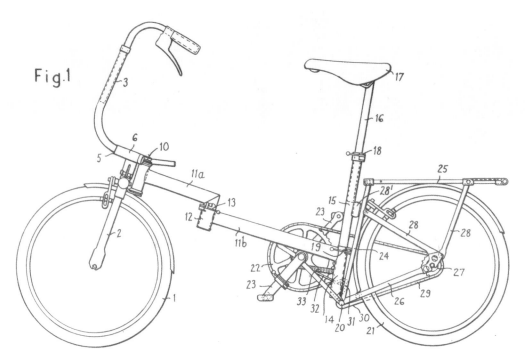

Technical illustration comes at the very end of the design process (or, technically, after it has ended) when the product either actually exists and is well into production or is at least fully specified in terms of appearance and geometry. It is a skill akin to still-life painting, in that the artist or illustrator (for it is not always cost-effective for the designer to be involved at this stage) has a tangible object—or at least a set of plans or 3D computer model—to look at and base the illustration on. A technical

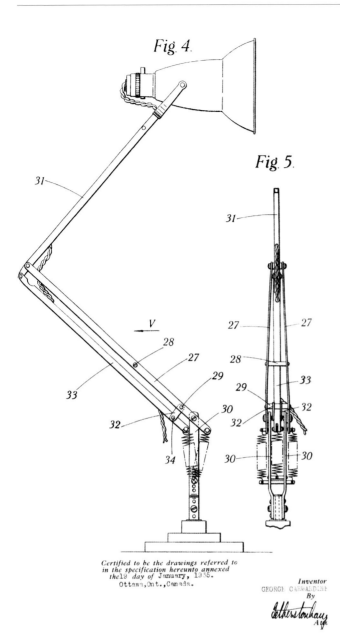

Fig. 4.

Fig. 5.

Certified to be the drawings referred to
in the specification hereunto annexed
the19 day of January, 1935.
Ottawa,Ont.,Canada.

Inventor
GEORGE CARWARDINE
By

Above 8.3 George Carwardine, Anglepoise lamp, 1935. Patent drawing. Accurate and functional drawings are essential documents in establishing patents. Courtesy Anglepoise Ltd, Waterlooville, Hampshire, England.

illustrator is an accessory after the fact. And the job of the technical illustration is to explain the mysteries of the designed object to those whose responsibility it will be to assemble, market, service and ultimately use the product.

In contrast to a 2D orthographic technical drawing, which is defined in ISO5456-2:1996 and divides the object into several independent views (*see* Chapter 7), a technical illustration combines all three sides of a workpiece in one pictorial representation, rather like a presentation drawing (Fig. 8.1). The demands of ISO9001:2000 with regard to technical documentation (called "product support")—product information plus all the services that manufacturers offer to their customers—can range from simple instruction manuals, maintenance manuals and spare parts catalogues, to the complete documentation of the product, which may also include bidding documents, advertising and training material. Technical illustrators are also responsible for the drawings that accompany patent applications (Figs. 8.2 and 8.3).

Assembly operators must be capable of maintaining and repairing even unknown machines and equipment, so the documentation must specify the order in which the machine components have to be assembled or dismantled and help to identify spare parts for repairs or repeat orders. A technical illustration will typically be a simplified 3D cutaway or exploded drawing (more later) in black line or shaded colour.

History

Technical illustration could be traced back to the earliest times, when perhaps a caveperson, wanting to explain the theory of the wheel to a sceptical colleague, scratched out a diagram in the sand. The drawings of Georgius Agricola from the *De re metallica* of 1556, showing the workings of such machines as the chain-and-dipper pump, are the precursors of today's cutaway and exploded diagrams that explain the inner mysteries of an assembly. Leonardo da Vinci, too, has left many examples of exploded diagrams, although whether these were of objects that really existed or mere fancies is open to conjecture.

Diderot's *Encyclopedia* in the eighteenth century created a requirement for "instructive" drawings, as did the many patent applications being made around the time of the Industrial Revolution. Technical illustrations can also trace their lineage from the "as-fitted" drawings of ships, usually undertaken by apprentices, and the "contract

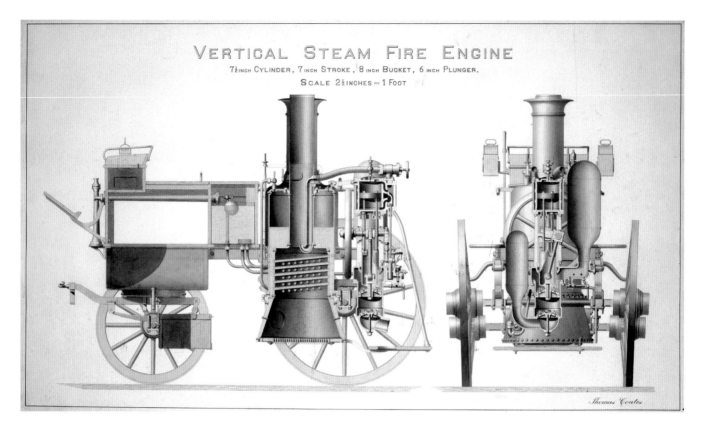

VERTICAL STEAM FIRE ENGINE
7½ INCH CYLINDER, 7 INCH STROKE, 8 INCH BUCKET, 6 INCH PLUNGER.
SCALE 2½ INCHES = 1 FOOT

Above 8.4   Thomas Coates, Shand Mason vertical steam fire engine, 1863. Ink with watercolour wash, 47 5/8 × 27 7/8 in (121 x 70.8 cm). This beautiful example of a technical illustration comprises a section halfway through the side elevation (with hidden details in dotted line) and the front elevation partially cut away to reveal the workings of the cylinder. Courtesy Science Museum, London.

drawings" of steam locomotives and other machines (Fig. 8.4), which were handed over to the client as part of the design contract, on completion of the work. It was the military, however, that revived the need for technical illustrations after the First World War, when manuals were produced to help keep all the equipment serviceable.

The skills of the technical illustrator have always been in demand in the aircraft and automobile industries, and the intricate cutaway diagrams that revealed the inner workings of the then "modern wonders" (Fig. 8.5) were once a popular feature of boys' comics such as *Eagle* and trade magazines, and remain popular in "how it works" books and websites aimed mainly at children.

"The job of a technical illustrator falls squarely between the artist and the engineering draughtsman", it states in the introduction to a "how to draw" book of the 1940s. "On one hand the artist generally draws an object as it appears to him personally, whilst on the other, the draughtsman proceeds with great pains to ensure an accurate reproduction complete with dimensions, to enable the craftsman to make the part with no possibility of error. The only way to do this is by orthographic projection, which is difficult for the layman to understand. The technical illustrator is the link. The technical illustrator's life-like portrayal, not only of the

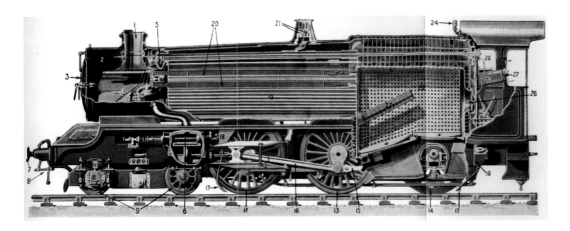

Above 8.5   Great Western Railway "King" class
4-6-0 locomotive, 1927. Cutaway drawings,
as in this fold-out, were once popular in children's
encyclopedias and comics such as *Lion* and *Eagle*.

component's exterior, but also of a comprehensive section
of the internal structure, make possible quick and easy
reading of a machine drawing."

The art of technical illustration

A good technical illustrator must be more than a good
artist. By his or her knowledge of how the product
functions, and a mastery of technique, the illustrator
will be able to simplify an engineering drawing, bringing
out the important details without sacrificing the overall
shape and form of the product (Fig. 8.6). The most
appropriate viewpoint must be chosen for clarity, making

Below 8.6   Henry Dreyfuss,
Polaroid Automatic 100 camera,
1962. Exploded assembly
perspective. Courtesy Cooper-
Hewitt National Design Museum,
Smithsonian Institution,
Washington, DC.

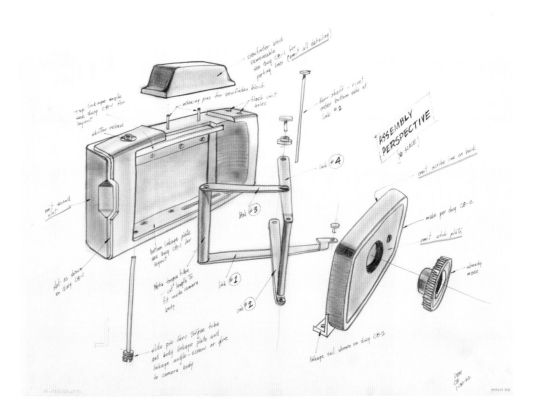

Right 8.7 Jan Frohm, Autorotor, 1960. The designer made this drawing in traditional airbrush, once the favoured medium for technical illustration.

Below 8.8 Torsten Neeland, Tank wall lamp, 2002. The designer used cross-hatching to denote a section. (*See also* figs. 7.19 and 7.21)

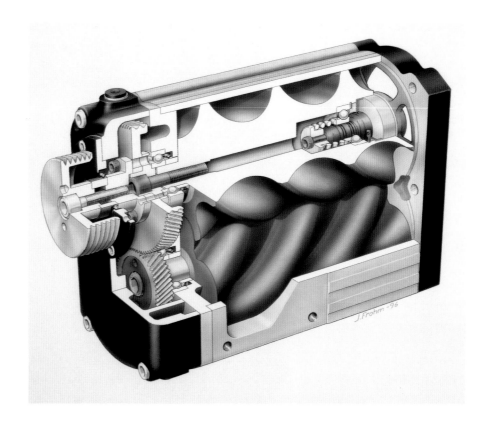

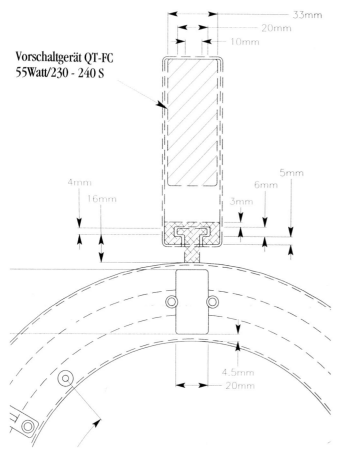

Vorschaltgerät QT-FC
55Watt/230 - 240 S

decisions as to what and how much "material" can be cut away whilst leaving the whole coherent and credible looking, and all the time aiming for an elegant and pleasing composition. The illustrator must have the insight and X-ray vision to generate drawings that would be impossible to produce by any other means (Fig. 8.7).

The constraints of printing technology have dictated the methods and media used by technical illustrators. Watercolour, gouache—even marker—have been used, but airbrush was always the favoured medium for colour work. For line work, intended for cheaply produced manuals often printed on poor quality paper, the illustrator turned to black ink on board or the unusual (elsewhere) medium of scraperboard (scratchboard), in which a sharp tool— a scalpel or proprietary cutter—is used to scratch away the smooth black surface of a specially coated board, revealing a layer of clay or chalk, resulting in white lines of great clarity and sparkle. Some illustrators preferred white board, which could be coated with black Indian ink where there were areas to be scraped out. Mistakes or areas for further detailed work could be scratched out or inked over, left to dry thoroughly and redrawn. Boards with a grained or stippled surface mechanically embossed into the material were also available.

Line drawings for technical illustration are, to aid execution and reading, almost as stylized in their way as comic-book illustrations. A single light source usually comes from the top left corner; shadows and shading are included only to enhance the three-dimensionality of the product being illustrated and are left out if they obstruct the view of some essential detail. The method of shading and cross-hatching must be consistent too (Fig. 8.8). As in engineering drawing, there are conventional ways of rendering such common objects as springs, screw threads and gear wheels.

Airbrush was used in technical illustration because of its capacity to make soft gradations of tone that subtly model 3D form and give a smoother finish than ordinary brushwork. Its precise "untouched by human hand" finish was ideal for the technological nature of the objects being depicted. Although the mechanical airbrush is all but obsolete, the technique lives on in computer programs such as Photoshop.

Airbrush—by hand or computer

Airbrushing, whether manual or computer, as a technique also has its conventions. Paradoxically, the aim of the airbrush illustration is not to attempt photographic realism (as does ray tracing a 3D computer model)

but to combine assumption and observation logically, to produce a seductive convincing image that is well defined and technically accurate, and which can also be easily assimilated by the buyer of the product.

Machines are shown in gleaming condition against pristine backgrounds, clean and unused (Fig. 8.9). Shiny and matte surfaces are kept separate and distinct, and the differences between them exaggerated. Reflections that might confuse a reading of the product's structure or which interrupt plain surfaces are avoided.

There is usually a constant balance of light and shade throughout the illustration, with edges defined by the sharp contrast between light and dark areas rather than by using delineation devices. In cutaways, light backlit edges are used to bring forms such as cylinders, shafts and bolts forward from the heavier tones behind.

A conventional airbrush illustration can take months to complete and it is not uncommon for one person to be responsible for the initial linework, while another is responsible for the colouring by airbrush. As well as being skilled in the techniques of airbrushing and competent at being able to read engineering drawings, the illustrator must develop a keen eye to judge tonal values and an efficient visual memory to retain a mental plan of the overall scheme as the work in progress is ever disguised

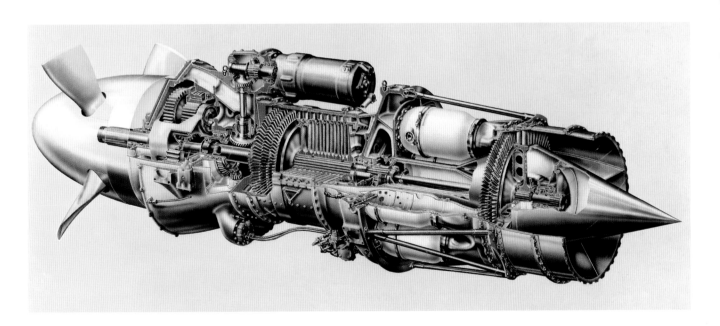

Above 8.9   Napier Eland aero engine, 1950s. Airbrush drawing on board, 43 1/3 x 24 in (110 x 61 cm). This is a classic cutaway as the designer has taken a quarter of the rotationally symmetrical shell away and coloured the cut metal in red. Note the ghosting and abbreviated propellers at the front end (left) and the jagged cut edge around the rear (right). Courtesy Institution of Mechanical Engineers, London.

by the many stencils and masks used in building up the picture.

Technical illustration is one of the older branches of illustration, but it is by no means a static technique. Present day illustrations tend to favour a "ghosted" look (Fig. 8.10), using subtle airbrushing (manually or by computer) to make the outer casing of the product look as if it were made of glass, resulting in a more coherent and solid drawing, rather than the more severe and hitherto conventional cutaway drawing that can have the effect of mutilating a form.

Technical illustration today is a lot freer than it once was, and is used in many more applications, mostly in marketing: in advertisements, sales brochures, posters and so on. Some technical illustrations are indistinguishable from presentation drawings—or even concept drawings— in their sketchiness, and there has been a vogue for reproducing "designer concepts" to spell out to a more design conscious public that this or that go-ahead company is actually employing design consultants (as they always did anyway!) on their "designer" products.

Techniques of technical illustration

Although at first glance looking similar, a technical illustration has a different role to a presentation drawing. The idea is to simplify the drawing, but at the same time focus attention on its salient features. In technical illustration, less is more—omitting some lines and emphasizing others can help to display the desired information more clearly.

An illustration is defined as an example that clarifies a concept. An illustrator aims to remove clutter and highlight those elements of the object which would be difficult to see in real life: cut away or with its component parts separated but still in the correct relation to one another. The illustrator aspires to produce a canonical view which is both revealing and memorable, that is, reduced to its simplest and most significant form possible without losing generality. Technical illustration is a balance of informative graphics and text, plus embedded data or intelligence, resulting in pictorial views that visually communicate and clarify critical product information to the end user or maintenance worker.

Thick and thin lines

The use of thick and thin lines is an important stylistic convention for depicting three-dimensional geometrical shapes by relatively simple line drawings (Fig. 8.11). It dispenses with extraneous detail and graphical information but, at the same time, allows the viewer to quickly grasp the form of the object shown in the illustration.

Thick lines are applied around the edges of an object and internally wherever surfaces border on other invisible surfaces. This can be a gap between separate but linked components or an aperture in a plane surface. Imagine being able to reach behind a line with your hand: if your fingertips could be obscured behind the part, then use a thick line. If you can see both adjoining surfaces, the border line is represented by a thin line. This kind of boundary, where both sides of the edge are visible, is also called a "crease".

Thin lines are used for changes of plane on a surface, such as angled edges, areas of concavity or the junction between interlocking components (Fig. 8.12). If the drawing is shaded or greyscale, the line of the crease can be depicted as a white "highlight" line, which adds to the three-dimensional effect. Thin lines are also employed for textural elements, such as grilles and other decorative details.

Lines drawn in black and white on a grey or coloured body suggest a light source and help fix the model's orientation. Shadows are only included when they do not occlude detail in other parts of the object. In 3D illustrations, adding a simple drop shadow on a ground plane, rather than the actual shadows cast by an object, may provide helpful visual clues without obscuring important details. It is not really necessary for these shadows to be highly accurate to provide information about the three-dimensional structure, especially in the spatial layout of a scene.

Above 8.12   co-lab* (Vibeke S. Vendena and Greg Vendena), *Your Guide to Making Tire Planters*. The designer uses thick and thin lines, though strictly speaking the incomplete circle on the wheel hub should be a thick line as it defines an edge behind which you could hide your hand. It is a digital print of an original drawing on Mylar, coloured in Illustrator and Photoshop.

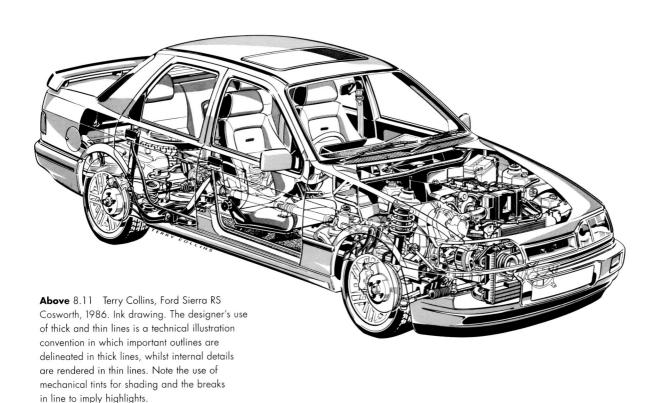

Above 8.11   Terry Collins, Ford Sierra RS Cosworth, 1986. Ink drawing. The designer's use of thick and thin lines is a technical illustration convention in which important outlines are delineated in thick lines, whilst internal details are rendered in thin lines. Note the use of mechanical tints for shading and the breaks in line to imply highlights.

For inking on board (paper or vellum), thin lines are usually made using a 0.25mm or 0.3mm technical pen; with 0.5mm or 0.7mm for the heavier line weight. On the computer this is equivalent to between 0.35pt (points) and 0.5pt for thin lines, and between 1pt and 2pt for thick. There may be a "house style" dictating the actual line weights used. The sizes used also depend on the scale of the drawing and how much reduction (if any) is to be applied when it is sent to print. A reasonable middle ground is 0.5pt for thin lines, and 1pt for thick lines, with annotation lines at 0.7pt.

An alternative method to thick and thin lines on perspective drawings is to taper the line thickness—make it heavier in the foreground and lighter in receding lines. This is called "perspective line" depth cueing. Sometimes lines in touch with the base plane are made thicker to "ground" the object and simulate a subtle shadow.

Below 8.13   This 2005 computer rendering of a 1.4l TSI-engine from Volkswagen is an exploded assembly with part of the central section cut away, using the convention of colouring cut metal red. Courtesy Volkswagen AG.

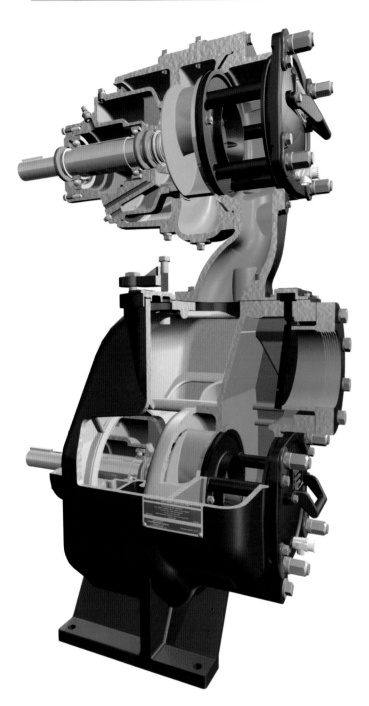

Above 8.14   Ken Radke, UltraMate pump,
2005. The designer used Solid Edge to design
this two-stage version for the company Gorman-
Rupp. The cut edges of the cutaway section are
shown as textured metal. Courtesy UGS.

Sections, cutaways and ghosting

A section is a simple cross-section, usually an orthogonal
view (plan or elevation), in which the cut edge forms the
outline of the object. It can be diagrammatic or may be
rendered to give internal components some degree of
three-dimensionality. A cutaway drawing is a true three-
dimensional view, in which a product is depicted as if a
chunk of the outer casing has been removed to reveal the
interior components and mechanisms (Fig. 8.13). It is
particularly suitable for subjects that are basically
cylindrical or have a central axis, such as pumps, valves
and filters, and the usual practice is to cut away a quarter
segment to expose the inner details while still maintaining
the external shape. The technique can be applied to any
subject, however, and the cutaway portion can be any shape
or size, providing it is clearly presented and the exterior
form is still recognizable.

If the object is of regular construction and the interior
structure continues along the full length of the object, then
a single cutaway section may suffice. Or one cutaway may
open up a deeper view, cutting through several interior
layers, revealing a more complex assembly of components.
It may be necessary to create many cutaway areas, or for
extra sections of details to be placed outside the main
illustration (Fig. 8.14).

The choice of viewpoint is crucial: the angle should
best illustrate the character of the internal workings yet
preserve a recognizable external view. It is best to imagine
the end user or person responsible for servicing the product
looking at the drawing. Give them a familiar view of the
product. The edge of the cutaway must be distinguished
from "real" edges, either represented smoothly, as if cut
by a knife or laser, or as a wavy or jagged line as if the piece
has been broken off. The thickness of the cut edge can be
represented in line work, for example, as finely stippled
or cross-hatched, with the surrounding planes left white.
In colour work, the convention is to make the cut edge a flat
flame red, to contrast with the shaded and modelled forms
in the rest of the illustration.

A ghosted (or phantom view) illustration was
developed by airbrush artists to reveal the internal
components of a product by rendering the exterior skin
of the object transparent. Both cutaways and ghosting can
be combined to create an illustration which eliminates the
cut edge, while in places leaving the interior clearly open
with no trace of surface covering. Ghosting is particularly
useful for products with complex styling, where it is
essential to retain the integrity of the external form.

Step by step 5:
A cutaway drawing
of a hammer drill
by Ryan Whitaker
supervised by
John Fox

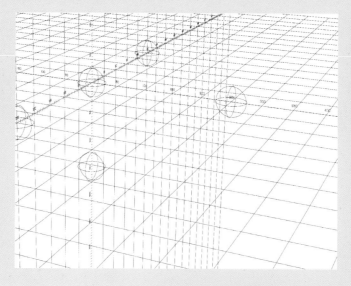

SS 5.1 Blackpool and The Fylde College, England, has a long tradition of technical illustration excellence. This cutaway of a hammer drill was produced by second-year technical illustration degree student Ryan Whitaker, under the supervision of John Fox. First, using a program designed and developed by Mark Swift at the college, they produced an accurate three-point perspective grid to meet the requirements of the artist's viewpoint.

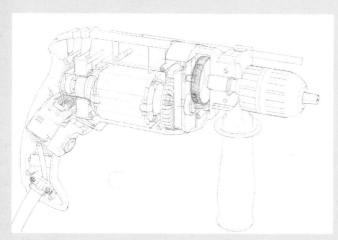

SS 5.2 They laid out this perspective on the drawing board and constructed a detailed pencil illustration from orthographic plans.

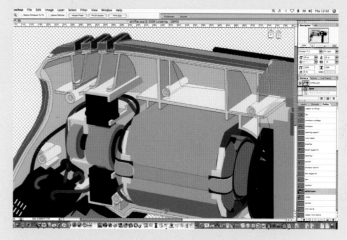

SS 5.3 They scanned the finished pencil stage into the computer. Using Adobe Photoshop, they carefully minimized the pencil lines and redrew the material as Photoshop paths, as shown in this screenshot.

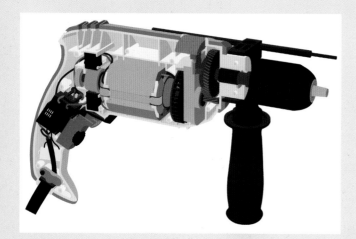

SS 5.4 They carefully minimized the paths as masks and guides for them to fill and develop three defined tones.

SS 5.5 Using a Wacom Intuos pad and their own skills, they added the final detailing.

As a technique, however, it can have the disadvantage of demonstrating the complexity of a machine or vehicle without instructing the viewer on the actual functions of the mechanisms depicted. The drawing has to suit the end use: a practical drawing for a maintenance manual will be different from one destined for a sales brochure designed to impress a lay audience.

Like cutaways, ghosting may be applied to small areas of an image or may extend along an entire form. Some of the most elaborate ghosted views are seen in the automotive industry to reveal what lies beneath the bodywork. Originally the internal detail would be rendered first, then the airbrush artist would place a fine spray of colour on top to represent the transparent and semi-transparent outer surface planes. Lines of black or white are used sparingly to identify exterior edges. Computer rendering makes the whole process much easier and controllable (Fig. 8.15).

Below 8.15   The 2007 Lincoln MKZ engine is a lightweight die-cast aluminium block with a 4-valve direct-acting-bucket valve. This drawing is a hybrid of a simple "blueprint" line drawing with the cutaway and ghosted parts of the image highly rendered.

Ghosting can also be used to show the workings of a moving part, with its resting position rendered solidly and alternate positions ghosted in different degrees of solidity. In line work, a ghosted edge is represented by a dotted line. Another convention is to place the company logo or product name with a faint halo of colour to establish an otherwise invisible foreground plane.

Components and exploded diagrams

An exploded view shows an assembly with its component parts expanding out from the main body, as if blown up, but still remaining in the correct relative order along their respective centrelines (Fig. 8.16). It is basically an explanatory catalogue of parts represented graphically

Above 8.16 Mario and Claudio Bellini, Palmhouse kettle, 2001. The designers used Rhinoceros to create this exploded rendering for Cherry Terrace.

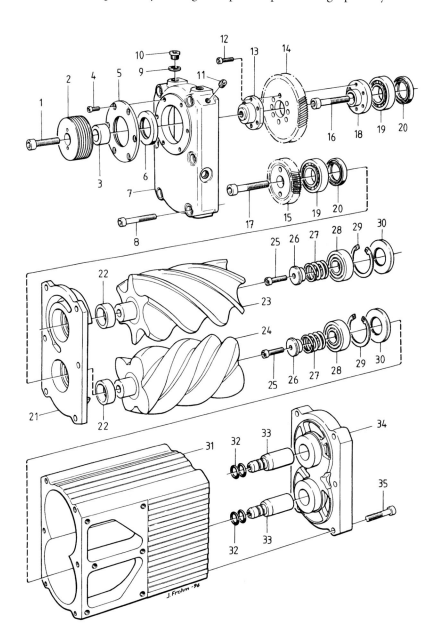

Right 8.17 Jan Frohm, Autorotor, 1996. Exploded drawing in thick and thin ink lines. This rendering would be too long to fit on the paper if the designer hadn't adopted the convention of bending the centreline back on itself to create three parallel assemblies.

and logically, and should be familiar to anyone who has attempted to assemble flat-pack furniture.

This technique can be used for a parts list where items need to be isolated from each other while still maintaining their sub-assembly groups. It is also ideal for showing the order of removal and assembly of components. Internal items such as O-rings and bolts, normally hidden, can be shown "threaded" along a central axis, or if the drawing becomes too long and narrow, this can be overcome by cranking the centreline into an S or Z formation, or by slightly overlapping each item (Fig. 8.17). Care should also be taken, however, not to make the drawing so fragmented that it is difficult to see how the various sub-assemblies fit together (Figs. 8.18 and 8.19).

Parts assembly is a sequential process, but engineering drawings do not present information in a step-by-step format (Fig. 8.20). Exploded view paraline (axonometric or isometric) or perspective illustrations, replete with BOM (bill of materials) data, sequential assembly operation notes and callouts convey manufacturing assembly instructions that visually guide the worker through the assembly process. A callout is an element (generally a circle with number inside) within an illustration that corresponds to some textual information elsewhere or another more detailed drawing placed in a circle or box away from the main illustration.

Below 8.18 Shaun Hauptli, Rollway RS20 pillow block assembly, 2005. The designer used Virtual Studio and Solid Edge to model this exploded image for Emerson Power Transmission. Courtesy UGS.

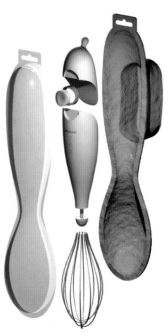

Below 8.19 Youmeus, Kenwood whisk, 2004. This exploded diagram was modelled using Autodesk Alias Studio (formerly Alias Studio Tools).

Step by step 6:
An exploded detail drawing of an electrical plug by James Wright

SS 6.1   James traces over a digital photo of the two main components, one suspended above the other in the desired positions. This provides an accurate starting point for his drawing. He draws in some more perspective lines, using a pencil so any mistakes can be erased.

SS 6.2   Using the two main components as reference points, he draws in the other components using the disassembled object, paying attention to their position, scale and perspective; drawing perspective lines helps. He is as accurate as possible at this stage, so as to avoid adjustments later on. He corrects as he goes along.

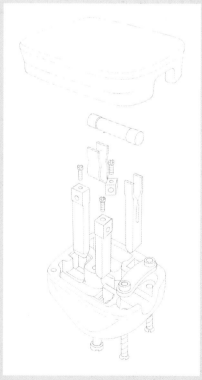

SS 6.3   James uses ellipse guides where necessary. Once he has corrected the image so that it consists of thin single lines only, he partially rubs out the lines so that they are faint and reveal less lead on the paper. This will improve the subsequent application of ballpoint pen lines over the pencil lines. With the ballpoint pen, he redraws over the whole image and erases any pencil marks. Alternatively, he could trace over the drawing using another sheet of layout paper.

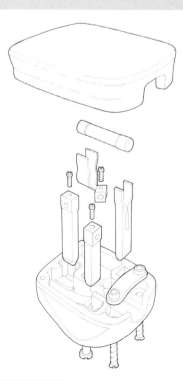

SS 6.4   Using a technical drawing pen that is thicker than the ballpoint pen, he draws around all the individual components. This helps emphasize the parts and makes the exploded diagram easier to understand. This technique is called "thick and thin lines".

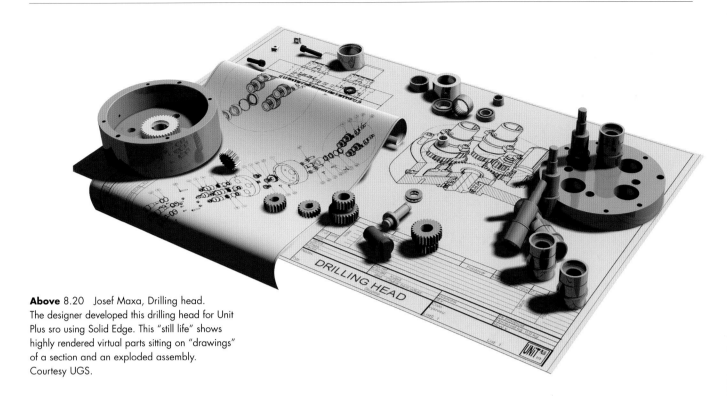

Above 8.20   Josef Maxa, Drilling head.
The designer developed this drilling head for Unit
Plus sro using Solid Edge. This "still life" shows
highly rendered virtual parts sitting on "drawings"
of a section and an exploded assembly.
Courtesy UGS.

Exploded views have to be the most accurate and unvariable form of technical illustration—the sequence of assembly cannot be altered for aesthetic reasons, so there is little artistic license available. Layout is dictated by the product's construction and component parts.

The central axis can be implied or depicted as a dot-dash line passing through the component parts, leading the viewer's eye through the assembly sequence. Large components or sub-assemblies can also be shown cutaway or ghosted. For objects with no obvious vertical or horizontal axis, there will be a point from which the exploded components radiate. A cubic object, such as a washing machine, can be exploded by pulling out each panel on a direct line from a common centre, with bolts and screws on minor axes passing through the centre of the holes into which they fit.

Exploded views are used in other key product support documents such as installation and operation guides, service orders, maintenance manuals and parts catalogues—all of which rely on the exact representation of parts and associated critical-fit conditions.

Photo-tracing

If the product actually exists, one of the most effective methods of creating a technical illustration is the photo-tracing technique. To create a line drawing from a photo,

you first need a photograph of the object taken from the required angle to use as a template. If drawing by hand, the outlines and main elements are traced in pencil or fibretip pen onto detail paper and then scaled up using a grid. Most computer graphics programs offer a background layer on which you can place your photo (or pencil sketch), which can be locked to prevent accidentally selecting, moving or deleting the photo. You can then begin to trace the photo on a second layer using the pen tool and Bézier curves.

Draw only as few details as necessary and be ever aware of the correct position of the elements. A badly drawn ellipse, for example, can destroy the overall impression of the illustration. An ellipse has a so-called "thrust-axis", running along the imaginary drilling direction or axle of a vehicle. The minor axis of the ellipse always lies on the thrust-axis, at right angles to the major axis. Cylindrical elements consist of at least two ellipses and two lines. It is important to ensure consistent perspective within such elements, and also to make sure that the element is placed in the correct perspective relative to its surroundings. As all elements in a photo will follow the rules of perspective, an individual component cannot simply be copied and moved to a different location—it won't look right—nor will you be able to apply standard library components or already drawn paraline elements. Such an illustration will be judged as not working, even though we may not be able to explain exactly why.

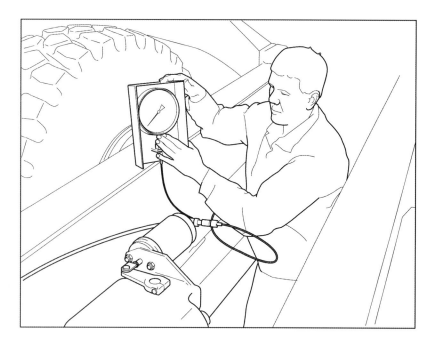

Left 8.21   Rob Woods, Photo-traced drawing, 2006. The designer used the commercial technical illustration software IsoDraw to photo-trace this illustration for Granthams from a photograph. Courtesy ITEDO & Granthams.

Photo-tracing produces realistic images quickly, but does require some skill (Fig. 8.21). Before you start tracing, take a moment to look at the photo closely, particularly the areas which will subsequently be the focal point of the information. Analyse and edit the forms that make up the product and assemblies. Note what kinds of materials have been used. A car's dashboard, for example, will be rounded with a soft covering. Make sure you understand how the parts you are depicting function; distorted or imprecise images may look as though they wouldn't work properly.

You can suggest radii merging into each other by means of small hooks at the ends of the curves. The drawing may need some improving away from the photograph—if you only use straight lines, your illustration will resemble an arrangement of disjoined lines rather than a depiction of an object.

You may often find that you have drawn everything correctly and got the perspective right, but your illustration still looks static and angular. It needs to be softened using lines with small gaps in them (known as inner edges). Be subtle: you do not need a line for every single edge.

Annotation and labelling

In technical illustrations, captions and/or callouts are often needed to identify specific parts or impart other information. There may be a house style for font and size, and so on, but to avoid your text being misrepresented or going awry, for example when the drawing is opened on another computer and the font you used is not installed, place the text so it cannot run into the illustration if the length increases, or transform the text into paths (lines) so it cannot be altered. If you do this, however, remember the text can no longer be edited, so keep an editable copy of it on a separate layer.

Reference lines are often used to assign text or position numbers to specific parts of an illustration. Since these lines will cross other lines in the illustration, it is important that they can be distinguished from the further lines that describe the object. The reference line should not disturb the displayed element. This can be accomplished by shadowing or haloing the lines, by creating a wide white line that lies beneath the reference lines, for example.

Computer-aided illustration

Using computers usually means that nothing has to be done twice. In theory, it should be possible to re-use or re-purpose drawings created earlier in the design process for the technical publications needed downstream of the design process. In practice, however, engineering drawings will contain too much information and are generally too complex and busy to reproduce well; concept/presentation drawings will inevitably be obsolete or too inexact. It will fall to the technical illustrator to create new drawings based on the latest update of the production drawings, or on the finished product itself.

These will be drawn from scratch specifically for the purpose, commissioned to illustrate an operating manual, for example.

Several computer programs are available for technical illustrations that are completely unrelated to programs for computer-aided design, although they do share some CAD features. The end product of a CAD system is the product; the end product of a computer-aided technical illustration program is a print-ready drawing, in a format that can subsequently be incorporated into a printed publication.

As explained in Chapter 6, there are two fundamentally different ways of producing illustrations, referred to as "draw" and "paint". A paint document is stored in the computer's memory as a bitmap, a one-to-one array corresponding to the pixels on the screen, and the best-known paint program is Adobe Photoshop.

A "draw" or vector program, such as Adobe Illustrator, is more akin to a CAD program, storing data in the computer's memory as a "display list" of the point and line coordinates plus formulae for the circles and curves that make up the drawing. This is also known as object-oriented graphics, because every "object"—a circle, line or curve—can be accounted for separately.

In practice, an illustrator will use a combination of programs to achieve the finished drawing, perhaps starting in a vector program, exporting the illustration to Photoshop using the EPS or PDF file formats or the "export paths" command, and finally touching up, airbrushing and softening the image in a paint program. As paint programs produce files that are resolution-dependent, Photoshop will ask you for information such as size, resolution and so on, during the rasterization of the vector image.

Interactive technical illustration

Traditional technical illustrations, whether drawn by hand or using computer tools, currently still do a better job of describing the shape, structure and material composition of objects than computer renderings created automatically from 3D solid models.

As we have seen earlier, a technical illustration is an abstraction that preserves and emphasizes some qualities of the product while sacrificing or suppressing characteristics that are not the immediate focus of attention. Most of this editing is done in the illustrator's head while drawing and requires a great deal of skill and

experience. But attempts are being made by computer scientists to match this process automatically.

In the book *Drawing on the Right Side of the Brain*, Betty Edwards lists five perceptual skills that an artist needs to produce drawings: the perception of edges, the perception of spaces, the perception of relationships, the perception of light and shadow and the perception of the whole or gestalt. An interactive technical illustration program would have to be able to handle line-weight depth cueing, shading and shadowing, light and highlight placement, and include a simplified method of representing materials such as metal.

Computer graphics rendering is usually concerned with photo-realism, that is, trying to emulate an image that looks like a high-quality photograph. This goal is useful and appropriate in many applications, but not in technical illustration, where elucidation of structure and technical information is the pre-eminent motivation. This calls for a different kind of abstraction in which technical communication is central, but art and appearance are still essential instruments toward this end.

The goal of an interactive technical illustration system would be to produce a clearer picture of shape, structure and material composition than that of traditional computer graphics methods, using algorithms for real-time drawing of silhouette curves using non-photo-realistic rendering (NPR) and lighting methods.

Commercial solutions

In some cases, however, it may be possible to produce simple technical illustrations directly from the 2D CAD drawings or a 3D computer solid model, and there is commercial software that aims to do that. IsoDraw (Fig. 8.22) from German company ITEDO (Ingenieurbüro für Technische Dokumentation und Illustration) is a program designed specifically to produce technical illustrations from CAD data and goes part way to achieving the above goals. The designer exports the 3D model from a CAD program such as Catia or Pro/Engineer in a format such as IGES or one of the AutoCAD formats. IGES (Initial Graphics Exchange Standard) is a format independent of any vendor or software that allows designers to transfer their design data from a CAD system (for example, Catia) to another CAD system (for example, Pro/Engineer) or to a graphics program (for example, IsoDraw).

Practically all CAD systems can create files with assembly information. The designer can thus export

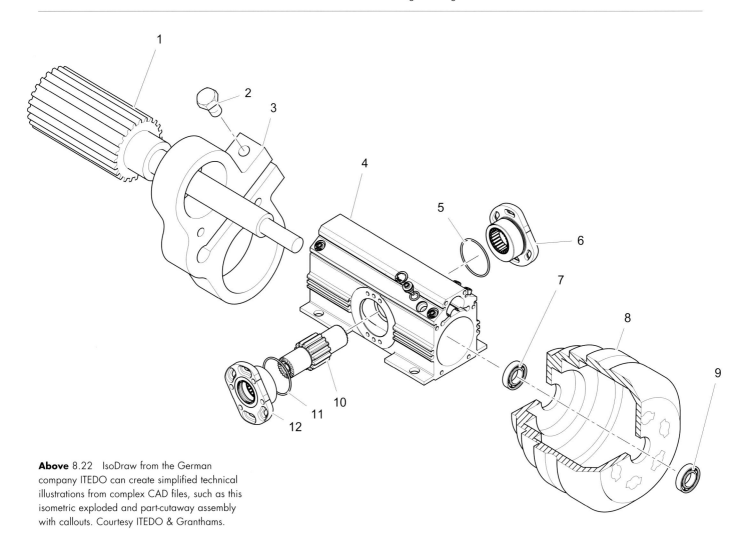

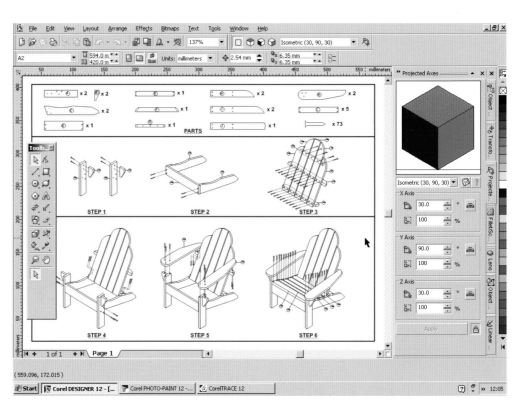

Above 8.22 IsoDraw from the German company ITEDO can create simplified technical illustrations from complex CAD files, such as this isometric exploded and part-cutaway assembly with callouts. Courtesy ITEDO & Granthams.

Right 8.23 Corel Designer is another commercial program aimed at aiding technical illustrators. This screenshot of a chair assembly is shown in isometric projection.

a complete assembly in one file, which is imported to IsoDraw using a program from the same company called CADprocess. The illustrator decides which assemblies/components to include. The 3D file can thus be broken down into individual spare-parts illustrations, a job which in the past had to be done by the designer. CADprocess deletes the hidden lines, sets the line thicknesses as required, and optimizes the elements. Individual line segments are connected and smoothed to Bézier curves or ellipses. Assemblies can be imported selectively and placed in different illustrations. All illustrations created with IsoDraw are shown automatically in thick and thin lines and there are tools available for manipulating the 3D data: explosion along any axes, cutaways, rotations and reflections.

The link to the CAD file stays intact, however, and any changes are updated automatically. This means that the illustrator can make a start on the documentation earlier in the design process and when the design is changed (as it will be), the illustrations are updated automatically. Corel Designer is another program aimed at technical illustration (Fig. 8.23).

Conclusion

While technical illustration is, strictly speaking, beyond the limits of the design-to-production cycle and is rarely undertaken by the designer of the product, it does fall within the product lifecycle and is most likely to be the image the consumer relates to the product. Airbrush used to be the dominant medium of the technical illustrator and a virtuoso illustration would take many hours to complete. Today the computer provides the "airbrush", but with the necessary intervention of the human illustrator. In the near future, however, the computer is likely to play a more active role in converting the data captured within a 3D solid model into a meaningful technical illustration. The designer will also be expected to embrace the World Wide Web and DVD/CD-Rom technology as a way of disseminating drawings to the end user.

Hot tip: Drawing hoses and tubes

In black line technical illustration, it is difficult to convey the three-dimensionality of hoses and tubes. These elements are technically made up of two parallel lines but, when looking at a tightly bent tube—the siphon of a wash basin for example—you will see that it is impossible to draw the contour of the inner line of the tube over the whole length. Instead, the contour line is running into the return surface of the tube. With a few carefully chosen line extensions and "hooks", the position of the tube in 3D space—is it coming forward or is it moving away?—can be made much more convincing (Fig. 8.24).

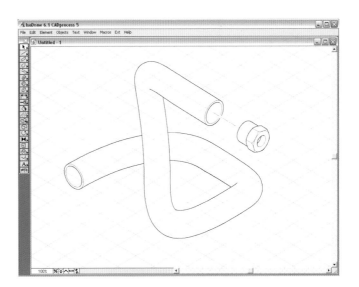

Above 8.24 Drawings of hoses or pipes in 3D space shown in isometric or perspective can be made more convincing by adding "hooks" or continuing the lines that indicate whether the images are coming forward or moving away. Courtesy ITEDO and Granthams.

"Drawings are witness to the creative process ... and more
immediately than published works give an insight into the
spiritual life of an artist. They are thus weighty documents
for the study and understanding of his activity."
Woldemar von Seidlitz in a treatise on Leonardo da Vinci, 1909

9 The future of the design drawing

Opposite Ron Arad, Blo Void rocking chair, 2003. The designer used a Cintiq graphics tablet and Corel Painter software to produce this expressive computer drawing.

Right 9.1   Karim Rashid, Exercise panel, 2006. This image took the designer's drawing into the realms of art for a 2006 show called "Kairotic" at the Townhouse Gallery in Cairo. The ease with which computers can step and repeat shapes and textures means that designers can quickly create visually rich non-photographic images. The designer used SolidWorks for 3D objects, Illustrator for the vector work, and Photoshop to combine them for presentation.

Product designers not only imagine the future, they create the future (Fig. 9.1). The objects being drawn at this moment by designers around the globe may not see the light of day for some years to come, by which time we will be amazed as these hitherto unknown objects of desire are revealed. Designers are striving to create a better world, improving and optimizing everyday products as well as devising new uses for cutting-edge emerging technologies—and it all begins with a simple sketch on paper. To summarize the role of drawing in the design process, look back at any of the case studies. The same sequence of concept sketches, followed by more finished presentation drawings and then detailed engineering drawings or a 3D computer model, will be seen in each case. Any differences in the design process highlighted in these case studies only serve to show that all design studios have broadly similar but practically different ways of working.

There have been many changes since I wrote *Drawing for 3-Dimensional Design* in 1990. First, personal computers—along with inexpensive scanners and printers—have become commonplace, both in the office and the home, and ever more powerful each year. Programs such as Photoshop, which would have brought a PC to its knees back then, are now routinely used in the home to retouch digital photographs and for making art. There is now a computer on every designer's desk. Once a virtual product has been described in the form of a

3D solid model, it can also be animated to show how it might look from all angles and how it might be assembled and used in the real world. The internet as a means of communication has made huge changes to society, not only enabling workgroups to be scattered all over the globe, but allowing drawings and animated videos to be disseminated to the end users simply and cheaply.

Furthermore, so many drawing products have disappeared: the mechanical airbrush is now a museum piece and even markers, once the mainstay of a designer's toolkit, are hard to find. On a trip to the graphic art supplies store you will more likely find inkjet cartridges and printer paper on the shelves that once stocked technical pens, Indian ink and ellipse templates. Most art supplies these days seem to be aimed at hobbyists and craftspeople, rather than design professionals. Fortunately, pencils are still in demand, and fibretip pens are becoming increasingly sophisticated and reliable.

Despite the changeover from manual tools to CAD, there is a growing interest in people wanting to see and buy designers' handmade drawings (Figs. 9.2 and 9.3). A collector such as New York-based Barbara Pine has

Above 9.2   Aldo Rossi, Press filter coffee maker with Doric column, 1985. Rossi led the way in making the designer's drawing more visible, as with this drawing of the Cupola coffee pot for Alessi. It was reproduced in a sumptuous book of drawings designed to appeal to the targeted consumers of the product.

Right 9.3   Aldo Rossi, Cupola coffee pot, 1985. Product shot for Alessi.

shown her drawings (mainly by architects/designers) in exhibitions around the world, most recently (in 2005) at Sir John Soane's Museum in London. Maybe this demand will encourage designers to keep and display their drawings, as Perry King and Santiago Miranda have done at the Milan Triennial.

"Doodles, Drafts and Designs" is a travelling exhibition, running at the time of writing, organized by the Smithsonian Institution in Washington, DC, with more than seventy original pencil sketches, ink drawings on linen, notebooks, patent drawings, trade literature covers and other documents illustrating consumer products such as Singer sewing machines, a Maidenform bra, Tupperware airtight food storage and Crayola crayons.

The internet is buzzing with designers, both professionals and students, sharing tips and tutorials on how to draw using all the latest software. Computers can't think, or design, for themselves—at least not yet—so there is still the need for the artistic expertise of a human who is well versed in manual methods as well as knowledgeable about graphics software, to make use of them for best effect. The role of the drawing in design is assured for some considerable time to come.

Drawing as communication

The drawing, as a means of externalizing ideas and communicating them to others, has been used by artists and designers since the beginnings of civilization. The Industrial Revolution, with its need to separate the designer from the maker, endowed the drawing with a new importance: that of a symbolic representation of the designed object that can be worked on, tested and approved before the final form is committed in an expensive model or prototype.

Until the 1930s, design theorists and the teachers of drawing were concerned with drawing as a formal and codified language. The European tradition of Modernism, refined at the Bauhaus, placed emphasis on harmony through geometry with its building blocks of circle, square and triangle. It was not so much "form follows function" as "form follows drawing style". (The expression "form [ever] follows function", for the record, could have been a quote from anyone at the Bauhaus, but it was in fact made by the American architect Louis H. Sullivan.)

From the end of the 1940s, product design has been carried out in group practices and consultancies, usually outside the organizational structure of the client company.

And despite the media's demand for "design stars", it is often difficult to attribute authorship of a particular design to a particular individual. Present-day design is a complex activity requiring teamwork and a range of skills. The Apple iMac, for example, is a virtuoso piece of 3D geometry in which the power supply, DVD drives and electronic circuitry inside are clearly integrated with the functional and aesthetically pleasing (and hence marketable) exterior. This was not a case of a stylist being brought in at a later stage to add the "cosmetics" to already "designed" machinery.

Out with the box

Ergonomics and psychological considerations are being added to the functional specifications of a product, and designers are studying the "semantics" of design, using simile, metaphor and hyperbole to help explain the function and operation of products spawned by the information technology age to "naive" users. These products, typified by the US-led "Cranbrook School" designers, have a cubist/organic look that has much in common with the "bio-form" designs of Luigi Colani. They are all breaking free from the Euclidean straightjacket of rectilinear boxes with rounded edges imposed by outdated drawing methods and manufacturing techniques (Fig. 9.4).

Drawing has always been about attempting to express the three-dimensionality of the real world on the flat two dimensions of paper. Inevitably, something will be lost, and the almost insurmountable difficulties inherent in describing complex "sculptural" shapes on a two-dimensional plane must, in the days before computers, have deterred many designers from even attempting to draw them. If a drawing for manufacture has to be complete and unambiguous, then it may as well be rectilinear, and the design theory can be retrospectively rationalized by using the geometric tenets of the Modern movement.

CAD is about more than just the slick visuals of ray tracing (Fig. 9.5) and the productivity increases of 2D drafting, as it enables the designer to explore new shapes and forms. With 3D solid modeling, a designer can "draw" in three dimensions, working on a virtual model that can be viewed from any angle. A designer can also be confident that, during experiments with form, any essential functional specifications, such as weight, strength, wall thicknesses, clearances and tolerances with pre-sourced components are ever adhered to. Ergonomic considerations can also be factored into the design (Fig. 9.6).

As computer hardware prices continue to fall, the CAD system has become just another tool available to the designer. CAD systems were first brought into the design office to handle the huge amount of 2D drafting required at the pre-production stages of the design process. Once they were installed, however, designers began to realize their potential for helping in the earlier stages of concept design and for producing presentation drawings. All designers now sit before a computer of some sort. Graduates of design schools, increasingly educated in the techniques of CAD, have come to expect these resources to be available to them in the workplace.

As flat LCD screens have replaced bulky CRT monitors, these too will eventually be replaced by video walls or even holographic displays. There have been many novel attempts to produce true 3D displays in the past. Head-mounted displays are commonplace in aviation, why not in design

Right 9.4   Mathias Bengtsson, *Slice* chair, 1999. A computer representation, such as this one modelled in Rhinoceros and rendered in Autodesk Alias Studio (formerly Alias Studio Tools), can open the designer's mind to new forms.

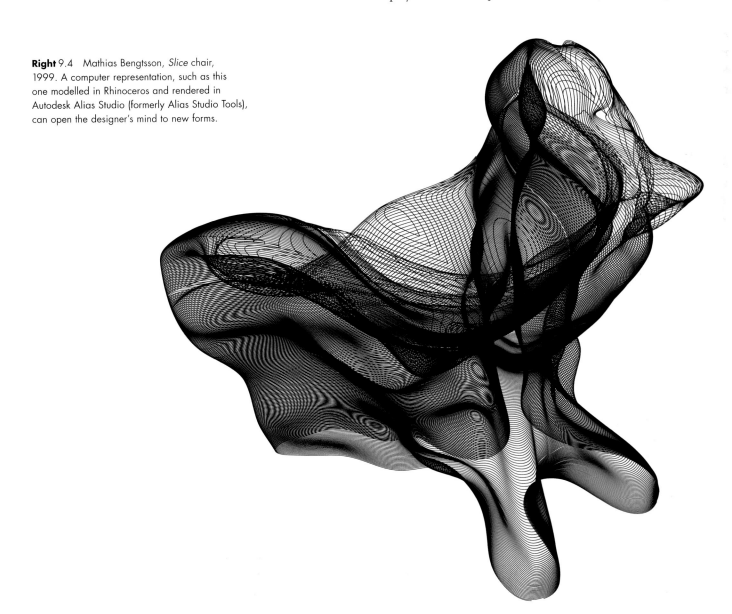

Right 9.5 Björn Holmgren, Multiflow valve body cast in brass, 2004. Computer visualizations, using techniques such as ray tracing, make virtual objects look as though they have been photographed. How long before we will be able to touch and handle designs using haptic devices? This valve body cast in brass for Tour Andersson AB won an award for the best part designed in Solid Edge using third-party rendering software (MicroStation). Courtesy UGS.

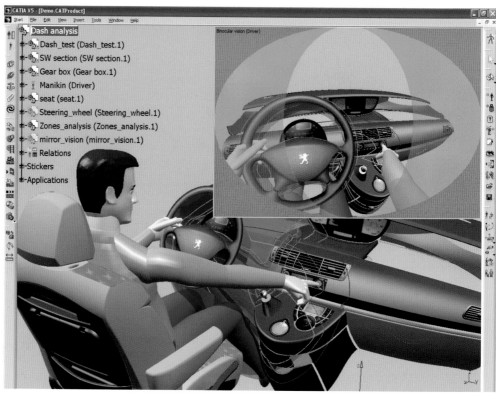

Right 9.6 The purpose of design is not just to make the surface of objects more attractive to the consumer; it is also to make products work better. Ergonomics programs such as Dassault Systèmes' Catia can be used to check that human users will be able to reach the controls in a car, say, and to check their visibility.

too? Already the client presentation, once done by flipcharts and holding up presentation drawings taken from a stack of boards, has been replaced by PowerPoint presentations projected from laptops, and full-colour printed documentation (remember when DTP was new?). Haptic devices for sculpting virtual clay have already been discussed, and these are likely to become more sophisticated, perhaps voice-controlled or glove-activated. Various forms of simulation and testing, such as finite-element analysis for stress and other forms of engineering analyses, have been around for many years and are beyond the scope of this book, but are likely to be used much more frequently for smaller projects.

Computer screens have replaced drawing boards, but the drawing will always be a necessary part of the design process. The idea of a paperless office has become something of a joke, as computerization has, in fact, created an enormous demand for paper. More data, in more and different forms, is the consequence of the information revolution. "If the computer can do it, then we want it" is the exhortation of management. Drawings, in the form of diagrams and charts, are helping make sense of all this "decision support" information, and computers aid the designer in all kinds of other ways: in producing illustrated reports, in project management, in marketing and in archiving previous designs. Just as Achille Castiglioni's studio contained a museum of inspirational objects, so can a present-day product designer have a DVD or hard drive full of instantly accessible source images at his or her fingertips. And search engines such as Google are always available to trawl the internet for inspiration.

Overcoming the fear of CAD

Some commentators, notably Mike Cooley in *Design after Modernism*, expressed reservations about the blind take-up of CAD, with consultancies buying into it to impress clients rather than to increase the quality (and quantity) of service. Cooley always argued that CAD would extend the division of labour (also known as Taylorism after Frederick W. Taylor [1856–1915], who evolved the theory of "scientific management", promoting the rationalization, standardization and automation of production to save labour) begun during the Industrial Revolution, to more intellectual activities, namely designing, during this "information revolution". The theory has symmetry and elegance, but has been overtaken by events.

Whether the teamwork seen in today's multidisciplinary design projects can be treated as white-collar Taylorism is debatable, and would happen whether CAD was involved or not. Shiftwork, introduced by large firms when the cost of CAD was outrageously expensive, was recognized to be counter-productive. The use of CAD-

trained operators, acting as technicians to reluctant Luddite designers, is likewise out of favour. The best work evolves when the designer has access to his or her own system to be used as and when necessary. Cooley's warnings that working with CAD or computer systems of any sort can be alienating, fragmented and stressful because of the ever-increasing tempo, have been received and understood.

Instead of subdividing the designer's traditional job description, CAD can expand a designer's conceptual span and give him or her a holistic view of the project, with more control over the span of the design-to-production process. It is conceivable that a computer-aided designer could tackle an entire large-scale project from conception to the generation of data to drive machine tools single-handed. CAD equipment has enabled many designers to set up one- or two-person practices with the minimum of office space but with the capacity to undertake quite complex projects.

Cooley is wary that "tacit knowledge" will be lost in rule-based and so-called expert systems; that designers will lose the ability to visualize, say, 3D objects from a plan and elevation. But just as calculators have removed the need to learn long division, so designers with CAD are, in theory, released to concentrate on the more creative aspects of the job. Thinking time, however, preferably away from the screen, must be allowed for, and it is a fool indeed who accepts uncritically that the computer is infallible. "Alternatives exist", says Cooley, after Dürer, "which reject neither human judgment, tacit knowledge, intuition and imagination, nor the scientific or rule-based method, and that we should unite them in a symbiotic totality."

The key word in computer-aided design is aided: a system should build on human skill rather than marginalize it.

Future CAD

John Frazer, international research co-coordinator for the Gehry Technologies Digital Practice Ecosystem, sees the future CAD system as an electronic muse and critic. It would be able to elicit from the designer the purpose of the present design activity and then discuss the approach being taken. When the designer cannot overcome a problem, the CAD system could helpfully suggest alternative strategies, find previous analogous approaches, or make random suggestions to help the designer clarify his or her ideas.

Current CAD acts as an amplifier or turbo-charger; it amplifies ability but also amplifies ignorance, indiscriminately. Rather than being stressful, in Cooley's sense, computers can cure designers of the boredom and lack of challenge that, according to Frazer, produced "the peripheral intellectual flippancy of Post-Modern styling". Rather than mimicking the "scruffy sketch, [CAD] mimics the process of juggling with ideas". In product design, programs should model not two- and three-dimensional form, but the *process* of manufacture and assembly that produces that form. This, says Frazer, re-establishes for the designer the power the craftsperson (a.k.a. designer/maker) has when designing a one-off craft object, overcoming the alienation and separation of designer and machine that has existed since the Industrial Revolution.

Collecting designers' drawings

As the artist's drawing achieved increased stature early in the twentieth century, and galleries sought out new media to fill the wallspace, so the designer's drawing

is finding the appreciation it deserves (Fig. 9.7). As well as giving an insight into the creative processes at work in design, designers' drawings are more and more being appraised as works of art in their own right, following the revival of interest in architects' and engineers' drawings as decorative objects. For example, a drawing by Afra and Tobia Scarpa of their *Miss* chair for Molteni, on sale at the Milan furniture fair in 1987, cost more than the piece of furniture illustrated.

According to Charles Hind, keeper of drawings at the RIBA and formerly of the London auctioneers Sotheby's, there are some problems for collectors of mainly nineteenth-century drawings, including the difficulty of telling hand-coloured copies from the genuine "original", and the fact that working drawings can often be marred with later annotations and alterations. If a drawing has been stored in reasonable conditions, however, it can be unaffected by light damage and glow with colour in a way rare in watercolours that have been hanging (and fading) for years.

Conclusion

Finally, here are some sobering words from the days
when designing meant nothing more than adding
ornamentation, which the practising product designer
would do well to heed. R.L.B. Rathbone wrote in the
metalworking section (the closest trade to today's product
design) of *Practical Designing: A Handbook on the
Preparation of Working Drawings* (1893):

> *It is generally worthwhile giving the workman a rough
> perspective sketch of the whole design, so that he may
> picture it in his mind more easily than he can do from
> plans and elevations alone. To avoid the dangers of
> subdivided labour, the designer should endeavour to
> obtain free intercourse with the workman who is going
> to actually carry out the design; but not until he has
> either had some practical manual training, or else has
> made himself as conversant with the construction and
> processes of metalwork as theoretical study will permit.
> Our British workmen are apt to hold the ideas and
> attainments of designers in high disdain, and perhaps
> even to take a certain degree of pleasure in
> overwhelming them with all the practical difficulties
> in the way of working out what looks so nice on paper
> … The designer who has had the patience to follow
> these dry, technical details, should now be able to
> avoid falling into those errors of construction which
> make the British (or other) workman scratch his head,
> and wonder why designers were created for the
> apparent purpose of setting him problems which he
> can never solve—errors which cause the enemy of the
> division of labour to blaspheme, not without reason.*

Below 9.8 Héctor Serrano,
Mundoeconomia, 2003. This
drawing is part of Serrano's
Netobjects project with Victor Viña,
a collection of everyday objects for
the home that present real-time
information from the Web.

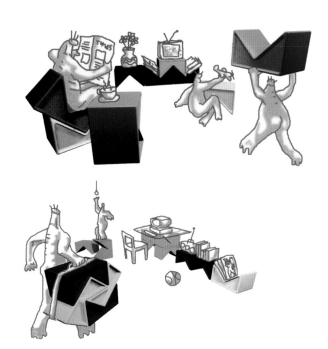

Above 9.9   El Ultimo Grito, Funktion stools and modular objects, 2001. This playful drawing for UEG combines realistic designed objects created in 3D Studio Max with cartoon-like users hand-drawn in Photoshop, and explains how the product could be assembled for different purposes.

Today's product designers may never even meet the workers responsible for manufacturing their designs—they may even be on the other side of the world—and so must be confident that the drawings, whether they be orthographic projections, more pictorial perspectives and paralines or a 3D computer-aided solid model, set out their aims and intentions, concerns and aspirations as explicitly and emphatically as the technology of drawing will allow. But above all, designers should enjoy the act of drawing (Fig. 9.8), one of life's exquisite pleasures: the ability to communicate an idea to another human being by means of a few choice lines on paper (Fig. 9.9). So, get out your pencil, and practise drawing every day. As Pablo Picasso said: "Inspiration exists, but it has to find you working."

Glossary

2½D A simplified version of 3D in which an x,y 2D profile is "extruded" in the z direction to generate a shape with no undercuts

3D printing A method of **rapid prototyping** in which layers of a fine powder are selectively bonded by "printing" a water-based adhesive from a inkjet printhead under the control of a CAD system

Auxiliary projection A view of the component taken from an angle which is not at right angles, and hence not orthogonal, to any of the three views in an orthographic projection, and which is usually included to help clarify the reading of a drawing

Axonometric projection A non-perspective pictorial method of representing a 3D object. It contains a true plan, 45° angles, and is the simplest metric projection to set up from orthographic drawings

Bézier curve A computer method for drawing freeform curves, invented in 1962 by French engineer Pierre Bézier, who used them to design automobile bodies for Renault. See also **spline**

Blueprint Once a copy made by the contact printing process of cyanotype of a drawing in ink or pencil on linen or Mylar film, but now synonymous with any engineering or architectural drawing and most likely nowadays to be a computer printout

Boolean operations (union, difference, and intersection) A system of logical operations, named after George Boole, for combining or subtracting 3D shapes to construct a form

B-rep (boundary representation) A type of solid modeler that keeps a list of all the faces, edges, and vertices of the model, together with the Euler topological and adjacency relationships between them

Cabinet projection An oblique projection in which the oblique lines emerging from the elevation are half the true length

CAD Computer-aided design, or more exactly in the case of 2D systems, computer-aided *drafting*. Computer-*automated* design is not here just yet—humans still have a place in the design process!

California chrome A convention of the airbrush artist for creating convincing reflections, which assumes that the shiny object being drawn stands surrounded by bright yellow sand under a deep blue sky that graduates to white at the horizon where it meets the dark desert

CAM Computer-aided manufacture—all the downstream shopfloor activities, such as **NC** and production planning, that can make use of a part's geometry as it is output from a CAD system

CADCAM Joining the two acronyms does not necessarily ensure integration, though nowadays the two types of system can be run on the same machine

Callout An element (generally a circle with a number inside) within a technical illustration that corresponds to some textual information elsewhere or another more detailed drawing placed in a circle or box away from the main illustration

CGI (computer-generated imagery) Term used in computer graphics to denote any virtual object or scene

CRT (cathode ray tube) An almost obsolete technology for making computer monitors

CSG (constructive solid geometry) A type of solid modeler that constructs objects by combining or subtracting **geometric primitives**

Cavalier projection An oblique projection in which the oblique lines emerging from the elevation are true lengths

Dimetric projection A form of **isometric projection** using "idealized" angles of 7° and 42° to the horizontal for the x and y axes such that two of the three axes of space appear equally foreshortened

Doblin perspective Jay Doblin developed a simplified method in 1956 using a cube as a basic perspective unit, which can be multiplied and subdivided to build up a framework for describing any shape of object

DWG (pronounced *drawing*) and **DXF** (Drawing Interchange Format, or Drawing Exchange Format) AutoCAD's de facto CAD data-exchange file formats

Dye-sublimation printer A printer technology mixing the ink while it is in gaseous form to produce near-photographic results

Extrusion Pushing or drawing a 2D profile through space to form a long 3D shape of a fixed cross-section, like forcing semi-liquid material through a die

FEA (finite-element analysis) Breaking down a component's geometry into a mesh of simple shapes that can be analysed for stress and thermal properties

Fractal A shape that is recursively constructed or self-similar at all scales of magnification and therefore infinitely complex—used in programs like Bryce to create natural-looking backgrounds and textures. The term was coined in 1975 by Benoît Mandelbrot, from the Latin *fractus*, meaning "fractured"

GA (general arrangement) drawings are the key to all the other detail, tooling, and assembly drawings needed for production. It is here that the final layout is decided, dimensions are fixed, ergonomic considerations resolved, and the methods of production finalized. Engineering drawings, which could run to hundreds, might be at different scales and are coordinated with reference to the GA

Geometric primitives The building blocks of 3D geometry: spheres, cubes, cones, and cylinders

Gouraud shading Method of rendering a 3D virtual object, invented in 1971 by Henri Gouraud to interpolate linearly the shading across each polygon, thus providing a smooth transition from one edge to the next. See also **Phong shading**

Haptic device From the Greek *haphe*, meaning pertaining to the sense of touch, a haptic device connected to a computer gives users the impression they are actually feeling and sculpting the virtual object

Hardcopy Drawings output from laser or inkjet printer

IGES (Initial Graphics Exchange Specification) A standard format for transferring a design between different CAD systems, superseded by **STEP**

ISO (International Standards Organization) The body for policing drawing conventions and coordinating the work of national bodies such as BSI (British Standards Institution) and ANSI (American National Standards Institute)

Isometric projection A non-perspective pictorial method of representing a 3D object, producing a less extreme drawing than the axonometric projection. Elevations are constructed using a 30° set square and as a result the "plan" is distorted

LAN (local-area network) The best-known means for connecting computers into workgroups is Ethernet

LCD (liquid crystal display) A technology for producing flat computer monitors

Metric projections Non-perspective pictorial methods of representing 3D objects, such as **isometric** and **axonometric**. Also known as **paraline** projections

Oblique projection A non-perspective pictorial method of representing a 3D object used where the front elevation of the object is of particular importance, in furniture design for example; the side and top views of an object are tacked onto the edges of the front face. The oblique lines emerging from the elevation can be any length: in a **cavalier** projection they are true lengths; in a **cabinet** projection they are half the true length

Orthographic projection The "engineering drawing" method of representing three dimensions on 2D paper by projecting three adjacent views—a plan and two elevations—of an object onto three orthogonal planes (i.e. at right angles to one another) and then "unfolding" those planes so that they lie on the same plane. A plan with the elevation of the front face drawn immediately above it and the end elevation to the right is known as **first-angle projection**. **Third-angle projection** has the views arranged such that one elevation is placed below the plan, with the end elevation to the left of the first elevation. This has the advantage of placing the features of adjacent views in juxtaposition, making it easier to project one view from another when drawing, and to associate these features when dimensioning or reading the drawing

NC Numerical control, as applied to machine tools, such as milling machines. **NC part programming** is the method of converting the geometry of a component output from a CAD system into an efficient toolpath for the appropriate machine tool to manufacture the part, and verifying that there are no clashes between the tool and the part's fixtures

NURBS (non-uniform rational B-spline) A mathematical model commonly used in **CAD** for generating and representing curves and surfaces

OOP (object-oriented programming) Software comprising tried and tested modules and components called "objects" which inherit the attributes of other objects

Package-constrained design Designing a product that has to contain a collection of pre-sourced components of specified geometry, such as motors and printed-circuit boards

Paint program Computer graphics software such as Adobe Photoshop, in which the image is stored in the computer's memory as a bitmap, a one-to-one array corresponding to the pixels (dots) appearing on the screen. See also **vector program**

Paraline see **Metric projections**

Parametric programming An almost automatic method of generating drawings of components that have a family resemblance by first defining a generalized component shape and subsequently inputting specific dimensions

PDS (product design specification) A detailed brief document that spells out all the requirements for the new product

Perspective A method of introducing systematic distortions into drawings to *symbolize* reality. Objects appear to diminish and converge as their distance from the viewer increases. The horizon is assumed to be infinitely distant, so that parallel lines meet at vanishing points. A perspective is a convention—in real life there will be many changing vanishing points as the designer's (two) eyes and head move and wander around a scene

Phong shading Method of adding specular reflection (highlights) to a 3D virtual object, invented by Bui Tuong Phong in 1973 based on an empirical observation that shiny surfaces reflect light unequally in different directions. See also **Gouraud shading**

Pixel Short for picture element, the size of a dot on a computer display. The resolution (sharpness) of a raster display is measured by the number of pixels horizontally by the number of scan lines vertically, e.g. 1280 × 1024

Radiosity An approach to rendering a 3D virtual scene that determines the light energy equilibrium of all the surfaces in a static environment, independent of the observer's position

Rapid prototyping Constructing physical objects using solid freeform fabrication, building up an object by **3D printing**, **selective laser sintering**, or **stereolithography**, as opposed to milling, which cuts away material from a solid block of wax, metal, or plastic

Ray tracing A technique for computing a photographically realistic visualization of an object and its environment by using the laws of optics. Each ray leaving a surface is the sum of varying contributions from three sources: diffusely reflected light, specularly reflected light, and transmitted or refracted light. Rays are traced back from the viewpoint (shot, in effect, through the pixels of the display's screen), bounced around the scene, and arrive eventually back at the light source

RSI (repetitive strain injury) See **WRULD**

Scrap view An enlarged close-up of a particular detail on a drawing requiring particular attention

Section A slice through a solid object to illustrate a profile or the interior of a part not made obvious by the orthographic projection; whole series of sections are needed to represent complex doubly curved shapes, such as car bodies

Selective laser sintering A method of **rapid prototyping** which uses a laser to fuse powdered metal under the control of a CAD system

Solid modeler (also known as volumetric or geometric modeler) A CAD system that produces a complete and unambiguous 3D model of the component that can be "weighed" and checked for interferences with other objects. Models are "sculpted" using **Boolean operations** (union, intersection, and difference) on primitive geometric shapes, such as cylinders, cubes, and spheres

Spline The computer equivalent to the French curve or piano wire, but more controllable—the most advanced type commercially available is called **NURBS**, for non-uniform rational B-spline. See also **Bézier curve**

STEP (Standard for the Exchange of Product model data) An international standard all **solid modelers** aspire to, formerly PDES (Product Data Exchange Specification)

Stereolithography A method of **rapid prototyping** which uses a laser under the control of a CAD system to solidify a liquid photopolymer on a movable table which is then lowered one layer's thickness into the vat of liquid

Surface modeler A 3D CAD program used for designing objects with complex doubly-curved surfaces, such as those defining turbine blades, automobile bodies, and telephone handsets

Sweeping Creating a 3D shape from a 2D profile by rotating it around an axis. Also called lathing, after the method of turning wood or metal

TFT (thin film transistors) Tiny switching transistors and capacitors in an LCD display

Theme sketch An initial expression of how a proposed design is intended to look, drawn with a free rein without the designer having to consider any internal constraints

TPD (Technical Product Documentation) The modern term for a set of engineering drawings, also known as TPS (Technical Product Specification)

Trimetric projection A form of **isometric** such that all of the three axes of space appear unequally foreshortened

Turnkey system A packaged and integrated assembly of hardware, software, and support once common for CAD systems, from suppliers such as Computervision and Intergraph

Vector program Computer graphics software such as Adobe Illustrator, in which the image is stored in the computer's memory as a "display list" of the points and lines that make up the illustration, plus the formulas for any circles, ellipses, and curves, using a language called PostScript (the same format used to describe the letter forms in a font)

Wireframe A "transparent" 3D representation of an object in which all lines can be seen, made up of lines and points, but no surfaces

WRULD (work-related upper-limb disorders) A disorder of the hands and wrists causing numbness, swelling, tingling, and ultimately complete seizure, also know as RSI (repetitive strain injury)

Bibliography

Resources:
Further Reading and Websites

Manual rendering

Ronald B. Kemnitzer, *Rendering with Markers: Definitive Techniques for Designers, Illustrators, and Architects* (New York: Watson-Guptill Publications, 1983). ISBN: 0823045323
Introduces dry markers and related sketching equipment. Demonstrates masking, blending and editing techniques, and shows how to simulate materials and special lighting conditions.

Mike Lin, *Drawing and Designing with Confidence* (Hoboken, NJ: John Wiley & Sons Inc, 1993). ISBN: 0471283908
With a teaching style that stresses speed and relaxation, the author covers all aspects of design, graphic composition, media, types of drawings and perspective techniques.

Richard M. McGarry, *Marker Magic: The Rendering Problem Solver for Designers* (Hoboken, NJ: John Wiley & Sons Inc, 1992). ISBN: 0471284343
Profiles top rendering pros, their techniques, and examples of their best work with 40 mini-lessons which demonstrate solutions to everyday rendering problems.

Dick Powell, *Presentation Techniques* (London: Little, Brown, 1994). ISBN: 0316912433
The definitive book on marker rendering, with historical drawings and how-to-do-it sequences, by a practicing designer. Unfortunately it is now out of print, but you may find it on eBay or in your library.

In the field of computer rendering, there are many books devoted to individual software products, such as Adobe Photoshop or 3D Studio Max – the ... *for Dummies* guides, for example – which either augment the manuals that come with the programs, or provide simplified introductions and tutorials. Few books, if any, compare and contrast the advantages and disadvantages of rival software packages. For that you need to consult the review pages of magazines, such as *Computer Arts* and *MacWorld*.

Technical drawing and illustration

Jay Doblin, *Perspective: A New System for Designers* (New York: Whitney Library of Design, 1956). ISBN: 0823074196
A simplified method for drawing perspectives specifically aimed at designers. Unfortunately it is now out of print, but you may find it on eBay or in your library.

Jon M. Duff and Greg Maxson, *The Complete Technical Illustrator* (New York: McGraw-Hill, 2003). ISBN: 007292229X
A comprehensive overview of technical illustration using software packages including Adobe Photoshop and Illustrator, AutoCAD, and 3D Studio Max. A CD-ROM included features a tool called AxonHelper, used to determine axonometric views.

Frederick E. Giesecke et al, *Technical Drawing* (Upper Saddle River, NJ: Prentice Hall, 2002, 12th edn). ISBN: 0130081833
Authoritative American text on engineering drawing, including manual design, CAD and solid modeling.

Robert W. Gill, *Perspective: From Basic to Creative* (London: Thames & Hudson, 2006). ISBN: 0500286078
Originally published as two separate books, this enlarged and combined volume provides a clear and simple explanation of the principles of perspective.

Judy Martin, *Technical Illustration: Materials, Methods and Techniques* (London: Macdonald Orbis, 1989). ISBN: 0356175669
Comprehensive survey of the manual methods of technical illustration, meaning mostly airbrush. The author has also written books on pastel drawing and coloured pencil techniques. Unfortunately it is now out of print, but you may find it on eBay or in your library.

Colin Simmons, *Manual of Engineering Drawing: To British and International Standards* (Oxford: Newnes, 2003). ISBN: 0750651202
A comprehensive guide to producing manual or CAD engineering drawings to BS8888:2002 which, being derived from ISO standards, is also valid internationally.

Drawing in general

Ken Baynes and Francis Pugh, *The Art of the Engineer* (Guildford: Lutterworth Press, 1997). ISBN: 0718825063
A lavishly illustrated book concentrating on the drawings of Victorian engineers, and restricted in content to modes of transport. Unfortunately it is now out of print, but you may find it on eBay or in your library.

Betty Edwards, *The New Drawing on the Right Side of the Brain* (London: HarperCollins, 2001). ISBN: 0007116454
The classic 'drawing for the apprehensive' guide. The left side of the brain is where words and numbers come from, but using the right side can unlock creative thinking, insight and visual literacy.

Keith Micklewright, *Drawing: Mastering the Language of Visual Expression* (London: Laurence King Publishing, 2005). ISBN: 1856694607
In this approach, drawing is seen as a flexible form of expression rather than a set of mechanical skills. There is no right way to draw creatively, the author argues, any more than there is one style of writing creatively.

Howard J. Smagula, *Creative Drawing* (London: Laurence King Publishing, 2002). ISBN: 1856693104
A lively, comprehensive introduction to the history and practice of drawing, handsomely illustrated throughout. Includes sections on individual artists and lots of projects for students.

Case studies

Ron Arad et al, *Spoon* (London: Phaidon Press, 2004). ISBN: 0714844551
Described as 'an exhibition in a book', it presents the work of 100 product designers, selected by ten critics, educators, designers and entrepreneurs, and includes many of their drawings.

Industrial Designers Society of America, *Design Secrets: Products: 50 Real-Life Projects Uncovered* (Gloucester, MA: Rockport Publishers, 2001). ISBN: 1564966380
Behind-the-scenes of 50 real-life product design projects, each illustrated in detail from concept to completion with original plans, sketches, visuals, interim drawings and presentations.

Industrial Designers Society of America with Lynn Haller and Cheryl Dangel Cullen, *Design Secrets: Products 2: 50 Real-life Projects Uncovered* (Gloucester, MA: Rockport Publishers, 2004). ISBN: 1592530710

A second volume of product design case studies, from the BMW Mini Cooper to the Segway Human Transporter.

Phaidon Design Classics: Pts 1, 2 & 3 (London: Phaidon Press, 2006). ISBN: 0714843997
Huge three-volume set of books, with its own carrying device, presents 999 industrially manufactured products, selected by a group of experts. It includes many drawings, many of them patent drawings mocked up to look like blueprints.

Ettore Sottsass, Milco Carboni (ed.) and Hans Hollein (ed.), *Sottsass: 700 Drawings* (Milan: Skira, 2005). ISBN: 8876240934
With 700 drawings from the Memphis designer, spanning his career in design and architecture from 1936 to the present, it includes furniture, ceramics, glass and jewelery.

Other coffee-table books and monographs from publishers such as Taschen, Phaidon and Rotovision (and of course Laurence King) on product/industrial design 'icons' and designers such as Philippe Starck and Ross Lovegrove often contain examples of their drawings.

Websites

The internet is a rich resource of information and tutorials, but web addresses do change, so check with a search engine such as Google if the links given here do not work. For information on commercial products, such as Adobe Photoshop, take a look at the vendor's website first.

Design at the Design Museum
www.designmuseum.org/design
Profiles of well known product designers, design groups and movements.

Doodles, Drafts, and Designs
www.sites.si.edu/exhibitions/exhibits/doodles/main.htm
A travelling exhibition documenting 200 years of American design with over 70 original drawings from the Smithsonian.

Product Design Forums
www.productdesignforums.com
Lots of tutorials and advice from other designers on this discussion bulletin board.

Wikipedia
http://en.wikipedia.org/wiki/Main_Page
A great source of concise technical information, with links to vendors' own sites and authoritative articles on any subject.

Websites of some of the contributors to this book

Alessi
www.alessi.com

Alvar Aalto
www.aaltosvoice.com

Ron Arad Associates
www.ronarad.co.uk

Nelson Au
www.nelsonau.com

Georg Baldele
www.georgbaldele.com

Bang & Olufsen
www.beoworld.co.uk

Bellini Studios
www.bellini.it

Bengtsson design
www.bengtssondesign.com

Oscar Tusquets Blanca
www.tusquets.com

Braun
www.braun.com

Brompton
www.bromptonbicycle.co.uk

co-lab*
www.co-labstudio.org

Michael diTullo
http://michaeld2lo.spymac.com

EL ULTIMO GRITO
www.elultimogrito.co.uk

Factory Design
www.factorydesign.co.uk

Thomas Gardner
www.kloss-online.co.uk

David Goodwin
www.david-goodwin.com

Isao Hosoe Design
http://85.18.123.118/isao/

Ora Ito
www.ora-ito.com

Georg Jensen
www.georgjensen.com

King and Miranda Design
www.kingmiranda.com

Torsten Neeland
www.torsten-neeland.co.uk

Pearson Lloyd
www.pearsonlloyd.co.uk

Philips Design
www.design.philips.com

Pilipili
www.pilipili.be

Priestman Goode
www.priestmangoode.com

Karim Rashid
www.karimrashid.com

Rio21Design
www.rio21design.com.br

Héctor Serrano
www.hectorserrano.com/

Seymourpowell
www.seymourpowell.com

Shin Azumi
www.shinazumi.com

Sottsass Associati
www.sottsass.it

Sowden Design
www.sowdendesign.com

Springtime-USA (Tucker Viemeister)
www.springtime-usa.com

Philippe Starck
www.philippe-starck.com

Marcel Wanders Studio
www.marcelwanders.com

Tokujin Yoshioka
www.tokujin.com/en/main.html

Youmeus Design
www.youmeusdesign.com

Index

Page numbers in *italic* refer to captions.